COMMUNICATING CAUSES

Non-profit organizations (NPOs) across the world are facing criticism alongside approbation. In order for NPOs to effectively support their causes, they require public trust. The editors of this book have persuaded PR experts from the UK and around the world, from a variety of PR specialisms operating across different organizational forms, to share their knowledge and experience. These contributions are scaffolded with authoritative academic and practical advice, as well as solutions.

The book starts with foundations that underpin communications for causes. These include arguments that support the importance of non-profits in civil society; lessons in corporate governance; and a new approach to issues management. PR planning subjects tailored, or specific, to the sector include: strategic global communications planning; agile digital communications; branding internal communications and the securing of meaningful outcomes. Corporate partnerships are examined with a new 'Fit to Partner Test' and consideration of the mandated corporate social responsibility (CSR) in India, corporate volunteering in Brazil, and CSR in South Africa. Relations between governments and non-profits are also considered, both generally and with a particular focus on China.

Communicating Causes looks at effective strategy and practice of PR in the modern non-profit. Including forewords by both John Grounds and Jon Snow, the expert perspectives offered in this book provide valuable support to current and future communicators.

Nicky Garsten is Senior Lecturer at the University of Greenwich, London. She directs the BA (Hons) in Public Relations and Communications, and is co-founder and leader of the module, 'Third Sector PR'. Coming from a background of senior roles in non-profit strategic communications, she publishes and presents academic research on non-profit communications.

Ian Bruce is President and Founder of the Centre for Charity Effectiveness at Cass Business School, City, University of London and Vice President Royal National Institute of Blind People (RNIB). Previously, he was CEO of RNIB & Volunteering England, assistant CEO of a London Borough and has authored four books, alongside many chapters and articles.

The expansion of the many forms of non-governmental organisations at local, national and international levels has created many challenges for communicators. Garsten and Bruce have brought together expertise from around the world to address key issues in this welcome and well-structured new volume.

Tom Watson, *PhD, Emeritus Professor, Faculty of Media &*
Communication, Bournemouth University, England

Nicky Garsten and Ian Bruce combine national and international examples with academic research to show how non-profits can communicate their cause in a clear, engaging and effective way, thus attracting support and changing society for the better. This book is an excellent read for the non-profit communications professionals who want to polish their messaging, understand their audiences better and improve how they measure the effectiveness of their communications.

Lynda Thomas, *Chief Executive, Macmillan Cancer Support, UK*

In our ever-congested world only those causes that truly resonate will be ultimately sustainable. Garsten and Bruce skilfully articulate both the justification and the benefits that accrue form the proper application of strategic public relations to the effective promotion of good causes. A 'must read' for all social marketers, campaigners, fundraisers and anyone concerned to get their message across in a clear and effective manner.

Dr Stephen Lee, *Professor of Voluntary Sector Management,*
Cass Business School, City, University of London

Non-profits operate in challenging environments, which call for highly skilled, strategic and adaptable communicators. *Communicating Causes* is a comprehensive guide grounded in theory, but brought to life with real-world examples. A thought-provoking read emphasising what we can achieve in the sector.

Beth Andlaw, *Head of Third Sector at The PHA Group*

Communicating Causes is an incredibly useful book for those wishing to gain a deeper understanding of the 'why' as well as the 'how' of strategic communications in the non-profit sector. It balances the theory behind the strategy with practical advice and case studies, addressing the major issues facing communications professionals in the current non-profit environment.

Fiona Young, *Head of Media & Communications, Social Enterprise UK*

COMMUNICATING CAUSES

Strategic Public Relations for the Non-Profit Sector

Edited by Nicky Garsten and Ian Bruce

Routledge
Taylor & Francis Group

LONDON AND NEW YORK

First published 2018
by Routledge
2 Park Square, Milton Park, Abingdon, Oxon OX14 4RN

and by Routledge
711 Third Avenue, New York, NY 10017

Routledge is an imprint of the Taylor & Francis Group, an informa business

British Library Cataloguing-in-Publication Data
A catalogue record for this book is available from the British Library

Library of Congress Cataloging-in-Publication Data
A catalog record has been requested for this book

ISBN: 978-0-8153-9400-6 (hbk)
ISBN: 978-0-8153-9401-3 (pbk)
ISBN: 978-1-351-02222-4 (ebk)

Typeset in Bembo
by Taylor & Francis Books

To communicators in the non-profit sector and to students of third sector PR

Nicky also dedicates this book to her mother and father, Elizabeth and Geoffrey; to her brother, Chris; and to her husband, Kevin

Ian also dedicates this book to Tina, Hannah, Jonathan, Tom, Gemma, Stevie and Lila

CONTENTS

FIGURES

TABLES

BOXES

CONTRIBUTORS

Joe Barrell is the Executive Director of communications agency, Eden Stanley, which has developed audience-centred strategies for more than 50 of the UK's leading non-profit organizations (NPOs). Eden Stanley's tracking studies focuses on public attitudes to international causes, public health, and disability rights. Joe entered the non-profit sector from a first career in journalism. His book, *Make it Matter: Creating Communications Strategies in the Non-profit-sector* (2014) is aimed at professional communicators. Joe was Communications Director for Save the Children (2005–2010).

Dalien Rene Benecke is a Senior Lecturer in the Department of Strategic Communication at the University of Johannesburg. One of her key interests is securing partnerships with various NPOs to address social issues. PR and Communication students are actively involved in experiential learning opportunities with these NPO partners. Some of their projects have earned them international and national awards.

Ian Bruce (CBE, CCMI, FCIM) is Vice President of RNIB (Royal National Institute of Blind People). He is also founder and President of the Centre for Charity Effectiveness at City, University of London's Cass Business School. It is one of the largest such university centres in the world. Previously Ian was Chief Executive of RNIB and Volunteering England; and Assistant Chief Executive of a London Borough and of Age Concern England; and a marketing manager with Unilever. He has written and broadcast extensively. His book, *Charity Marketing* is in its fourth edition and his academic writing has been widely cited. He has founded or co-founded 12 local, national and international non-profit organizations and is the founder and chair of the Chartered Institute of Marketing's non-profit interest groups. He was the first UK charity chief executive to be made a Companion of the Chartered Management Institute and the first to be given the Outstanding Achievement Awards of both the National and UK Charity Award organizations.

Colin Byrne is a writer. He was UK & EMEA CEO of Weber Shandwick, the world's second largest PR network, and the most award winning. During his 23 years with the firm Colin led the London public affairs practice, the UK business and then EMEA. Previously Colin was a senior PR professional with The Prince's Trusts and The Labour Party amongst others. He has worked with many NGO clients, including The Gates Foundation and War Child, and is a trustee of Action Aid UK.

Gustavo Carbonaro graduated in journalism and is pursuing a Ph.D. in Communication Sciences at University of São Paulo. He is senior partnership officer for Latin America at King's College London. Previously he was the International Manager of the Brazilian Association for Business Communication (Aberje).

Elizabeth Chamberlain heads NCVO's policy and public services work, having first joined the policy team in 2008 as an expert on charity law and regulation. Elizabeth has acted as secretariat for a number of specialist policy projects, including the review of fundraising regulation, and NCVO's independent review of the Charities Act. Before joining NCVO, Elizabeth worked for the vice president of the European Commission in the cabinet for Justice, Liberty and Security.

Nupur Chaturvedi heads marketing communications for Genesis Burson-Marsteller as well as supporting the company leadership for their content requirements in India. She was earlier leading GBM's Content & Design Bureau. She has over 18 years of editorial and content management experience, which include six years as an entrepreneur running her own editorial agency, and over five years as a technology journalist in a leading technology media group.

Caroline Diehl, MBE, is Chair and Founder of the UK Community Channel. She was founder chief executive of the Media Trust until 2017. Caroline recently launched the Social Founders Network, connecting founders across the charity and social enterprise sector. Caroline is a social entrepreneur in residence at INSEAD, a director of the Creative Diversity Network, and an Associate of Newnham College, Cambridge. She is an EY Social Entrepreneur of the Year, and a winner of both the Cannes Chimera Award and the PRCA Charity Communications Award.

Sir Stuart Etherington was appointed Chief Executive of NCVO in 1994. Throughout his career he has been involved in the leadership of voluntary organizations and policies surrounding them. Stuart is a member of the Economic and Social Committee of the European Union and the Chair of London United. He is Chair of the Trustees of the Patron's Fund and chaired a cross-party review looking at the structure of the regulation of fundraising. He is also an Honorary Fellow of the Institute for Employment Studies.

Liam FitzPatrick is a senior consultant at Quiller Consultants and is managing partner at Working Communication Strategies. He has worked in PR and change communications for nearly 30 years. He has supported corporates around the world as well as NGOs such as the International Committee of the Red Cross and World Food Programme. In the UK, he has worked with The Childrens' Society and Plan International. His writing includes *Internal Communications: A Manual for Practitioners* and chapters on internal communications in several textbooks including the 4th edition of *Exploring Public Relations* edited by Ralph Tench and Liz Yeomans.

Nicky Garsten (Ph.D. SOAS, University of London) is Senior Lecturer at the University of Greenwich, London, where she directs the BA (Hons) in PR and Communications. There, she is co-founder and leader of the specialist undergraduate course, 'Third Sector PR'. She is an editorial board member of *Public Relation Review: A Global Journal of Research and Comment*. Her research interests include non-profit communications, PR specializations and Singaporean studies. She is a member of the PRCA's Charity Committee, a Fellow of the Royal Society of Arts and a Senior Fellow of the Higher Education Academy. Previously, Nicky was a healthcare journalist and went on to run the Press Office at the Royal National Institute of the Blind. She later had strategic consultancy (Publicis Groupe) and non-profit roles. She co-directed campaigns with clients at the British Heart Foundation and the Health Education Authority that won national PR awards. At the Media Trust, she set up Community Newswire with the Press Association.

Orla Graham is a Senior Client Insights Manager at Gorkana, where she has developed and led PR evaluation programmes for global and national non-profit organizations alike, including UNICEF, UK Department of Health, Marie Curie, UK Department for Digital, Culture, Media and Sport (DCMS), Vodafone Foundation and BBC Television Licensing. Her work with UNICEF and DCMS has seen success at the AMEC evaluation awards, and she is co-chair of the AMEC Young Leaders Group.

Lida Holtzhausen (Ph.D.) is a Senior Lecturer and currently Acting Director in the School for Communication Studies of the North-West University (Potchefstroom Campus) South Africa. She teaches corporate communication, marketing communication and marketing management. Her research within the discipline of Corporate Communication, focuses on Integrated Marketing Communication and Corporate Branding. She has published both nationally and internationally and has presented numerous conference papers.

Rama Iyer, Founder of White Kettle, is one of the pioneers of CSR in India. Identified among '15 Emerging Leaders in India' by Dishaa, a platform initiated by the British PM, she has also been nominated 'Expert Trainer CSR' by the Dutch Government. Partnering lead Indian corporates in developing and implementing sustainable CSR solutions, across verticals and amongst multiple stakeholders, Rama continues to set new benchmarks in Indian CSR. Rama advises state governments, speaks at industry forums, and is a mentor in the non-profit sector.

Brian Lamb, OBE, is a campaigns and policy consultant. He previously held senior director positions in the voluntary sector with responsibility for communications, campaigning, research, and public policy. He was chair of NCVO's Campaign Effectiveness Advisory Group for 10 years. He has written two books on campaigning in the voluntary sector and is Visiting Professor of Special Educational Needs and Disability at Derby University. He is also chair of Achievement for All, a charity he helped to found, to improve outcomes for disadvantaged children.

Sean Lang (郎希宇LANG, XIYU) is Greenpeace's East Asia Deputy Programme Director. He is responsible for the organization's communications and digital strategy design. Sean is also responsible for programme work in mainland China and Hong Kong. He leads local and global teams to implement more than 20 projects. Before Greenpeace, Sean worked in the international business sector as marketing specialist and marketing director. Sean graduated from Peking University with a major in political science.

Patrick Law is Director of Communication and Stakeholder Relations at the Guinness Partnership, one of the largest and oldest housing associations in England. For nine years he was director of corporate affairs at Barratt Developments, Britain's largest house builder. He has also held senior communications and public affairs roles at British Gas and Centrica. He was a trustee of NEA, the fuel poverty charity, for seven years and in 2017 he became a trustee of the Hyde Charitable Trust.

Ann Longley is a strategy and transformation expert whose career in digital spans 20 years. She has worked across sectors and continents modernising organisations through the strategic and innovative use of digital platforms, tools and technologies. She successfully introduced new digital services and ways of working with the DEC, Hays, and countless consumer-facing brands. She has pioneered in the area of social media insight, content and community engagement creating award winning work and a legacy of relevant cultural change. Ann is an RSA fellow, conference speaker, and visiting lecturer in Communications with the Business School at Greenwich University.

Hannah Myers is a non-profit PR and crisis communications specialist. She holds a Bachelor's degree in English Literature from St. Mary's College of Maryland and a Master's degree in Promotional Media from Goldsmiths College, University of London. Her dissertation is titled '*#IStandWithPP: Planned Parenthood's Crisis and Reputation Management in the 21st Century*'. She has previously worked with small non-profits in the USA and UK and currently works in social impact PR in Washington, D.C.

Paulo Nassar is Senior Assistant Professor at the School of Communications and Arts of the University of São Paulo, Brazil. He holds a postdoctoral degree from

IULM (Italy) and is CEO of the Brazilian Association for Business Communication (Aberje).

Tove Nordström is Communications & Coordination Lead at Social Entrepreneurship Forum (SE Forum), based in Sweden, working with entrepreneurs worldwide. Her background is in strategic communications from the UK covering PR, digital and branding, with a particular focus on social entrepreneurship, responsible business and social innovation. Tove holds a first-class BA in Public Relations from University of Greenwich and won the EUPRERA Award for best communications BA dissertation in Europe.

Michaela O'Brien is Principal Lecturer at the University of Westminster, London. She is course leader, and co-founder, of the pioneering MA in Media, Campaigning and Social Change. She also leads the Media and Society cluster of eight MA programmes. Michaela previously worked in consultancy and strategic communications roles for non-profits including Business in the Community, Gingerbread, Amnesty International, War on Want, Carers UK, British Library and the Refugee Council. Her research interests are power and the history of campaign communications.

Kevin Read is Founding Director and Chief Executive Officer at Pembroke and Rye. He is an experienced PR advisor having worked for more than 25 years for leading communications consultancies. He is a specialist on new business, pitching and thought leadership. His sector expertise encompasses non-profits. He is a Visiting Fellow at the University of Greenwich. He is a fellow of the Chartered Institute of Public Relations and the RSA. He was chief examiner in public relations for the CAM Foundation for many years.

Prema Sagar founded Genesis PR in November 1992 when the public relations industry was at a nascent stage. Over the last two decades, the company, which was acquired by Burson-Marsteller in 2005–2006, has mirrored the journey of India's public relations and public affairs landscape. Today, Genesis Burson-Marsteller is a full-service integrated communications firm, delivering innovative and integrated solutions across multiple geographies and practices. Prema is also Vice Chair for Burson-Marsteller Asia-Pacific as well as a member of the BM's Global Leadership Team.

David Horton Smith (Ph.D. Sociology, Harvard) founded ARNOVA (www.arnova.org), *Nonprofit and Voluntary Sector Quarterly*, and the organized global field-discipline of voluntaristics. Co-recipient of the first (1993) ARNOVA Award for Distinguished Lifetime Contribution to Nonprofit and Voluntary Action Research, he has bios in the *International Encyclopedia of Civil Society* (Springer, 2010) and in Marquis' *Who's Who in the World* since 2001. Founder-President of ICSERA (www.icsera.org), Editor of *VOLUNTARISTICS REVIEW,* and Research-Emeritus Professor at Boston College, Smith has authored/edited 21 published books and 150+ articles-chapters.

Nigel Stanley was Head of Campaigns and Communications at the Trades Union Congress (TUC) from 1997 to 2015, having been appointed the TUC's first parliamentary officer in 1995. He started his career in Labour Party linked jobs, working first for Robin Cook MP and then Bryan Gould MP. This was followed by a period freelancing in journalism, public affairs and campaigning. He is currently chair of the Members' Panel of NEST, the government sponsored pensions scheme and a board member of the Pensions Quality Mark.

Natália Tamura is pursuing a Ph.D. in Communication Sciences at University of São Paulo and has a masters in Education, Art and History of Culture from Mackenzie University, São Paulo. She is a consultant for Communication and Sustainability, and a PR lecturer at Anhembi Morumbi University.

Mazia Yassim (Ph.D.) is a Senior Lecturer in Social Marketing at the University of Greenwich and also holds a research associateship in the charity sector. Her research interest is in not-for-profit and social marketing, consumer behaviour, as well as sports and arts marketing. She has published widely and also acts as a reviewer for academic journals.

FOREWORD

Jon Snow

The non-profit sector has always been close to my heart. I started out as a volunteer in Uganda with VSO and on my return, directed the New Horizon Youth Centre. Since becoming a journalist, I have worked in a voluntary capacity as Chair, Trustee, or patron to organizations ranging from New Horizon itself, to the Tate, the Media Trust, Prisoners Abroad and others. So despite appearances, I do feel part of the vibrant non-profit sector both in the UK and internationally. I have communicated on its behalf and have actively encouraged other journalists to do so through the sterling work of the Media Trust.

Non-profit organizations of all sizes and types need strong voices to help shape the societies in which we work. When we advance a cause, we need to engage many different types of supporters from on-line advocates, to donors, to beneficiaries or clients. This is complex, particularly in ever-shifting digital, and increasingly global, environments. The contributors of this book offer strategic guidance that is tailored to, and/or specifically created for, the non-profit sector. This counsel ranges from different aspects of communications planning to corporate partnership development.

The millions of non-profits around the world need credibility to get their voices heard. In this book, Lamb argues that value of non-profits needs to be clearly articulated to governments of different political persuasions. Non-profits also need strong and open leadership. The importance of building trust in civil society through different aspects of public relations is stressed. Sadly, society has become increasingly divided in many countries. Non-profits provide paths across those divides. But the public has to believe in the value of non-profits for those paths to be maintained and to become thoroughfares.

This is a go-to book for anyone working in communications, or studying public relations, with a specific interest in the non-profit sector. Firstly, the contributors offer sound advice that is specifically related to non-profits. Secondly, the expertise, whilst largely being based in the UK, comes from a wide range of areas in the sector: from NGOs to housing associations; from social enterprises to trade unions; from China to South Africa, and from India to Brazil.

The non-profit sector faces many communication challenges and this book will help organizations steer an effective, ethical path. I am delighted it has been published; it is much needed.

Jon Snow
Newscaster, Channel 4 News

FOREWORD

John Grounds

The not-for-profit sector has a long and rich history. Its roots can be traced to Egypt, Greece and Rome, through the medieval era where the Church, public authorities, guilds and noble families combined to help those in poverty and need, to Queen Elizabeth I's Statute of Charitable Uses in 1601 which arguably laid the foundation for the concept of charities as we know them today. However, the real expansion of the sector began in the 19th century, reflecting in part the rapid economic growth of that period and some of its less palatable consequences. In that century, too, we saw the beginnings of what we now recognise as the effective use of marketing and communications to raise awareness of causes, attract support and encourage action.

The use of striking images of children in poverty in 1860s London by Dr Thomas Barnardo – perhaps exploitative by modern standards – drew attention to the important work of the organization we now know as Barnardo's. Combined with written material, Barnardo provoked both emotional and rational responses and, as we would describe it today, took people on a journey through awareness and understanding to a change of attitude and behaviour – through giving money to help children and seeking changes in the law to protect them. Other charities with their roots in the 19th century including the NSPCC and RSPCA, offer similar fascinating historic examples.

Today, with a large and influential sector in the UK and increasingly mature sectors all over the world, marketing and communications are the life blood of our relationship with charities and a platform for the achievement of their purpose. They inspire us to give and show our support. They connect us to the beneficiaries. Levels of sophistication in identifying and engaging with audiences are increasing exponentially. Even very small charities and campaigning groups recognise the significance of brand distinctiveness, clear, consistent messages and the power of a personal story.

Successful marketing and communication depend on a few fundamentals – above and beyond budget, the skills and experience of individuals or the current public resonance of a particular cause. Is there an inspiring vision of the world our organization wants to create? Is our specific purpose or mission clear and believable? Is there a focused strategy and objectives that reflect our vision and purpose? Is there a distinctive sense of brand; not just visual identity but the real essence of who we are, what we say and how we say it, what we do and what we feel like to those we wish to engage? Is there a narrative that reflects our beliefs, our values and the change we want to achieve, that can inform our messages, images and stories? Are our staff, volunteers and stakeholders informed and motivated? Do we know who we need to engage with to achieve our purpose; do we understand how best to encourage audiences to think, feel or do something that will help the beneficiaries of our cause? Can we measure and communicate our impact? Can we do this all with honesty and integrity?

These are the challenges that are being addressed by not for profit organizations day in, day out, as they seek to achieve support or change for people, animals and environments all over the world. This book is a valuable resource for all those seeking to understand and perhaps one day join their remarkable efforts.

John Grounds
Independent consultant to charities, Chair of CharityComms and
Chair of Forster Communications

INTRODUCING *COMMUNICATING CAUSES: STRATEGIC PUBLIC RELATIONS FOR THE NON-PROFIT SECTOR*

Nicky Garsten and Ian Bruce

The 21st century, predicted former UN Secretary-General Kofi Annan (Lang 2013) is the 'era of the NGO'. In many parts of the world, there has been an upsurge of interest and growth in the non-profit sector in the late 20th and early 21st centuries. For the non-profit sector to maintain its current role in societies around the world, it must be perceived to have legitimacy.

An 'explosion' of growth in the non-profit sector has occurred on international and national levels (Lang 2013: 1). For instance, there were 32 International Non-Governmental Organizations (INGOs) in 1874 (Anheier 2006 citing Chatfield 1997). Today, there are over 20,000 (Davies 2013). Some single INGOs have members that exceed many national populations. For instance, the International Cooperative Alliance (*ibid.*: 1), 'unites a billion co-operators in ninety-one countries'. The growth in national non-governmental organizations (NGOs) has occurred in many parts of the world. For instance, in China, there were about 700,000, or more, government-registered non-profits in July 2017 (Smith and Zhao 2017). This total has more than doubled that from a few years ago (see chapter 15). Nevertheless, growth across the sector is not uniform. For instance, in OECD countries, trade union density (the number of members relative to the number of workers) declined from 21 per cent in 1999 to 16.7 per cent in 2014 (OECD n.d.). In the next chapter, Lamb discusses reasons for the overall growth in the sector and newly identifies PR strategies to support these justifications.

Many non-profit organizations are small. For instance, in the UK, nearly half (48%) of voluntary organizations have incomes of below £10,000 (NCVO 2017). Non-profit organizations of all sizes face many challenges. These include increasing scepticism about the legitimacy of the sector, financial and human resourcing challenges, and technical change (Waters 2014).

This book provides support to current and future communicators in non-profits. Growth in the sector fosters worthwhile career opportunities that can encompass advocacy, fundraising and service communication roles. Communication specialisations range from digital to policy development. Their geographic scope varies from working at local to international levels.

Purposes of this book

The need for strategically driven, legitimising PR is important in the expanding non-profit sector. This is not only for the survival of individual non-profit organizations (NPOs) that provide crucial advocacy and/or services to advance specific causes, but also for the good of civil society. Scarce resources need to be raised and spent responsibly. Public trust and confidence in non-profits has to be enhanced. Moreover, communications need to operate in an always-on, open digital world.

This book's expert contributors examine thoughtful PR practice in the non-profit sector. To date there has been no other textbook on non-profit communications that studies PR in as many different types of non-profit organizations (NPOs, NGOs, INGOs, trade unions, social enterprises and housing associations); whilst encompassing the examinations of non-profits in countries from four continents; and whilst also relating communications in the non-profit sector to as many different areas of PR specialist practice (such as digital communications, internal communications, issues management and evaluation).

Expert perspectives on strategic public relations in the non-profit sector are offered in this book. The major themes in this book, outlined in the section below, support strategic practice.

PR and communications are strategic when they support the delivery of NPOs' missions and goals; be they related to advocacy, income generation and/or service delivery. These missions need to be understood in the context of the contribution to civil society (chapter 1) and in relation to codes concerning corporate governance in the non-profit sector (chapter 2). Corporate strategies (which can include digital strategies) then need to be translated into communications strategies. These communications strategies are multi-faceted. They include, for example, harnessing digital technologies (chapters 4, 13, 15); engaging internal stakeholders (chapter 8 and 4); branding (chapters 6, 10, 13 and 16); representing the views of human beneficiaries with respect (chapter 7), and evaluating communications using outcomes-based measures (chapter 9). For INGOs specifically, communications strategies need to support organizational strategy on both an international level and through support of national communications (chapter 13).

The editors seek to build on strong existing works relating to non-profit communications and to avoid duplication. There are guides to different overall areas of strategic PR practice, like Barrell's (2014) book on strategic planning and Lamb's (2011) guide to campaigning and influencing. Nevertheless, when considering PR planning there is little written specifically on how some specialist areas of PR planning, like internal communications, applies to non-profits. Kanter and Fine's (2010) important book on networked non-profits' connections with social media is referred to often in this book, and Miller's (2013) book on *Content Marketing for*

Nonprofits is most useful. Nevertheless, digital communication is constantly evolving which is why there is a chapter on it. There are also fine books and chapters in books from American non-profit specialists that examine non-profit communications in the US. For instance, Waters (2014) important edited collection of scholarly essays that apply theories to communications practice principally (although not exclusively) in the US. Therefore, this book does not have a chapter on the US.

Much can be learned from non-profit communications around the world. This book continues, and furthers, work by others in this field (for instance, Tkalac and Pavicic 2009) by considering INGO communications planning, and by having national perspectives from countries in four continents. Those included are from China, India, Brazil and South Africa. All these countries have important non-profit sectors and their communications work deserves recognition so that learning can applied in other countries. In addition, there are case studies from around the world, including campaigns not only from the UK but also from Azerbaijan, Nepal and West Africa, and INGOs like UNICEF, Save the Children, and Water Aid. Nevertheless, there is potential for many more textbooks in this arena.

A key strength of this book is that it brings together the expertise of practitioners and academics. The importance of bringing together practitioners and academics has been strongly advocated by leading PR academic James Grunig (Waddington 2016) and some prominent practitioners. Stephen Waddington, former President of the Chartered Institute of Public Relations, and Chief Engagement Officer at the global PR consultancy, Ketchum states that 'the relationship between practitioners and academics is critical to public relations becoming more professional' (Waddington 2014). Further, academic scholarship is advanced when grounded on practice according to Grunig (Waddington 2016). Critical PR theorists warn that scholarship risks losing criticality if academia and practice become too interlinked. This is indeed a real risk, but does not preclude mindful collaboration that advances scholarship and understanding.

Career communicators who specialise in the non-profit sector should be supported with current, relevant literature. The work of communicators who specialise in the non-profit sector is extremely demanding. Notably, the *European Communications Monitor* report of 2012 (Zerfass et al. 2012: 24) found that communicators in NPOs reported to have more ethical dilemmas than those in the commercial or public sectors. Dedicated, poorly resourced communicators, operating in the 24/7 communications world can suffer from burn-out (Anonymous 2015). Knowledge builds confidence that in turn helps stress management. Communicators who work in the field of CSR (Corporate Social Responsibility) and sustainability also have pressurised roles. They may, at times, feel torn between loyalties to corporations and causes.

The collection of chapters in this book is designed to contribute to non-profit strategic communications, marketing and business studies pedagogy. Growth in public relations, marketing and business degrees has expanded worldwide. For example, a public relations degree was first introduced at Boston University in 1947, and degree programmes were later introduced into Asia (for instance Japan in

1951 and Taiwan in 1963), Australia (mid-1970s) and in parts of Eastern and Western Europe in the 1980s and 1990s (Watson 2017: 13). PR degree programmes in the UK only numbered four in the late 1980s (Watson 2017). At the time of writing, these have expanded to over 50 recognised degrees by the Chartered Institute of Public Relations (CIPR 2017). There have been sustained calls for non-profit PR to feature more in university curricula. This is from the renowned PR academics, Cutlip, Center and Broom in 1999 (cited by Tkalac and Pavicic 2009); to 21st century critical PR theorists. As marketing and PR come closer together (CIPR 2016) it is helpful for marketing students to gain a deeper understanding of the strategic value of PR. Similarly, business students need to understand the sector too for how can cross-partnerships be built without mutual understanding? For students wishing to go into the sector, or conduct undergraduate or postgraduate research in it, it is important that they can access the perspectives of experts.

Themes in the book

Some of the major themes that span different chapters include the increasing importance of: building trust; NGO relations with the state and corporates; the importance of relationship building across multiple channels; and the pressure on non-profits to demonstrate legitimacy.

The need for non-profit legitimacy in a climate of declining trust

The **legitimacy** of the sector cannot be taken for granted warns Lamb in the next chapter. Legitimacy essentially means the licence to operate and is often used in the context of individual organizations (for instance, by Cornelissen 2014). However, the legitimacy of the non-profit sector has come under increasing scrutiny (Walton et al. 2016; Waters 2014). Further, when corporate organizations' interests jar with campaigns that non-profits run for the benefit of society, corporates can seek to undermine those specific NPOs' legitimacy, states O'Brien in chapter 3.

Trust, as Bruce observes (2011: 201), is 'the source' of the charity sector's 'legitimacy' and as such requires 'vigilance'. Many contributors of the book highlight declining levels of trust in the non-profit sector. Opinion research surveys by Edelman (2017) show declining global trust in NGOs. Specifically, in the US, China, Japan, the UK and Germany, trust levels fell to below 50 per cent in that research. Surveys by Eden Stanley in the UK show that one quarter of the UK public (27%) now believe INGOs are 'open and honest', states Barrell in chapter 13. The findings show, he says, that '75% of the UK's INGO supporters believe, … that corruption prevents aid reaching the people that need it most'. Meanwhile, Sagar et al. observe that journalists in India, perceive NPOs to be disorganised or corrupt (see chapter 14). The levels of trust in NGOs are declining in the UK (Charity Commission 2016), where there is media criticism about issues of corporate governance including fundraising practice and executive pay in the UK, note Chamberlain and Etherington in chapter 2.

Measures to address this creeping scepticism are offered in this book. Lamb outlines arguments that support legitimacy of the non-profit sector and argues that the non-profit sector's role needs to be vigorously espoused. O'Brien identifies different arguments that can be used to undermine NPOs' legitimacy during campaigns about social issues. Having an awareness of these arguments can help non-profit communicators with their issues management. The importance of brand in building trust is discussed in chapter 6. In chapter 16 it is related to the NPO brand histories in South Africa in an era of de-colonising.

The legitimacy of some specific sectors within the non-profit sector has come under fire. For instance, in chapter 10, Law, when considering the communications of housing associations in the UK, points out how housing associations were 'under attack' in the UK in 2015. He then shows how the housing association movement repositioned itself, after research with stakeholders to demonstrate how generating profits supported their social purpose.

The need to make public relations more accountable (Waddington 2014) and the communications non-profits more accountable and transparent has been called for (Kanter and Fine 2010; Kelly 2001). Longley and Nordström (chapter 4), identify how technology, within a corporate digital strategy, can be used to make NPOs more accountable. This is, for instance, with the use of blockchain that releases donations only when specified levels of impact are achieved. Then, in the chapter about case studies (chapter 7), it is argued that there are opportunities for authenticity in the way that NGOs present case studies about the impact of their work.

Nevertheless, much of the criticism of NGOs has been fuelled by issues that related to organizational behaviour, like the way that money has been raised or spent, as Chamberlain and Etherington point out in chapter 2. Management and leadership have an important influence on the development of organizational culture (Mullins with Christy 2016: 542). Hence, reputational management is part of trustees' responsibilities, state Chamberlain and Etherington. Usefully, Chamberlain and Etherington outline lessons in corporate governance. The editors of this book believe that communicators can only systematically influence the way that organizations behave if they are given roles on executive boards – be it as trustees or executives. If communications advice is dependent on 'having the ear' of the chief executive this is more discretionary than debates within a board. Further, relationships between directors of communication and chief executives often vary with the comings and goings of different people who fill those positions.

Relationships with the corporates and the state

Kofi Annan also declared (UN 1999) that with a partnership between NGOs, the private sector, international organizations and governments, 'there is nothing we can take on that we cannot succeed in'. Such partnerships, he predicted, would also involve 'testing … boundaries … in the years ahead'.

The importance of working with the business community was expressed by Annan (UN 1998) with the rationale that 'Markets are global, while governments remain local'. This approach has been taken forward by UN Sustainability Goals for 2030, as Barrell points out in chapter 13 when observing the increasing importance of corporate partnerships with INGOs. At a specific national level, these goals have, in part, encouraged the growth in corporate volunteering programmes in Brazil (see chapter 17 by Nassar, Carbonaro and Tamura). Many large Brazilian companies have invested millions of dollars in these initiatives. The authors also point out that, volunteers from the corporates can act as conduits between society and businesses, thereby increasing mutual understanding. The importance of a good fit between corporates and NGOs is highlighted both in chapter 17 and in the chapter on corporate partnerships. Indeed, 'a test to fit' is introduced by Read and Diehl in chapter 5. These authors also identify the wide range of different corporate partnership types. Ground-breaking legislation in India, which mandates that companies over a certain size invest in CSR, is explained by Sagar et al. in chapter 14. Social enterprise PR is explored in chapter 12 where Nordstrom argues that social enterprises sit 'between the non-profit and the business sectors'.

However, relationships with corporates carry risks and may be antagonistic. Potential problems of partnerships are identified by Read and Diehl in chapter 5. Given these risks, Chamberlain and Etherington, in chapter 3, highlight the importance of trustees vetting such partnerships. Furthermore, the risk of corporates undermining NGO legitimacy when non-profits campaign about social or environmental issues that present uncomfortable truths for big business, is examined by Michaela O'Brien in chapter 4.

Lamb identifies different perspectives on the rationale for and against state support in chapter 1. These perspectives vary according to political orientation, and an understanding of these perceptions will help communicators when lobbying politicians. The relationship with the state is also explored in China (chapter 15).

Relationship management across multiple channels

Extending reach and deepening relationships is intrinsic to many of the chapters. Both the chapters on agile digital communications and the communications in China highlight the importance of using the digital sphere to build and nurture meaningful relationships with supporters, and to amplify impact through influencers' channels. The role of digital media in building relations with the public at large is considered in a variety of chapters. This is significant given that Lang (2013: 1) believes 'the most salient source of legitimacy of the non-government sector is public engagement'. Edelman's Trust Barometer 2018, identifies the need to 'create a sense of community', to address an overall decline in trust in NGOs.

The importance of digital communications for INGOs is outlined by Barrell in his chapter on INGO communications planning in chapter 13. He notes that

> Promoting good practice, offering skills training, or providing content, have been more effective strategies than more 'top-down' rigid approaches. The

benefits of this approach are obvious in the case of social media, which relies on the energy and engagement of individuals who need the freedom to find their own way in to the online conversations.

Digital innovation is highlighted across the globe. For instance, in Brazil, the Scout movement launched the *Play the Call* game (Alencar 2012), that rewards children for changing the world for good. Players can share their completed tasks via social networks.

As well as highlighting the importance of digital communications, the contributors also identify how off-line channels can be effective. In India, fascinating use of folk cultural traditions has been made to boost grass-root communications, as is identified in chapter 14. In China, face-to-face meetings with officials are crucial.

Pressure to prove: outcomes-based evaluation for legitimacy

An ability to get things done more effectively than states also fosters confidence in NGOs (Lang 2014). A key role of public relations is to communicate the benefits of NPOs' activities (Barrell 2014; Brill and Marrocco 2012). The legitimacy of non-profit work, has to be communicated to stakeholders ranging from external audiences like state officials and journalists; to connected stakeholders like donors and beneficiaries; to internal stakeholders like staff and volunteers. Sustainable communications need careful resourcing and planning.

The impact of communications also needs careful measurement. The importance of evaluated attitudinal and behavioural change that results from communications, rather than the outputs of communications (such as posts or press releases) is stressed by Orla Graham in chapter 10 on evaluation. The guiding principle is relevant for internal communications (IC) measurement, states Liam FitzPatrick in chapter 8.

Acknowledgements

We thank Amy Laurens, Routledge's senior editor for her belief in, and encouragement of, the concept of the book. We thank Routledge's anonymous reviewers who helped shape the structure of the book. We also thank Sophia Levine, Olivia Hatt, Kris Wischenkamper, Jess Harrison, Alex Atkinson and Laura Hussey at Routledge. We are also most appreciative of recommendations from Professor Anne Gregory, Vicky Browning, Adam Powell and Kate Steele.

This book would not exist without the expert contributions of our distinguished authors. We thank our contributors for generously sharing their expertise from around the world and from different parts of the Third Sector. We also thank their families and friends who, in turn, supported this endeavour.

Thanks also go to all lecturing contributors to, and students of, the 'Third Sector PR' at the University of Greenwich. Guest lecturers who particularly informed the structure of the book included Kate Sloan on branding, and David Hamilton on internal communications. Tove Nordström, who has contributed two chapters to this book, is one of the course's alumni. Professor Stephen Lee has added to the authors' broader marketing approach.

We have also appreciated the support of many people including: Beth Andlaw, Alan Anstead, Lynn Appelbaum, Ezri Carlebach, Bruce Cronin, Denise Fairhurst, Kevin Kwok, Alistair Morrison, Jane Ray, Noah Shaw, Jon Sibson, Jason Suttie, Roger Trollope and Simon Wheale.

We warmly thank our respective spouses, Kevin and Tina, for their insightful editorial advice and caring support. Nicky also thanks her former teachers including: Mrs Doris West, Dr Rachel Harrison and Professor Ulrich Kratz.

References

Alencar, V. (2012, 4 December). A brincadeira é a única maneira de mudar o mundo. Available at: http://porvir.org/a-brincadeira-e-unica-maneira-de-mudar-mundo

Anheier, H. (2006) *Nonprofit Organizations: Theory, Management, Policy.* London and New York: Routledge.

Anonymous (2015) I Live and Breathe my Charity Work, but Burnout was a Wake-up Call. *The Guardian.* Available at: www.theguardian.com/voluntary-sector-network/2015/jul/26/live-breathe-charity-work-but-burnout-wake-up-call

Barrell, J. (2014) *Make it Matter: Creating Communication Strategies in the Non-profit Sector.* London: CharityComms.

Brill, P. and Marrocco, C. (2012) Not-for-profit Public Relations, in A. Theaker, *The Public Relations Handbook.* 4th edn. London and New York: Routledge, (Chapter 18) pp.387–410.

Bruce, I. (2011) *Charity Marketing: Delivering Income, Services and Campaigns.* London: ICSA.

Charity Commission (2016) Public Trust and Confidence in Charities. Available at: www.gov.uk/government/uploads/system/uploads/attachment_data/file/532104/Public_trust_and_confidence_in_charities_2016.pdf

CIPR (2016) CIPR Reports on the 'State of the Profession' in 2016. Press release. 23 March. Available at: http://newsroom.cipr.co.uk/cipr-reports-on-the-state-of-the-profession-in-2016/

CIPR (2017) University Course List. Available at: www.cipr.co.uk/content/training-qualifications/cipr-recognised-degrees/university-course-list

Cornelissen, J. (2014) *Corporate Communication: A Guide to Theory & Practice.* 4th edn. Los Angeles; London; New Delhi; Singapore, and Washington DC: Sage.

Davies, T. (2013) *NGOs: A New History of Transnational Civil Society.* London: Hurst.

Edelman (2017) Edelman Trust Barometer 2017: Executive Summary. Edelman. Available at: https://www.edelmanergo.com/fileadmin/user_upload/Studien/2017_Edelman_Trust_Barometer_Executive_Summary.pdf

Edelman (2018) *Edelman Trust Barometer 2018: Global Report.* Edelman. Available at: http://cms.edelman.com/sites/default/files/2018-01/2018_Edelman_Trust_Barometer_Global_Report_Jan.PDF

Kanter, B. and Fine, A. (2010) *The Networked Nonprofit: Connecting with Social Media to Drive Change.* San Francisco: John Wiley & Sons.

Kelly, K. (2001) Stewardship: The Fifth Step in the Public Relations Process, in R. Heath, *Handbook of Public Relations.* Thousand Oaks; London, and New Delhi: Sage.

Lamb, B. (2011) *The Good Guide to Campaigning and Influencing.* London: NCVO.

Lang, S. (2013) *NGOs, Civil Society and the Public Sphere*. Cambridge and New York: Cambridge University Press.

Miller, K.L. (2013) *Content Marketing for NonProfits: A Communications Map for Engaging Your Community, Becoming a Favorite Cause, and Raising More Money*. San Francisco: Wiley.

Mullins, L.J., with Christy, G. (2016) *Management & Organisational Behaviour*. 11th edn. Harlow, England: Pearson.

NCVO (2017) Top Facts about Small Charities: Results from the Almanac 2017. NCVO. 21 June. Available at: https://data.ncvo.org.uk/wp-content/uploads/2015/06/Almanac_2017_Top_facts_small_charities_final.pdf

OECD (n.d.) OECD.Stat: Trade Union Density. Available: https://stats.oecd.org/Index.aspx?DataSetCode=UN_DEN. Accessed 3 September 2017

Smith, D.H. and Ting Zhao, with Jun Xu (2017) Post-Mao Chinese Nonprofit Legitimation Strategies. Paper presented at ARNOVA Asia Conference, Beijing, China, 6–7 June.

Tkalac, A. and Pavicic, J. (2009) Nongovernmental Organizations and International Public Relations, in K. Sriramesh and D. Vercic (eds) *The Global Public Relations Handbook: Theory, Research and Practice*. New York and London: Routledge, pp.807–821.

UN (1998) Secretary-General Describes Emerging Era in Global Affairs with Growing Role for Civil Society Alongside Established Institutions. Press release SG/SM/6638. 14 July. Available at: www.un.org/press/en/1998/19980714.sgsm6638.html

UN (1999) Secretary-General Calls Partnership of NGOs, Private Sector, International Organizations and Governments Powerful Partnership for Future. Press release SG/SM/6973. 29 April. Available at: https://www.un.org/press/en/1999/19990429.SGSM6973.html

Waddington, S. (2014) Academia and Practice: Working Together Hallmark of Maturing Profession. 6 May. Blog. Available at: www.bledcom.com/archive-news/blog-stephen-waddington

Waddington, S. (2016) Exploring the Relationship between Public Relations Academics and Practitioners. 27 June. Available at: http://wadds.co.uk/2016/06/27/exploring-relationship-public-relations-academics-practitioners/

Walton, O., Davies, T., Thrandardottir, E. and Keating, V. (2016) Understanding Contemporary Challenges to INGO Legitimacy: Integrating Top-Down and Bottom-Up Perspectives. *Voluntas*27: 2764–2786.

Waters, R.D. (ed.) (2014) *Public Relations in the Nonprofit Sector: Theory and Practice* (Vol. 6). London and New York: Routledge.

Watson, T. (2017) Public Relations Origins: Definitions and History, in R. Tench and L. Yeomans (eds), *Exploring Public Relations: Global Strategic Communication*. 4th edn. Pearson, pp. 3–19.

Zerfass, Z., Verčič, D., Verhoeven, P., Moreno, A. and Tench, R. (2012) *European Communications Monitor: Challenges and Competencies for Strategic Communication. Results of an Empirical Survey in 42 Countries*. Brussels: EACD/EUPRERA.

PART I

Civil society, governance and issues

1

NON-PROFIT PR AS THE VOICE OF CIVIL SOCIETY?

Brian Lamb

Introduction

A crucial component of civil society is the non-profit sector. Public relations (PR) contributes to the understanding of the role of non-profits in society by communicating the mission, values and aspirations of non-profits to the public, government and market.

In reflecting the needs and aspirations of civil society PR practitioners need to understand the role of the non-profit sector, how this has developed, and why non-profits' future role cannot be taken for granted. PR practitioners also need an awareness of the sector's values and debates about the ethos and impact of social marketisation.

By drawing attention to social problems PR practitioners highlight unmet need, raise public awareness and mobilise public opinion to achieve positive social and political change. Effective PR creates the conditions for securing additional services, legal rights, resources and improved conditions for non-profits' beneficiaries and ensures entitlements are claimed and maintained.

To achieve this PR needs to establish the legitimacy of non-profits as civil society's organized voice. PR promotes the effectiveness of non-profit provision to meet the need it has identified and provision it has created through enhanced entitlements. It also secures acceptance of the sector's moral legitimacy through mobilising and reflecting the values of civil society.

The concept of civil society can be viewed as having three elements. One is **an associational life** of people coming together in groups separate from state and markets, which is central to the debate about why the sector exists at all and its role. A second is the notion of developing the **good society**. The third is the idea of a **public sphere**, where debate and deliberation about what constitutes a good society and the public interest takes place (Edwards 2009, 2011). Defining the role of non-profits and their relationship to civil society is a major area of debate (Wagner 2012) and as Garton (2009: 23) argues, 'there is no single purpose, form or mode of behaviour which captures the essence of the sector'.

Non-profits' role and the contribution of Public Relations

How we think of the definition and role of non-profits in relation to civil society will significantly influence how we see a good society being achieved and how it is promoted. One of the most influential definitions of the non-profit sector (Salamon 2014) suggests that to be part of civil society an organization must be:

self-governed;
private, independent from the state, market and informal sector;
creating social value but not be non-profit making or reinvest profits in producing social value;
non-compulsory.

Further, as (Garton 2009) notes, if it is a charity it should be *non-party political*.

There are different views of the definition of the non-profit sector. Salamon (2014) defines the sector mainly in terms of its economic contribution. Others have built on the idea of democratic civil renewal as non-profits' unique and defining contribution to public life in civil society though associations (Putnam 2000; Edwards 2009; Wagner 2012). In the UK charities have been the predominant organizational expression of the non-profit sector (Garton 2009) and 'values driven', in that they are 'primarily motivated by the desire to further social, environmental or cultural objectives rather than make a profit' (Cabinet Office 2006: 8). Often the concepts of third sector, voluntary organization and social enterprise have been used interchangeably and in doing so have created confusion (Wagner 2012).

Growth of the non-profit sector

Salamon (1987) and Garton (2009) have summarised the main **theories for nonprofit sector growth** from which this author has derived **associated PR strategies** (see Table 1.1).

Non-profits' expanding role

Most characterisations of non-profits agree that they should not been seen as residual, simply filling in the gaps left by state and market (Kendall 2009). Hybrid organizational forms that span elements of civil society, market and state are not easily defined as belonging to any one category, having developed in response to the changing demands of government and markets. Billis (2010) argues these different hybrid organizations can still be considered part of the sector as they still

TABLE 1.1 Theories of Non-profit Growth and PR Strategies

Theory (from Salamon and Garton)	Potential PR strategy for the non-profit sector (from Lamb)
Market failure – public goods are not easily provided for by the market which the non-profit sector steps in to provide.	Focus on the gap in provision/market failure for public goods and how the sector can fill this. Focus will be on stressing how non-profit values and approach differ from private market solutions.
Contract failure – non-profits are thought not to have been corrupted by the profit incentive or are a better proxy for demand and therefore are more trusted to provide public goods.	Focus on the unique role of the sector in not being driven by the profit motive and build public trust and confidence in providing public services with added value.
Government failure – public goods are not provided by the state or there is a failure of social rights to fully meet need.	Focus on the gaps in provision, what is needed to fill this by enhancing rights, regulation or provision and promote the sector's role as a change and delivery agent which then delivers the services commissioned as a result.
Voluntary failure – the state steps in to support the sector only after voluntary sector responses on their own have failed because of the lack of capacity to deal with the problem as part of civil society.	Focus on the need for greater state or private sector support so that the sector can support civil society and increase social goods. Civil society does not have the capacity to address issues on its own but needs to work with the state as a partner.

Ideas about non-profits' origins often reflect one or a number of these theories but only taken together do they suggest a complete explanation of the development and role of the sector (Garton 2009).

encapsulate values in service provision organizations which also reflect wider civil society values not just market or state driven ones.

The dichotomous approach which assumes 'thickening state' equals 'thinning civil society' (Eberly 2000: 13) is not really consistent with the development of the sector. Recent historical studies have argued for a 'moving frontier' between state and non-profits in which 'the state and the voluntary sector have complemented one another' (Hilton et al. 2010: 1). The UK non-profit sector has largely been defined by its relationship to the development of state provision (Alcock 2010). There are also good reasons to expect state and non-profit provision to grow in parallel. Both are responses to the same social pressures for expanding public goods. The state brings the ability to generate resources while the non-profit sector the capacity to deliver services, support and expertise (Salamon 1996; Murdock 2009).

Growth in different directions

Salamon (2012: 15) has characterised non-profit activity as potentially being pulled in different directions. This is summarised and reframed to draw out the PR implications in the third column of Table 1.2.

TABLE 1.2 Voluntary Sector Impulses

Type of impulse	Context	Strategy and style of organization and support groups relevant for PR practice
'Voluntarism'	Social problems rooted in disadvantage. Support to overcome individual problems.	PR stress on self-help, and mainly pastoral care and support on a temporary basis. Dependant on volunteers, donors or members.
'Civic activism'	Social problems are a result of power structures which can be challenged with the support of the sector which engages with citizens.	PR stress on participation and advocacy. Community organizing though citizens and community assets.
'Professionalism'	Social problems rooted in particular individual's challenges and problems which are addressed through the sector providing services and support.	PR stress on culture of performance management, stress professionalism in messaging and governance by professional regulation. Established services as part of statutory infrastructure. Often supported by government contracts or funding.
'Commercialism'	Problems rooted in ineffectiveness or inefficiencies in current markets for care or support.	Market mechanisms to achieve social positive social outcomes. PR stress on sound business management and social entrepreneurship are harnessed to social ends through the production of social revenues using optimum business practices.

PR strategies to promote greater voluntarism or civic activism may differ markedly to those promoting professional service delivery or social enterprise. However these activities are not necessarily mutually exclusive as human service organizations following a professional impulse may also be involved in civic activism (Han 2017; Hasenfeld et al. 2014).

Values in the non-profit sector and civil society

Across the spectrum of non-profit activity there is evidence of values which reflect the ethos associated with civil society. Survey research in the USA found that advocacy and service organizations share values such as being 'productive, effective, enriching, empowering, responsive, reliable, and caring' (Salamon et al. 2012: 4) which appeal to civil society sentiment of respect for the individual and their welfare. Edwards (2009) also argues that whichever notion of civil society is subscribed to, all share a notion that collective, creative, and value-based action provides an essential counterweight to individualism, cynicism, and the overbearing influence of state authority. These values are so powerful in appealing to public sentiment that different groups with different visions of the good society will contest for ownership of them as Salamon (2014: 5) argues: 'Diverse and often conflicting interest groups, from left-wing social movements to conservative think tanks, claim proprietorship of the third sector concept because of the emotively desirable connotations it evokes, such as public purpose, freedom, altruism, civic initiative, spontaneity, or solidarity.'

Critiques of the non-profits' role in social marketization

The role of non-profits in promoting civil society values has been questioned where social marketisation, through contracting out state services to non-profits, has been perceived to undermine voluntary ethos including the following.

1. **Lack of public accountability** with '(t)he tendency, especially for service provision organisations to lack accountability to the public and be driven by staff and funder interests' (Calhoun 2011: 318)
2. **Compromised capacity to advocate**. In service organizations 'Advocacy goals are focused primarily on brokering resources and promoting the organization rather than substantive policy change or client representation' (Mosley et al. 2012: 841)
3. **Undermined independence**: professionals working in human services fear a greater engagement with state commissioned services necessitates subservience and a lack of independence to advocate for their clients (Glennon 2017)
4. **In-equality of voice**: 'individuals and groups who have fewer resources or who are already less advantaged in society are less likely to become involved in voluntary associations to promote their interests, satisfy their needs, or make changes in policy favourable to them' (Kamerāde 2015: 2)
5. **Lack of enhanced political participation**: 'a very fragile empirical basis' (Decker 2014: 45) for the assumption that countries with higher levels of third sector participation also have higher levels of political participation generally.

Does social marketisation shackle non-profit advocacy?

Overall there is little evidence that social marketisation – in the form of contracting for services – reduces advocacy in human service providers. An empirical study of non-profit advocacy in the UK concluded that 'social marketization is positively related to the influence of third sector organisations on government policies, and can strengthen the development of civil society, rather than erode it' (Han 2017: 1223). Hasenfeld and Garrow (2012: 93) found that the 'degree of reliance on government funding does not predict whether organizations will engage in social-benefit advocacy, organizational advocacy, or both'. Similar research from the USA and UK confirms this view (Smith and Pekkanen 2012; Lamb 2014). Human service organizations have been slower to use advocacy but are now finding it a 'necessary way of coping with the uncertain, complex environments in which they operate' (Almog-Bar and Schmid 2014: 28). Further larger organizations with greater numbers of staff and volunteers can be more active in advocacy and PR because more resources equal greater capacity. Government funding has also provided an incentive to advocate as a means to protect funding (Mosley 2010: 71).

The role of the state; and making markets through advocacy

The state sets specific legal boundaries and regulates the limits of engagement in the political process for charities through charity law and the regulation of advocacy and campaigning which can be seen in countries with common law jurisdictions such as the UK, USA, Canada and Australia (Garton 2009). Therefore the overall regulatory context, contracting regimes and the acceptability of advocacy within specific legislatures will influence the range and focus of issues taken up, style of advocacy and campaigning undertaken and willingness to risk upsetting funding arrangements (Hemmings 2017; Hasenfeld and Garrow 2012; Lamb 2014; Mosley 2012). What is allowed as acceptable activity will change depending on the relative power relationships between the sector and state fought over through different concepts of the role of non-profits in civil society (Garton 2009; Lamb 2014).

As Macmillan (2015) suggests, there is an active process of 'making markets' or claiming political space. Actors with different positions, values and power, including the state, private sector and non-profits will seek to construct and shape markets for services and political space to their best advantage. PR can play a crucial role in supporting and advocating for new rights, protections and regulations which result in obligations to provide public goods or entitlements which the non-profit sector can then meet through its service provision or expertise (Lamb 2010; Salamon and Geller 2008).

Therefore non-profits advocating for their particular beneficiary group can also lead to the sector collectively enhancing the public realm through expanding the case for services, including non-profits providing them; and further, by improving the quality and accountability of public policy through public scrutiny of social problems (Fung 2003; Lamb 2010). While there may often be tactical tensions and contractual issues between pursuing enhanced rights and providing services there is no insurmountable conflict between advocacy and service provision. PR plays a crucial role in creating the political and public will for change.

Role of non-profit in mobilising public opinion and securing legitimacy and moral authority

Mobilising opinion

Social problems are constructed through the mobilisation of public opinion, as Mauss and Wolfe (1977: 2) argue:

There is no such thing as a social problem, until enough people, with enough power in the society, agree that there is. Social problems are produced by public opinion, not by particular social conditions.

Mobilising public opinion in civil society requires a central role for PR in promoting social issues but also the sector's role in then addressing the problems it has identified; 'since it is usually through voluntary organizations and the media that citizen's carry on their conversations' (Edwards 2009: 83). As Calhoun (2011: 316) argues 'Public communication shapes which civil society organizations are formed, from health clinics to Girl Scout troops, and what issues they address, from poverty to the environment.' Political consensus is often needed to secure and deliver significant social reforms and PR will play a crucial role in shaping that debate and securing the political or public will necessary, especially where there is diversity of opinion in civil society. Confronting society-wide issues often requires a greater mobilisation of public and political will than can be leveraged by civil society acting on its own (Edwards 2011).

Competing value sets in areas such as social entitlements, rights, environmental and animal welfare may make it difficult to deliver a public consensus on some issues, however. Therefore as well as providing the social glue for civil society non-profits can also be part of its polarisation where non-profits have taken diametrically opposed positions on fundamental issues (Grønbjerg 2017). Cutting across these different discourses has been a strong civil society purism, echoing de Tocqueville, which sees civil society as 'a market free zone', comprising 'a non-governmental space of associations in which a complex plurality of individuals, groups, organisations, civic initiatives and social movement cultivate virtues' (Keane 2005: 26). Within this debate the left has often seen civil society discourse reflecting the voice of the oppressed and as a forum for social solidarity with a critique of market and state failures. While the right has rested more on a Hayekian view (Macmillan 2013) in which the individual should be left free to pursue their own needs and in doing so help civil society achieve wider social cohesion through the creation of a spontaneous social order separate from the state.

At times it may therefore be in the competition between ideas and values that non-profits' contribution to public debate is made rather than in securing a singular uncontested vision of the good society (Edwards 2011) or being its only voice.

Building the legitimacy and moral authority of non-profits

A crucial element of any communication strategy is the legitimacy and moral authority of the non-profit organization. Xu and Ngai (2011) examined how **moral resources and political capital** promote civic values, which can inform an understanding of how to gain public support for non-profits. Moral resource relates to the available values which could be chosen by non-profits. Political capital is the earned credibility that will improve or enhance the NGOs' status, position or access to resources in the existing political system.

MORAL RESOURCE AND POLITICAL CAPITAL

Xu and Ngai (2011) identify two types of moral resource available to non-profits.

Moral Resource I: Kant's central insight that morality consisted of the question 'What ought I to do?', Moral Resource-I is the basis of NGOs' confidence to act on the basis of its values and is self-chosen.

Moral Resource II: refers to the morals or values that are well accepted by the given society and therefore important for the sector to be aligned with to gain salience with the public or commissioners of services.

Two types of political capital are identified.

Political Capital I refers to the political capital mainly ascribed to the status that the NGOs inherited throughout history or what in PR terms might be termed their underlying brand value.

Political Capital II refers to the political capital that the NGOs earned through their current work, which in PR terms could be seen as their current reputational value.

'[T]he combined force of Moral Resource I and Political Capital I and II may enhance an NGO's ability to promote the public sphere and thus contribute to the development of civil society' (Xu and Ngai 2011: 261).

Moral Resource 1 is important but needs to align with Moral Resource II to gain leverage in society. Moral Resource II also helps grassroots organizations with little Political Capital I to win Political Capital II, which is a crucial factor for their growth by showing they are consonant with prevailing civil society values and can authentically represent them. This will entail appealing to commonly held values (Common Cause Foundation 2016) in civil society to create the public will to act.

Threats to the legitimacy of the non-profit sector

Legitimacy and support for the sector can be undermined if the non-profit ethos of independence from special interests is undermined (Tonkis and Passey 1999). Disputes about Chief Executive remuneration, fundraising practices, contracting for services, and the limits and role of campaigning are informed by underlying assumptions about the appropriate role of non-profits and their ethos. Because non-profits interface with the state and market, the sector 'cannot afford to be captured by these other institutions if it is to hold them accountable for their actions and fulfil its role as the carrier of different norms and values' (Edwards 2011: 8). It has therefore been argued that 'the ability of civil society to advocate on behalf of poor and vulnerable populations hinges on two factors: the extent to which the public sphere is independent of government and the extent to which civil society is protected from market forces' (Hasenfeld and Garrow 2012: 318).

Concepts of civil society

A brief examination of modern concepts of civil society which emerged in the late 18th century through Smith, Kant and Hegel, though the idea stretches back through Locke and Hobbes to Aristotle (Laine 2014), can inform current PR practice. Concepts of civil society reflect a recognition of the importance of an arena of human interaction separate from the state, market and family. Hegel argued that civil society was separate and balanced the diverse range of human needs which are separate from the family and state (Laine 2014). From Hegel there is a divergence of thinking about civil society with very different conceptualisations of its role and values.

Alexis de Tocqueville focused on the importance of civilian and political associations as a counterbalance to the individualism of the market and the centralization of the state (Laine 2014). The effectiveness of civil society was as an 'independent eye of society' (de Tocqueville 2014 [1844]), an aspiration which has been echoed in many justifications for the non-profit role in holding government and markets to account. Putnam (2000) supported de Tocqueville's stress on social associations as the core of civil society and thus of democracy. Social capital created by these associations is an essential element of any society as civic virtue is fostered when embedded in a network of reciprocal social relations (Putnam 2000).

Putnam argues that voluntary associations (wider than just non-profits) are distinctive in their capacity to function as repositories for social capital. They are involved in a virtuous circle by establishing trust as they instil habits of co-operation, solidarity and public spiritedness, which helps develop the skills required for political activity (Putnam 2000). Associations also provide a place for those without power and resources to promote their interests and thus protect themselves from the 'tyranny of majority' (de Tocqueville 2014 [1844]: 114). This concept of civil society has underpinned the debate about the role of civil society as an independent force (Wagner 2012).

Conversely Marx saw civil society as separate but also an expression of bourgeois class interest which works with the state to oppress the rest of society (Laine 2014). Gramsci (1971) later defined a greater space for ideology in securing acceptance of and justifying capitalist hegemony in civil society. In doing so he provided the basis for seeing civil society as more than the transmitter of a dominant ideology but a public space which could be contested and stressed the importance of understanding how a common culture underwrites consent to the prevailing values and norms in society.

Habermas (1991) developed Gramsci's ideas, conceiving civil society as a 'public sphere', a coercion-free arena for discussion and mutual learning, detached from the state and the economy. People came together to form a common discourse and in doing so compel the state to justify itself before public opinion. The mobilisation of public opinion becomes a critical force on behalf of civil society through promoting discussion and criticism.

Early English socialist thinking, with roots in the co-operative and trade union movements, saw working people self-organizing as a counterbalance to capitalist society. Through friendly societies and trade unions they sought to create an alternative civil society promoting self-help and protection from and reform of the market using their collective power and voice (Alcock 2010). Later Socialism and Labourism sat alongside Liberal reform movements in seeing the state as a potentially helpful tool in achieving the needs of civil society not met by the market; even though socialist and working class organizations were critical of specific aspects of Edwardian Liberal reforms of social conditions (Gladstone 1999).

The Keynesian reform of the welfare state recognised a key role for the state exemplified through the Beveridge Report (Beveridge 1942) introducing enhanced social insurance measures. Civil society laid claims on the state and market by ameliorating its worst elements and providing protections. Beveridge saw a continued role for voluntary action coupled with state action but also that independence was central to organizations performing this role adequately (Beveridge 1948). Post Beveridge, Keynesian demand management of the economy (Diamond 2004) was used as a means of reconciling economic efficiency with social rights, as well as legal and political ones (Marshall 1950) and gave a positive role to the state in securing civil society's needs. The post war welfare consensus, and its associated notion of a rapprochement between the state and civil society, came under threat from the 1960s as the post war consensus on state welfare started to unravel (Timmins 1995; Gladstone 1999). The welfare consensus was challenged by a *neo-liberal tradition* which wanted to see a reduced role for the state and a return to a greater focus on individual responsibility, with non-profits as an alternative to state bureaucracy and a stress on voluntarism from the 1970s onwards (Crowson 2011).

Two differing concepts of non-profits' role in civil society have developed from elements of these traditions. A *partnership model* (left of centre) which sees civil society and the state working together to mitigate the effects of the market and a *neoliberal model* (right of centre) which envisages civil society as fundamentally separate from the state with a stress on market solutions and a focus on individualism.

These different concepts are vital background knowledge for PR in crafting representations to governments depending on whether they are left or right of centre.

There are at times overlaps and tensions between these approaches as partnership approaches have used market mechanisms and neo liberal approaches have continued state support (Alcock et al. 2012, 2016; Kendall 2009) but the distinction captures an emphasis in the state's relationship towards the sector (see Table 1.3).

Conclusion

Non-profit PR can help shape and mobilise public and political will to secure major change while promoting non-profits' role within civil society as its organized voice. However if the public loses faith in non-profits' championing of a civil society ethos and feels the sector has lost connection with the communities it represents then the legitimacy to be the voice of civil society will become more

TABLE 1.3 Different Models of Non-profits' Role

Partnership model emphasis	Neoliberal model emphasis
A social investment state working with civil society to meet needs (Giddens 1998), leading to a partnership between state and sector (Deakin 1996) with an emphasis on what works, not who provides. Exemplified by the early years of the UK New Labour Government 1997–2010.	'Big Society'" as an expression of civil societies caring and associative impulse – but this is separate from the state. Exemplified by the UK Coalition Government in 2010–2015 with a greater stress on the concept of civil society not third society (Alcock 2016)
Non-profits and state work together in a partnership with a strategic unity within the sector around this enhanced role (Alcock 2010).	The State, by dint of its desire to regulate and centralise, disables the creativity, self-reliance and the drive of individuals (Macmillan 2013) and their desire to support others in the community.
Relationships with the sector characterised as 'hyperactive mainstreaming' (Kendall 2009) because of integration of non-profits into major areas of service provision and democratic renewal.	Greater emphasis on non-service providing organizations as the authentic voice of the sector. A reduction in core financial support, (Glennon et al. 2017; Lamb 2014), with more contracts and fewer grants (Crowson 2011).
Non-profit sector is embedded in civil society and therefore trusted in the delivery of social welfare and widening participation. State works with the sector to identify and address social needs and extending rights.	Civil society and voluntary activity is undermined by close association with the state. State encourages market based approach to commissioning or supports self-help (Crowson 2011).
Civil society needs help to articulate and represent those without a voice and solve problems. Government has a role to support non-profits to articulate social issues and help meet them (HM Treasury 2005).	Partnership between sector and state reduces non-profits to a mouthpiece of the state which pays to lobby itself and interest group's secure greater access to public goods at the expense of others.
Implemented through an expanded definition of charitable activity (Garton 2009), the expansion of grants, but also more contracting and a supportive partnership regime through the Office of the Third Sector. Voluntary sector compact to help support and regulate the new partnership, some delegation to local accountability (Kendall 2010; Alcock 2012).	Implemented by rolling back state support to the sector through contracts for services, reduced funding (Eikenberry 2009, Hasenfeld and Garrow 2012). Office of Civil Society. Greater focus on 'authentic voluntary' civil society partners, delegation to local structures and less national accountability.

contested. Non-profits need to understand, support and shape the vibrant dissatisfaction of civil society when confronted by social injustice and unmet need. In doing so the sector supports the development of new entitlements and services central to the achievement of this aim. The challenge for non-profit PR is to successfully frame that conversation so that the sector's role and contribution is understood and the basis for its future growth and impact is sustained and supported by the public, state and market. This is the fundamental role for PR within the context of modern non-profit development and practice.

Discussion questions

1. Can non-profits be the voice of civil society?
2. Why does how we define civil society matter for PR?
3. How could the theory of moral resources be relevant for how we think about PR strategies?
4. Can we define a core set of values or ways of working which define non-profit organizations?
5. Do you think that civil society organizations should work with the state or independently from them?
6. Are service provision and advocacy compatible for non-profit organizations?

References

Alcock, P. (2010) A strategic unity: Defining the third sector in the UK. *Voluntary Sector Review*, 1(1): 5–24.
Alcock, P., Kendall, J. and Parry, J. (2012) From the Third Sector to the Big Society: Consensus or contention in the 2010 UK general election? *Voluntary Sector Review*, 3(3): 347–363.
Alcock, P. (2016) From partnership to the Big Society: The third sector policy regime in the UK. *Nonprofit Policy Forum*, 7(2): 95–116.
Almog-Bar, M. and Schmid, H. (2014) Advocacy activities of non-profit human service organizations: A critical review. *Nonprofit and Voluntary Sector Quarterly*, 43(1): 11–35.
Beveridge, W. (1942) *Social Insurance and Allied Services*, Cmd. 6404 and Cmd. 6405. London: HMSO.
Beveridge, W. (1948) *Voluntary Action: A Report on Methods of Social Advance*. New York: Macmillan.
Billis, D. (2010) *Hybrid Organizations and the Third Sector: Challenges for Practice, Theory and Policy*. London: Palgrave Macmillan.
Calhoun, C. (2011) Civil society and the public sphere. In Edwards, M. (ed.), *The Oxford Handbook of Civil Society*. Oxford: Oxford University Press.
Common Cause Foundation. (2016) *Perceptions Matter: The Common Cause UK Values Survey*. London.
Crowson, N. J. (2011) Introduction: The voluntary sector in 1980s Britain. *Contemporary British History*, 25(4): 491–498.
Deakin, N. (1996) *Meeting the Challenge of Change: Voluntary Action into the 21st Century- Report of the Commission on the Future of the Voluntary Sector*. London: NCVO.
Decker, P. (2014) Tocqueville did not write about soccer clubs: Participation in voluntary associations and political involvement. In Freise, M. & Hallmann, T. *Modernizing Democracy? Associations and Associating in the 21st Century*. New York: Springer, 45–58.
De Toqueville, A. (1956 [1844]) *Democracy in America*. Heffner, D. (ed.) Mentor Edition.
Diamond, P. (ed.) (2004) *New Labour's Old Roots*. Imprint Academic.
Edwards, M. (2009) *Civil Society*. Cambridge: Polity.

Edwards, M. (ed.) (2011) *The Oxford Handbook of Civil Society*. Oxford: Oxford University Press.

Eberly, D. E. (2000) The meanings, origins, applications of civil society. In Eberly (ed.) *The Essential Civil Society Reader: The Classic Essays*, pp. 3–29. Maryland: Rowman & Littlefield.

Eikenberry, A. M. (2009) Refusing the market: A democratic discourse for voluntary and non-profit organizations. *Nonprofit and Voluntary Sector Quarterly*, 38(4): 582–596.

Fung, A. (2003) Associations and democracy: Between theories, hopes, and realities. *Annual Review of Sociology*, 29: 515–539.

Garton, J. (2009) *The Regulation of Organised Civil Society*. Oxford: Hart Publishing.

Giddens, A. (1998) The Third Way. *The Renewal of Democracy*. Cambridge: Polity Press.

Gladstone, D. (ed.) (1999) Before Beveridge: Welfare before the welfare state. *Civitas*, 47.

Glennon, R., Hannibal, C. and Meehan, J. (2017) The impact of a changing financial climate on a UK local charitable sector: voices from the front line. *Public Money & Management*, 37(3): 197–204.

Gramsci, A. (1971) *Selections from The Prison Notebooks*. New York: International Publishers.

Grønbjerg, K. and Prakash, A. (2017) Advances in research on non-profit advocacy and civic engagement. *Voluntas*, 28: 877.

Habermas, J. (1991 [1962]) *The Structural Transformation of the Public Sphere: An Inquiry into a Category of Bourgeois Society*. Cambridge: MIT Press.

Han, J. (2017) Social marketisation and policy influence of third sector organisations: Evidence from the UK. *Voluntas*, 28: 1209.

Hasenfeld, Y. and Garrow, E. E. (2012) Nonprofit human-service organizations, social rights, and advocacy in a neoliberal welfare state. *Social Service Review*, 86(2)(June): 295–322.

Hasenfeld, Y. and Garrow, E. E. (2014) Institutional logics, moral frames, and advocacy: Explaining the purpose of advocacy among nonprofit human-service organizations. *Nonprofit and Voluntary Sector Quarterly*, 43(1): 80–98.

Hemmings, M. (2017) The constraints on voluntary sector voice in a period of continued austerity. *Voluntary Sector Review*, 8(1) (March): 41–66.

Hilton, M., Mackay, J., Crowson, N. and Mouhot, J-F. (2010) 'The Big Society': civic participation and the state in modern Britain. *History and Policy Papers*, no. 103.

HM Treasury. (2005) *Exploring the Role of the Third Sector in Public Service Delivery and Reform: A Discussion Document*. London: HM Treasury.

Kendall, J. (2009) The third sector and the policy process in the UK: ingredients in a hyperactive horizontal policy environment. In Kendall, J. (ed.) *Handbook of Third Sector Policy in Europe: Multi-level Processes and Organised Civil Society*. Cheltenham: Edward Elgar.

Kendall, J. (2010) Bringing ideology back in: The erosion of political innocence in English third sector policy. *Journal of Political Ideologies*, 15(3): 241–258.

Kameräde, D. (2015) Third Sector impacts on human resources and community. TSRC Working Paper Series, No. 134.

Keane, J. (2005) Eleven theses on markets and civil society. *Journal of Civil Society*, 1(1): 25–34.

Laine, J. (2014) Debating Civil Society: Contested Conceptualizations and Development Trajectories. *International Journal of Not-for-Profit Law*, 16(1), September/59.

Lamb, B. (2010) *The Good Guide to Campaigning and Influencing*. NCVO.

Lamb, B. (2014) Is charity campaigning under threat from the coalition government? *Voluntary Sector Review*, 5(1): 125–138.

Macmillan, R. (2013) Decoupling the state and the third sector? The 'Big Society' as a spontaneous order. *Voluntary Sector Review*, 4(2) (July): 185–203.

Macmillan, R. (2015) Starting from elsewhere: Reimagining the third sector, the state and the market. *People, Place and Policy*, 9(2): 103–109.

Marshall, T. H. (1950) *Citizenship and Social Class and Other Essays*. Cambridge: Cambridge University Press.

Mauss, A. and Wolfe, J. (eds) (1977) *This Land of Promises: The Rise and Fall of Social Problems*. Philadelphia, PA: Lippincott.

Murdock, A. and Lamb, B. (2009) The impact of RNID on auditory services in England: Borrowing lawnmowers and the price of salt. *Journal of Social Enterprise*, 5(2).

Mosley, J. E. (2010) Organizational resources and environmental incentives: understanding the policy advocacy involvement of human service non-profits. *Social Service Review*, 84(1): 1–17.

Mosley, J. E. (2012) Keeping the lights on: How government funding concerns drive the advocacy agendas of non-profit homeless service providers. *Journal of Public Administration Research Theory*, 22(4): 841–866.

Cabinet Office, Office for the Third Sector. (2006) *Partnership in Public Services: An Action Plan for Third Sector Involvement*. London: Cabinet Office.

Putnam, R. (2000) *Bowling Alone*. New York: Schuster and Schuster.

Salamon, L. M. (1987) Of market failure, voluntary failure, and third-party government: Toward a Theory of government-non-profit relations in the modern welfare state. *Non-profit and Voluntary Sector Quarterly*, 16: 29.

Salamon, L. M. (1996) Partners in public services: Government-nonprofit relations in the modern welfare state. *The Journal of Sociology & Social Welfare*, 23(1) Article 23.

Salamon, L. M. (2012) *The State of Non-profit America*. 2nd edn. Brookings Institute.

Salamon, L. M. and Geller, S. L. (2008) *Non-profit America: A Force for Democracy?*Johns Hopkins University.

Salamon, L. M. and Sokolowski, W. (2014) The third sector in Europe: Towards a consensus conceptualization, *TSI Working Paper Series*, No. 2.

Smith, S. R. and Pekkanen, R. (2012) Revisiting advocacy by non-profit organisations. *Voluntary Sector Review*, 3(1): 35–49.

Snowdon, C. (2012) Sock puppets: How the government lobbies itself and why. *IEA Discussion Paper*, No. 39.

Timmins, N. (1995) *The Five Giants, A Biography of the Welfare State*. Harper Collins.

Tonkiss, F. and Passey, A. (1999) Trust, confidence and voluntary organisations: Between values and institutions. *Sociology*, 33(2): 257–274.

Wagner, A. (2012) 'Third sector' and/or 'civil society': A critical discourse about scholarship relating to intermediate organisations. *Voluntary Sector Review*, 3(3): 299–328.

Xu, Y. and Ngai, N. (2011) Moral resources and political capital: Theorizing the relationship between voluntary service organizations and the development of civil society in China. *Nonprofit and Voluntary Sector Quarterly*, 40(2): 247–269.

2

GOVERNANCE IN THE NON-PROFIT SECTOR

The role of trustees in reputation management

Elizabeth Chamberlain and Stuart Etherington

Recent governance issues and the responsibilities of trustees: Introduction

The UK non-profit sector has recently faced a troubled period, during which governance and the responsibility of boards has come under scrutiny. From fundraising to corporate partnerships, campaigning and political affiliations, trustees have been blamed to a large extent for their role in ensuring their charities' activities meet the public's expectations (Neville, 2016). Trustees' fulfilment of their duties has sometimes been found wanting, leading to strong criticism from politicians and the media (Laville and Butler, 2016). The negative stories, generated by these weaknesses have had an impact on the public's trust and confidence in the non-profit sector (Shawcross, 2016).

The latest research by the Charity Commission (2016b) found that public trust and confidence in charities had fallen to the lowest recorded level since monitoring began in 2005: from 6.7 out of 10 in 2014, to 5.7 in 2016. This chapter provides an analysis of the recent governance issues that have affected the sector. The authors stress the importance of governance and consider the changing regulatory landscape. They draw out lessons for trustees, and identify what steps need to be taken to address the problems that have come to light. The authors then consider the future of governance and outline the characteristics of good governance. They conclude that a culture of good governance is essential. They argue that this is one that goes beyond regulatory requirements and a rules-based approach; it is informed by values and ethics.

The importance of governance

Non-profits have been the subject of considerable media and public scrutiny, often leading to strong criticism and a loss of public confidence (Charity Commission,

2016b). Beyond the headlines and the immediately visible problems, poor or inadequate governance is the common thread linking the recent events that have brought non-profits under the spotlight, and ultimately trustees have been singled out for having failed to meet their responsibilities (Charity Commission, 2016d).

CASE STUDY 2.1: PROBLEMATIC GOVERNANCE AT ATLANTIC BRIDGE

A case that demonstrates the extent of trustees' responsibilities, and the potential consequences if they are not fulfilled, concerned the Atlantic Bridge Education and Research Scheme. The Charity Commission's interest related to whether the organization was acting improperly under charity law by promoting or aligning itself with a particular political party.

The Commission concluded that, although Atlantic Bridge was correctly established as a charity and was capable of operating for the public benefit, its educational objects had not been advanced by its activities. This was because of the way in which it had promoted a 'Special Relationship' between the US and the UK (Charity Commission, 2010). Although it is legitimate for a charity to study, research or educate the public about an issue, it is not permissible for a charity to promote a particular political point of view. As a result, Atlantic Bridge was ordered to cease its activities immediately, and the following year the organization was wound up voluntarily by its trustees.

Despite the organization's closure, the controversy continued. The Charity Commission looked into the possibility of exercising its statutory powers to recover funds from Atlantic Bridge's trustees which had not been used to support its charitable aims. Hence, the trustees could have been personally held accountable to repay such funds to the charity if they had been found by the Commission to be in breach of trust. Ultimately, the Commission's further review found that whilst some of Atlantic Bridge's funds had been applied to carry out non-charitable activities, no evidence could be found that the trustees had acted in bad faith. It therefore decided not to pursue any of the trustees personally.

Although the outcome for the former trustees of Atlantic Bridge was positive, the case brought to light some important legal and reputational issues for all trustees to consider (Newton, 2011). In particular, the Charity Commission's investigation uncovered a network of relationships between Atlantic Bridge's founder (Conservative MP and future cabinet minister Liam Fox) and senior executives, and a group of US businessmen of neoconservative thinking (Neate, 2011; Doward, 2011). This was seen as causing a blurring of the separation between the Conservative Party and Atlantic Bridge, and the independence of the charity from party politics was deemed to be questionable. Whilst there is nothing wrong in politicians acting as trustees or becoming involved with non-profits, all non-profits registered as charities must observe the requirement that they are independent from party politics. Any politicians who act as trustees should therefore have regard to this legal duty and put aside any political bias when fulfilling their role, and must not use the organization as a vehicle to express or promote their political views (Charity Commission, 2008).

The Atlantic Bridge case also highlighted that trustees can be held personally accountable by the Charity Commission if, as a result of their breach of duty, the charity's funds are allowed to be applied for non-charitable purposes. This is because trustees are responsible for the overall control and management of organizational administration. In addition, trustees need to consider reputational issues that might arise if they are subject to an investigation, since this could have negative implications for their organization's image and brand.

The changing regulatory landscape

The regulatory landscape for non-profits in the UK, and in particular in England and Wales, has undergone a number of changes over the last few years, leading it to be a much more challenging one for trustees.

New legislation not immediately directed at non-profits has had an impact on the sector. For example, the so called Lobbying Act (HM Government, 2014), aimed at controlling the expenditure of campaigns that influence voters' decisions ahead of an election, has caused what many refer to as a 'chilling effect' on the campaigning activities of non-profits (Harvey and Asthana, 2017).

Specific legislation aimed at non-profits has also come into force, mainly the Charities (Protection and Social Investment) Act (HM Government, 2016). This provides the Charity Commission with a range of new powers to prevent and address abuse in non-profits, in particular a power to disqualify trustees (Charity Commission, 2016c). Another change made by the Act is the introduction of a new category of reasons that lead to the automatic disqualification of trustees. Previously, individuals were automatically disqualified from acting as trustees if they were guilty of convictions for offences related to dishonesty and deception. Now there is a much wider range of offences that lead to automatic disqualification, including for example unspent convictions for terrorism or money laundering (Mott, 2016).

There have also been a number of changes in regulation following a systematic review by the Charity Commission of its key pieces of guidance. The prime example of this is the Essential Trustee guidance (Charity Commission, 2015) which is the key piece of guidance for charity trustees, explaining the fundamental responsibilities and duties they undertake. The guidance has always used the approach of distinguishing between the terms 'must' and 'should': 'must' indicating a legal or regulatory requirement that trustees must comply with, and 'should' indicating good practice requirements that the Commission expects trustees to follow and apply.

The new version of the guidance proposes a redefinition of 'should' and what it means if trustees fail to follow the 'should' recommendations: trustees are warned that they may be in breach of their legal duties and be guilty of misconduct or mismanagement if they do not follow the 'should' requirements without good reason. So, the Commission now expects trustees to follow its 'should' recommendations of good practice, and if it is looking into concerns raised about a particular charity, it will not be enough for its trustees to say that they have complied with the minimum legal requirements. The Commission will want to know if they have also followed and applied the recommended good practice. If not, trustees have to be able to explain and justify their reasons.

Non-profits and their trustees are also facing considerable regulatory uncertainty as a result of Brexit, since so much EU legislation has introduced into UK law rules and safeguards that are fundamental to the work of non-profits. Their preservation and full transposition into UK law is therefore of the utmost importance to non-profits, which are therefore looking to the legislative changes that will follow Brexit with understandable concern (Asthana, Steward and Walker, 2016).

Recent governance issues: fundraising, corporate partnerships, chief executives' pay, campaigning and the closure of the Kids Company

Fundraising

More than anyone else, trustees were singled out by the Public Administration and Constitutional Affairs Committee in its inquiry into fundraising practices (21 January 2016, HC 431). The inquiry was announced following a series of scandals involving non-profits and their fundraising practices during the Summer of 2015, many of which attracted negative media coverage and caused considerable public concern.

The Committee's final report concluded that trustees are ultimately responsible for every aspect of their charity's activity, including fundraising, and that trustees were to blame for the failures in fundraising that had been uncovered. In particular, there was consensus both within the Committee's members and witnesses to the inquiry that trustees had failed in their duty to extend their governance role to fundraising.

This resonated with one of the key findings made a few months earlier by the Review of Fundraising Regulation. The review, although tasked with looking at the framework of fundraising regulation, had identified trustees as key in ensuring compliance with existing rules, and concluded that trustees had too often been absent from discussions on fundraising practice and how this reflected their organizations' values (NCVO, 2015).

The clear message to trustees from both the Committee and the review was that trustees must not only ensure their organization complies with the law relating to fundraising, but they also have a responsibility to think carefully about the impact their fundraising methods will have on public opinion and the reputation of their organization.

Corporate partnerships

The media has also critically looked at non-profits' engagement in commercial partnerships. Sometimes these agreements allow companies to use the names and logos of non-profit organizations to promote their own products or services. In return, non-profits may receive a proportion of the income, or other benefits, generated from the promotion of those products.

Relevant Charity Commission's guidelines recognise the potential benefits of successful corporate partnerships. In particular, they acknowledge that charities have much to gain from entering into commercial partnerships with companies, from increased opportunities for fundraising to augmented brand awareness (Charity Commission, 2013).

However, over the years, some deals have also raised controversy and have caused damage to the profile and reputation of the non-profit involved. For instance, Age UK had a deal with the energy company E.ON which involved marketing a special gas and electricity tariff to the charity's beneficiaries. When it was claimed that Age UK's enterprises division was overcharging its customers, and was receiving a significant commission to promote this particular tariff when there were other less expensive ones available, both organizations found themselves in the centre of a media storm (Lamden, 2016).

The case is a strong reminder for trustees about the importance of ensuring that the right decision-making processes are in place when working with businesses, and that appropriate oversight and review need to be exercised (Brignall, 2016). Given the inherent risks in such arrangements to the brand and reputation of a non-profit, as well as to its assets, the role and responsibilities of trustees are essential to ensure their brand values and long-term mission are properly considered alongside income generation and name promotion (Charity Commission, 2016a). The case also highlighted how media coverage of a non-profit's commercial operation is likely to resonate with the public. Most people do not know how a specific non-profit's commercial arm works and can feel uncomfortable about the scale of some non-profits' commercial operations (Ruddick, 2016).

Chief executives' pay

The amount that non-profits spend on senior executives' salaries has been the subject of extensive media coverage. The controversy reached its peak in Summer 2013, following a series of media stories highlighting chief executive pay in some large non-profits (Hope, 2013; Spencer, 2013). This generated a heated public debate about the appropriate amount that should be paid, and whether or not salaries in the non-profit sector should be capped.

As a response, the sector's representative body, the National Council for Voluntary Organisations (NCVO), set up an independent inquiry panel. The group was tasked with exploring the appropriate levels of pay for non-profit senior executives and how these levels should be set. The inquiry also considered the relationship between salary levels and public trust and confidence in the sector as a whole (Rimmer, 2013).

The inquiry clearly stated that each board of trustees has the responsibility of setting levels of staff pay. This is part of trustees' organizational responsibility.

Decisions about the appropriate level of pay must be made very carefully, and inevitably present challenges to trustees. Each decision will be based on the specific needs and interests of the individual organization. It requires trustees to consider the best interests of a charity and its beneficiaries. Trustees want to attract and retain the best talent and necessary skills. Simultaneously, they also need to be mindful of the charity's reputation among the public and donors; staying true to their values and making sure the public understands the contribution they make to society (NCVO, 2014).

Campaigning

Recently there has not only been scrutiny about how funds are raised and spent but also on non-profits' campaigning activities. In particular, there has been media and public attention over the question whether campaigning by non-profits has become too 'political' (Morris, 2015).

CASE STUDY 2.2: OXFAM'S 'PERFECT STORM' TWEET

Oxfam's 'Perfect Storm' tweet was part of a social media campaign leading up to the publication of a report on food poverty produced jointly by Oxfam, Church Action on Poverty and the Trussell Trust (Cooper, Purcell and Jackson, 2014).

The tweet, and the image that accompanied it, led to a complaint about the campaign being overtly political and aimed at the policies of the existing government (Hope, 2014; Williams, 2014).

In response to the complaint, the Charity Commission opened an investigation to explore whether the tweet sought to influence public opinion in a party-political sense, and whether the concerns raised were founded. The final report exonerated Oxfam from the alleged question about its political affiliation, although it also concluded that the text of the tweet and the embedded picture did indeed give rise to speculation and varying perceptions about the tweet's purpose, and consequently could be misconstrued by some as party-political campaigning (Charity Commission, 2014).

The investigation's attention therefore turned to the organization's governance arrangements, to consider the trustees' decision-making processes in relation to campaigns and their communications, and highlight the importance of their oversight and responsibilities in these matters.

The Perfect Storm tweet case, and in particular, its referral to the Charity Commission, was viewed by many (Butler, 2014) as proof that campaigning by non-profits is being increasingly perceived as a political issue. This has important implications for trustees, who will have to take a number of steps to protect themselves. While ensuring that all legal and regulatory requirements are complied with, trustees also need to be able to show that they have acted properly, demonstrating what steps they have taken, the safeguards in place and how campaigning decisions have been arrived at.

The case also shows how campaigns can present communication challenges for trustees and how they need to consider the prospect of a more adversarial relationship with some of the media. In particular, if the campaign could be seen as political by the media, the public, or politicians themselves, trustees need to have robust messaging in place.

Therefore, the case was a strong reminder for the whole non-profit sector about the essential need for trustees to have clear oversight of the campaigning work of their organization. Trustees have the duty to take particular care to ensure that any material does not damage their organization's reputation or impact on public trust and confidence; that messages are appropriate and in furtherance of the non-profit's objectives, and that any risk of being misinterpreted or perceived as being party political is properly managed.

Kids Company

In the UK non-profit sector a high-profile case in which governance has been criticised is the collapse of the organization Kids Company in August 2015. Previously, Kids Company enjoyed a high profile and strong support from senior politicians, with successive governments providing grants of up to at least £42m (National Audit Office, 2015). When it first closed, the stated reason was that the finances had become stretched because of the number of children pouring through its doors for help. However, media stories appeared claiming that the organization had existed by heavily relying on public money, and that donors had been steadily withdrawing support because they had been alarmed by stories of alleged mismanagement (Gosden, 2015; Wright, 2015).

There followed a series of investigations into the organization and its management. The Metropolitan Police examined claims that incidents involving young people who used the charity had not been passed to police (Rayner, 2015). The National Audit Office investigated the government's funding of the organization (National Audit Office, 2015) and the Charity Commission opened a statutory inquiry. The Public Administration and Constitutional Affairs Select Committee also initiated an inquiry and once again focused on the role of trustees. It concluded (House of Commons, 2016) that the primary responsibility for the collapse of the organization rested with the trustees.

The Committee's final report was highly critical not only of Kids Company's trustees, but also of the organization's whole governance arrangements. In particular, it noted that Kids Company's demand-led operating model carried the constant risk that the non-profit organization would be unable to ensure that its commitments would be matched by its resources. The Committee found that the trustees had failed to address this risk, allowing their judgement to be swayed by the dominant personality of the founder and chief executive, and not demonstrating the leadership or the expertise required by their role.

Lessons for charity trustees

The memories of Kids Company and of the fundraising scandals are unlikely to go away anytime soon. The biggest lesson of all is the need for good governance. The priority, moving forward, is to identify key elements of good governance from these episodes. This is so trustees of all non-profits can ensure they have the necessary governance arrangements in place and follow the right behaviours. Indeed, despite the widely held view that none of the cases outlined above are indicative of how non-profits operate generally, it would be unwise to assume that lessons cannot be drawn or that improvements cannot be made. Six lessons are proposed below.

1. Risk management and sharing lessons learnt

There is a legitimate and understandable concern that the recent failures in governance and the wider regulatory developments will lead to risk aversion. Yet trustees need to be able to take measured risks if this will help them achieve their charitable purposes.

Trustees should be supported when things go wrong, and encouraged to be honest about what has happened and to share this in their annual reports, drawing out the lessons they have learnt on how they will do things differently next time and what they have changed. Whilst no two situations are the same, this would ensure that many general lessons could be drawn from the collective experience across organizations of various sizes and with different missions.

2. Openness

Trustees still tend to be concerned about sharing business beyond the board room. In reality, the majority of board decisions should be communicated to staff, volunteers and other key stakeholders. The public's trust that a non-profit is delivering on its mission is fundamental to its success and the wider non-profit sector. Making accountability and transparency real, through genuine and open communication that celebrates successes but also demonstrates willingness to learn from mistakes will help to build this trust and confidence, and will earn greater legitimacy.

Trustees therefore need to consider how they 'open their boardrooms' up and share their discussions and information in digestible formats so that stakeholders can scrutinise their work.

3. Proper oversight and regular review

A common theme throughout the governance failures of the recent years is the weakness of trustee oversight systems. Ultimately this weakness has inhibited, and in some cases prevented, the trustees' ability to fully discharge their legal duties.

It is imperative that boards and trustees exercise proper oversight. They need to have appropriate systems to maintain scrutiny and control. A board that not only adopts effective governance arrangements, but that also regularly reviews those arrangements, is better positioned to spot behaviours and activities that undermine the good name of the organization, and is more aware of the potential impact this will have on public trust and confidence. Trustees should set and regularly review their organization's aim and mission, set a strategic direction, review performance and hold the employed executive to account.

The board is ultimately responsible for the decisions and actions of the non-profit. However, the board cannot, and should not, do everything. Trustees must know their boundaries and not stray into operational activities. The issue is therefore for the board to make sure that its decision-making processes are informed, rigorous and timely, and that effective delegation, control and risk assessment systems are set up and monitored. When doing so, trustees need to be mindful that they are delegating authority, not responsibility, so they need to implement suitable controls to make sure they oversee the delegated matters. Trustees should also regularly review their decision-making framework and the matters over which they have exercised their powers of delegation.

4. Diversity: thinking differently

Diversity, in the widest sense, is essential for boards to stay informed and responsive, and for them to navigate the fast-paced and complex changes facing their organizations. Boards whose trustees have different backgrounds and experience are more likely to encourage debate and to make better decisions.

However, it is unlikely that different types of trustees can be attracted unless organizations start doing things differently. Achieving more diversity will not just happen through recruitment: it also requires improving accessibility and making opportunities more attractive. The timing, location and atmosphere of meetings; the format of relevant information, and the training and support offered, all need to be taken into account.

5. Skills and expertise

A review of the board itself should also be a regular exercise. In particular, the board needs to have, and regularly consider, the skills, knowledge and experience it requires to govern, lead and deliver the organization's purposes effectively. A refresh of the trustee board is an opportunity to bring different backgrounds and experiences, and therefore different points of view to a discussion. This in turn can help think of new ways of doing things, such as new ways in which to reach beneficiaries, new ways to raise funds, and new ways to make use of technology.

6. Reputation management

Trustees have ultimate responsibility not only for the charity's funds and assets, but also – and perhaps especially – its reputation. A non-profit's reputation is one of its greatest assets. Donors, beneficiaries and supporters all invest their trust in the non-profits they are involved with, and that trust is inextricably linked to the reputation that the non-profit enjoys. Negative media coverage can cause huge amounts of reputational damage for any business, but for non-profits, many of which are almost entirely reliant on public donations, it can be devastating. Not only can it severely affect their capacity to raise funds, but it can also have an impact on their ability to attract high quality staff and to forge vital partnerships. Loss of reputation leads to loss of trust and can ultimately lead to a charity's demise.

It is therefore no surprise that the Charity Commission now makes it very clear that trustees' duty to manage their non-profit's resources responsibly includes protecting and safeguarding the non-profit's reputation (Charity Commission, 2015). This means that trustees have to ensure that there is adequate consideration of the impact on their organization's reputation in relation to all activities.

Therefore, the most important lesson of all is that trustees are and should see themselves as guardians of their non-profit's brand and reputation. Trustees are charged with the good governance of their organization, and safeguarding the reputation of non-profits is intrinsic to good governance.

The future of governance

The case for good governance in non-profits led by committed and engaged trustees with an understanding of their role, appropriate skills and ability to lead, has never been clearer. This is not only as a consequence of the regulatory cases outlined above. It is also because of the public's changing expectations of non-profits, their values, and how they operate in accordance with these values. Meeting expectations, and not simply complying with the legal requirements, must be the basis for the future of the non-profit sector's governance.

This is the approach that has been taken by both the House of Lords Select Committee on Charities, and by the sector itself in revising the Charity Governance Code. The Committee's final report (House of Lords Select Committee on Charities, 2017) reiterates the fundamental role of good governance for a strong non-profit sector and makes a number of recommendations on how to improve the development and performance of boards, and on ensuring trustees have the right skills and experience that can lead to better governance. Over the coming years these will be a roadmap for both the sector and government towards making trusteeship more accessible, increasing diversity among trustees and improving governance. The new edition of the Charity Governance Code (2017) also reflects the universal concerns about improving governance in all organizations, and sets out the recommended good practice charities need to implement.

Its recent revision was in response to the governance failures that have come under the spotlight, but also a demonstration of the sector's collective commitment to strengthening governance. The code now sets new, and higher, standards for boards and their trustees, placing a greater emphasis on values, accountability, transparency, probity, maintaining control, leadership and the need for diversity of opinions and skills. Its premise is that boards must be able to maintain a strategic focus, commit to board development and stay true to the organization's purposes.

Conclusion: the importance of culture, values and ethics

The majority of the reactions to the recent governance failures have been to look at the regulatory environment and how this can be strengthened. Addressing long-standing challenges in the governance sphere is however more difficult, particularly as many challenges fall under the heading of cultural and behavioural change. Regulators and policymakers, and the sector itself, have come to appreciate that a rules-based compliance approach will not, on its own, deliver healthy governance behaviour. This is because behaviour is determined not only by rules but also by the culture of the entity concerned.

Both the House of Lords Select Committee on Charities and the Code of Good Governance also recognise that the culture and behaviours of the non-profit and its board are as important as its governance structures and processes.

A rules-based compliance approach will not on its own deliver healthy behaviour: rules can determine behaviour only to a certain extent. Governance involves the proportionate, sound and effective balance of appropriate rules, regulations and behaviours. It is therefore apparent that culture is crucial to the effective governance of an organization, and in turn its success.

Over the following years, it will most likely be the culture change within trustees that will determine whether the rules will be followed in the first place, ensuring compliance with the regulatory framework. But most importantly, it will be trustees' culture and the values they believe in that will make the difference between doing things rightly and doing the right thing, only the latter of which will restore the public's confidence in the sector.

Discussion questions

1. What are the key elements of good governance?
2. What are the key skills that a board of trustees should include?
3. What are the key issues that trustees should regularly review at board meetings?
4. What should the priorities be when trustees are deciding whether to enter into a corporate partnership?

5.   What are the key considerations trustees should make before approving the launch of a campaign?
6.   What questions should trustees be asking when discussing their charity's fundraising strategy?

References

Asthana, A., Steward, H. and Walker, P. (2016) 'Brexit: civil service facing its largest task since WWII, says union'. *Guardian*, 15 November 2016. Available at: https://www.theguardian.com/politics/2016/nov/15/brexit-civil-service-facing-its-largest-task-since-wwii-says-union

Brignall, M. (2016) 'Age UK criticised over E.ON partnership'. *Guardian*, 19 April 2016. Available at: https://www.theguardian.com/money/2016/apr/19/ofgem-criticises-age-uk-over-tariff-deal-with-eon

Butler, P. (2014) 'Campaigning charities that expose inconvenient truths must not be silenced'. *Guardian*, 17 June 2014. Available at: https://www.theguardian.com/society/2014/jun/17/oxfam-advert-campaigning-charities-stifled-by-government

Charity Commission (2008) *Campaigning and Political Activity Guidance for Charities (CC9)*. Available at: https://www.gov.uk/government/publications/speaking-out-guidance-on-campaigning-and-political-activity-by-charities-cc9/speaking-out-guidance-on-campaigning-and-political-activity-by-charities

Charity Commission (2010) *Regulatory Case Report: The Atlantic Bridge Education and Research Scheme*. Available at: https://www.publications.parliament.uk/pa/cm201012/cmselect/cmstnprv/1887/188710.htm

Charity Commission (2013) *Charities: Working with Companies and Professional Fundraisers*. Available at: https://www.gov.uk/guidance/charities-working-with-companies-and-professional-fundraisers

Charity Commission (2014) *Operational Case Report: Oxfam (202918)*, 19 December 2014. Available at: https://www.gov.uk/government/publications/oxfam-case-report

Charity Commission (2015) *The Essential Trustee: What you Need to Know, What you Need to Do*. Available at: https://www.gov.uk/government/publications/the-essential-trustee-what-you-need-to-know-cc3/the-essential-trustee-what-you-need-to-know-what-you-need-to-do

Charity Commission (2016a) *Regulatory Alert to Charities Engaged in Commercial Activities*. Available at: https://www.gov.uk/government/news/commission-issues-alert-to-charities-engaged-in-commercial-activities

Charity Commission (2016b) *Public Trust and Confidence in Charities*. Available at: https://www.gov.uk/government/uploads/system/uploads/attachment_data/file/532104/Public_trust_and_confidence_in_charities_2016.pdf

Charity Commission (2016c) *Explanatory Statement – The Discretionary Disqualification Power: Power to Disqualify from Being a Trustee*. Available at: https://www.gov.uk/government/publications/the-discretionary-disqualification-power

Charity Commission (2016d) *Tackling Abuse and Mismanagement: 2015–16*. Available at: https://www.gov.uk/government/publications/tackling-abuse-and-mismanagement-2015-16/tackling-abuse-and-mismanagement-2015-16-full-report

Charity Governance Code (2017). Available at: https://www.charitygovernancecode.org/en/

Cooper, N., Purcell, S. and Jackson, R. (2014) *Below the Breadline: The Relentless Rise of Food Poverty in Britain*. Church Action on Poverty, Oxfam GB and Trussell Trust. Available at: http://policy-practice.oxfam.org.uk/publications/below-the-breadline-the-relentless-rise-of-food-poverty-in-britain-317730

Doward, J. (2011) 'Liam Fox's Atlantic Bridge linked top Tories and Tea Party activists'. *Guardian*, 15 October 2011. Available at: https://www.theguardian.com/politics/2011/oct/15/liam-fox-atlantic-bridge

Harvey, F. and Asthana, A. (2017) 'Chilling Lobbying Act stifles democracy, charities tell party chiefs'. *Guardian*, 6 June 2017. Available at: https://www.theguardian.com/politics/2017/jun/06/chilling-lobbying-act-stifles-democracy-write-charities-party-chiefs

Gosden, E. (2015) 'Kids Company founder Camila Batmanghelidjh denies mismanagement after charity goes bankrupt'. *The Telegraph*, 6 August 2015. Available at: http://www.telegraph.co.uk/news/politics/11786639/Kids-Company-founder-denies-mismanagement-after-charity-goes-bankrupt.html

HM Government Great Britain (2014) *Transparency of Lobbying, Non-Party Campaigning and Trade Union Administration Act 2014*. Chapter 4. London: The Stationary Office.

HM Government Great Britain (2016) *Charities (Protection and Social Investment) Act 2016*. Chapter 4. London: The Stationary Office.

Hope, C. (2013) '30 charity chiefs paid more than £100,000'. *The Telegraph*, 6 August 2013. Available at: http://www.telegraph.co.uk/news/politics/10224104/30-charity-chiefs-paid-more-than-100000.html

Hope, C. (2014) 'Oxfam: MPs shocked by "disgraceful" political campaigning'. *The Telegraph*, 10 June 2014. Available at: http://www.telegraph.co.uk/news/politics/10888966/Oxfam-MPs-shocked-by-disgraceful-political-campaigning.html

House of Commons Public Administration and Constitutional Affairs Select Committee (2016) *The 2015 Charity Fundraising Controversy: Lessons for Trustees, the Charity Commission, and Regulators*. HC 431, Third Report of Session 2015–2016. Available at: https://www.publications.parliament.uk/pa/cm201516/cmselect/cmpubadm/431/431.pdf

House of Commons Public Administration and Constitutional Affairs Select Committee (2016) *The Collapse of Kids Company: Lessons for Charity Trustees, Professional Firms, the Charity Commission, and Whitehall*. HC 433, Fourth Report of Session 2015–2016. Available at: https://www.publications.parliament.uk/pa/cm201516/cmselect/cmpubadm/433/433.pdf

House of Lords Select Committee on Charities (2017) *Stronger Charities for a Stronger Society*. HL Paper 133, Report of Session 2016–2017. Available at: https://www.publications.parliament.uk/pa/ld201617/ldselect/ldchar/133/133.pdf

Lamden, T. (2016) 'Energy firm E.ON "paid £6m to Age UK in return for the charity promoting expensive tariff to pensioners"'. *Daily Mail*, 4 February 2016. Available at: http://www.dailymail.co.uk/news/article-3431006/Energy-firm-E-paid-6m-Age-UK-return-charity-promoting-expensive-tariffs-pensioners.html

Laville, S. and Butler, P. (2016) 'MPs blame "negligent" trustees for Kids Company collapse'. *Guardian*, 1 February 2016. Available at: https://www.theguardian.com/uk-news/2016/feb/01/kids-company-collapse-mps-pacac-report-blame-negligent-trustees

Mott, N. (2016) 'How will the new Charities Act affect your charity?' Charity Commission blog, 20 May 2016. Available at: https://charitycommission.blog.gov.uk/2016/05/20/how-will-the-new-charities-act-affect-your-charity/

Morris, D. (2015) 'Too political? Charities and the legal boundaries of campaigning'. Voluntary Sector Studies Network. Available at: http://www.vssn.org.uk/paper/too-political-charities-and-the-legal-boundaries-of-campaigning/

National Audit Office (2015) *Investigation: The Government's Funding of Kids Company*. Available at: https://www.nao.org.uk/wp-content/uploads/2015/10/Investigation-the-governments-funding-of-Kids-Company.pdf

NCVO (2014) *Report of the Inquiry into Charity Senior Executive Pay and Guidance for Trustees on Setting Remuneration*. Available at: https://www.ncvo.org.uk/images/news/Executive-Pay-Report.pdf

NCVO (2015) *Regulating Fundraising for the Future: Trust in Charities, Confidence in Fundraising Regulation*. Available at: https://www.ncvo.org.uk/images/documents/policy_and_resea rch/giving_and_philanthropy/fundraising-review-report-2015.pdf

Neate, R. (2011) 'Charity created by Liam Fox axed after watchdog issues criticism'. *Guardian*, 5 October 2011. Available at: https://www.theguardian.com/politics/2011/oct/05/charity-liam-fox-axed-watchdog

Neville, S. (2016) 'Charity trustees to blame for fundraising scandals, say MPs'. *Financial Times*, 25 January 2016. Available at: https://www.ft.com/content/a7f4aa80-c2a c-11e5-808f-8231cd71622e?mhq5j=e1

Newton, S. (2011) 'The lessons of Atlantic Bridge'. *Guardian*, 16 October 2011, Available at: https://www.theguardian.com/commentisfree/2011/oct/16/lessons-atla ntic-bridge-questioning

Rayner, G. (2015) 'Kids Company faces Met Police investigation'. *Telegraph*, 30 July 2015. Available at: http://www.telegraph.co.uk/news/politics/11774431/Kids-Company-fa ces-a-Met-Police-investigation.html

Rimmer, A. (2013) 'National Council for Voluntary Organisations launches inquiry into chief executive pay'. *Third Sector*, 11 October 2013. Available at: http://www.thirdsector. co.uk/national-council-voluntary-organisations-launches-inquiry-chief-executive-pay/ governance/article/1216031

Ruddick, G. (2016) 'Age UK chair defends controversial E.ON pensioner tariff'. *Guardian*, 12 February 2016. Available at: https://www.theguardian.com/society/2016/feb/12/a ge-uk-chair-defends-controversial-eon-pensioner-tariff

Shawcross, W. (2016) 'Trust in charities is at an all time low. Time to change'. *Guardian*, 28 June 2016. Available at: https://www.theguardian.com/commentisfree/2016/jun/28/ trust-charities-low-charitable-work-public

Spencer, B. (2013) 'Charities accused of bringing good causes 'into disrepute' after it is revealed 30 bossed earn more than £100,000'. *Daily Mail*, 6 August 2013. Available at: http://www.dailymail.co.uk/news/article-2385120/Charity-bosses-earning-100-000-a ccused-excessive-pay-rises.html

Williams, R. (2014) 'Oxfam "perfect storm" poster attacked as "shameful" by Conservative politicians'. *The Independent*, 11 June 2014. Available at: http://www.independent.co.uk/ news/uk/home-news/oxfam-perfect-storm-poster-attacked-as-shameful-by-conserva tive-politicians-9526661.html

Wright, O. (2015) 'Kids Company: The truth behind the collapse of Camila Batmanghe- lidjh's charity'. *Independent*, 6 August 2015. Available at: http://www.independent.co.uk/ news/uk/home-news/kids-company-the-truth-behind-the-collapse-of-camila-batmanghe lidjhs-charity-10444401.html

3

NON-PROFIT ISSUES MANAGEMENT

A new approach to resist the label of 'risk'

Michaela O'Brien

This chapter looks at the principles behind issues management theories, explores case studies from the non-profit sector and suggests a new approach that challenges the dominant corporate-centric theories and is more appropriate for non-profit organizations.

Introduction: am I at risk, or am I the risk?

Many core public relations theories, from ethics to stakeholder management, assume a corporate subject and overlook the specific reality of working in the non-profit sector. Issues management theory shares this approach and is often presented from the business perspective (Jaques 2014; Regester and Larkin 2008; Deegan 2001). Issues management models may omit non-profit organizations altogether, or feature them primarily as creating risks or issues for the 'legitimate' (business) organization. This corporate-centric approach within mainstream issues management models reduces their usefulness for non-profit organizations in three ways. Firstly, it sets up an oppositional dynamic between business and non-profits that seeks to undermine non-profits. Secondly, the models may focus on issues that pose risks for businesses, but are less of a concern for non-profit organizations. Thirdly, they have an organizational rather than a societal focus. Issues management is seen as a way of protecting the reputation of a business, and issues are considered only in terms of their potential (negative) impact on that business, rather than on their potential impact on society. By contrast, non-profit organizations need to consider both the societal and the organizational impact of issues.

While some aspects of issues management apply across all sectors, existing models do not adequately address the specific challenges facing the non-profit sector.

Defining issues: a sectoral approach

Issues can be defined in a number of ways. Many authors (Jaques 2014; Cornelissen 2011; Regester and Larkin 2008) take a corporate-centric approach. They define issues in terms of reputational risk, and as factors that may damage a company's reputation. In their view, issues are often caused by that company's own activity. These issues include public concern about manufacturing processes or working practices, product failure or product recalls, or other business activity that poses harm to society or the environment – and may therefore result in public policy that adversely affects that business.

Another corporate-centric approach is to define issues as attacks on businesses by non-profits, including charities, pressure groups, trades unions or non-governmental organizations (NGOs). Regester and Larkin (2008) position NGOs as one of the key risks facing organizations, having 'the power to inflict long-term damage on companies' (2008: 12) and stating that 'global companies are the main targets' and 'direct action campaigns clearly pose threats to reputation risk' (2008: 13). Jaques (2014) also conceptualises issues in terms of conflict between NGOs and business. He categorises the 'qualities' of issues (2014: 302–303) as: 'ambiguous', 'external', 'emotive', 'high risk', 'policy', 'ongoing', of 'media' appeal, 'contentious', and 'controversial'. In particular, two of these, 'emotive' and 'controversial', are revealing about the way NGOs are conceptualised in issues management.

Of particular interest is the quality 'emotive', which Jaques unpacks as 'emotions rather than facts and figures often prevail'. This is key, because NGO challenges to corporate activity can be presented as emotional or factually inaccurate, when they may simply be querying the accuracy of facts presented by the business. Regester and Larkin (2008: 29) claim that NGOs are emotional but businesses' decision-making processes are rational, technical and scientific. Jaques's example of a property developer in conflict with the local residents association describes the property developer's approach as technical and based on fact, while the residents association are described as emotional and depending heavily on opinion. However, while residents associations may draw on their experience of living in a property, they commonly also use technical references to planning and property law. Challenges to fracking and other environmental degradation can be dismissed as emotive, though environmental NGOs point to scientific evidence to support their claims. This framing of the different qualities embedded in non-profits as opposed to businesses helps to inform the corporate positioning of NGOs as a troublesome emotional risk.

The quality 'controversial' is also pertinent. Many non-profit activities necessarily involve challenging corporate or government policy around issues that are sensitive: production chains that are exploitative or damage the environment, for example, or products that may cause health risks. These may certainly be controversial. However, issues management theory tends to focus on that controversy and not on the ethics of the controversial business policy or practice, or the alternatives to it. By labeling issues as controversial, businesses focus attention on conflict between different stakeholders, rather than on examining how business activity has created the issue.

Other authors take a broader view of issues. Cornelissen (2011: 180) acknowledges that issues such as obesity or executive pay can exist independently of businesses and be of public concern 'before they become connected to an organisation'. The implication, though, is that these are latent issues and do not require action until they pose a risk to the business. Heath and Palenchar (2009: 27–28) list a number of types of issue that impact business, such as international trade discussions, regulatory standards, workplace regulations and health and safety standards. Several of these impact organizations across sectors. They also identify broader socio-economic issues; for example changes in financial practices, lifestyle, public opinion and infrastructure.

Alternatively, L'Etang (2009: 75) defines issues through a societal rather than purely organizational lens, in terms of public discourse: 'An issue can be defined as a topic of debate, a trend or a recurring theme that moves from the private sphere into the public sphere and on to the media agenda.' Rather than defining issues as risks to a business, she identifies core topics with resonance for large parts of society, in which organizations from each sector may have a stake or a preferred policy approach. She includes issues such as child obesity, smoking in public places, world hunger and corporate governance in her discussion.

Overall, issues can be defined as involving change. The emergence of new knowledge or technologies; changes in lifestyle or quality of life; changes in public attitudes, priorities or understanding; or changes in political or organizational strategies. This broader definition of issues is more relevant to non-profits.

Issues management: a body of literature designed to neutralize NGOs

Most issues management models focus on the management of issues by business (Jaques 2014; Regester and Larkin 2008) and are characterised by their focus on the organization and its reputation, rather than on the issue itself. They also tend to conceptualise NGO activities as a risk to business, as an issue to be managed, rather than as activities that proactively address societal issues. Both the models and the proposed corporate responses rarely involve scrutinising or changing policies and practices that are called into question by NGO activities.

Issues management originated in the 1970s, its development prompted by 'the lack of corporate capacity to respond to the influence of activists and other non-governmental organizations' (Jaques 2014: 301). For instance, the 1970s saw the emergence of Greenpeace, which aimed to hold governments and businesses to account for policies and practices which threatened the environment. This may help to explain the focus within issues management theory on a business as the protagonist managing issues, with NGOs portrayed as creating those issues. Influential early theorists such as Howard Chase crystallised this idea, explicitly positioning issues management as a tool to help business influence public policy (Chase 1984 cited in Jaques 2014). L'Etang states that the early literature in this field had 'something of a corporate bias' in which opponents of corporate goals were 'positioned as organisational threats and *othered* as "activists" with the implication that they were illegitimate' (L'Etang 2009: 84).

Focus on the organization

Drawing on Chase, Heath and other early architects of issues management models, Jaques describes issues management as 'a management approach to dealing with potential threats and ... a system of proven tools and processes' (2014: 311). He outlines three different approaches to understanding issues. The first focuses on conflict and the other two are purely organizational:

1.   A contested matter, where policy differences lead to social or political dispute;
2.   An expectation gap, where the behaviour of an organization falls short of what its stakeholders expect;
3.   And impact, where an issue can significantly affect an organization's operations.

For Jaques, contestation or dispute is problematic because it could jeopardise the way a business operates. His focus is on the business, not the issue itself. This organizational approach is also evident in Regester and Larkin (2008: 44) who define issues management more narrowly as a business activity carried out to close the expectation gap: 'an issue represents "a gap between corporate practice and stakeholder expectations"'. Heath and Palenchar (2009: 12) define issues management more broadly as 'a multifunctional discipline that includes the identification, monitoring, and analysis of trends in key publics' opinions that can mature into public policy'. This definition could be applicable to all sectors, as the authors acknowledge, though they consider that non-profit organizations engage in issues management primarily when they hold corporate actors to account.

Key to understanding issues management literature is the concept of the lifecycle of an issue – there are different models for this, but all include an early opportunity for the proactive researcher who keeps abreast of trends to spot a potential issue and manage it, often through strategic communication, before it builds to a crisis. The difference between issues management and crisis management is acting early and, ideally, preempting the crisis. Indeed, it is common to consider crisis as one stage of issues management. This fits the organizational-focus of corporate issues management models, but is less helpful for considering the societal impact of issues.

How organizations manage issues

Also central to the literature is the process by which organizations manage issues. Jaques (2006: 410) describes this process as being well defined by academics over

30 years as: 'monitoring the environment; early identification of issues; classification and prioritization; taking pre-emptive action; formal planning; setting realistic goals; organizing an effective process; building coalitions; and assembling and focusing resources'. Heath and Palenchar (2009: 28–29) outline four stages of issues management which foreground the role of the public relations (PR) practitioner as a strategic manager, placing issues management in an organizational planning context:

1. Strategic business planning – understanding the environment in which the organization operates and setting goals
2. Strategic issue monitoring – identifying and understanding issues and their implication for the organization
3. Strategic corporate responsibility adjustment – addressing the legitimacy gap between what an organization does and the expectation of its stakeholders
4. Strategic communication – using rhetorical and dialogic approaches to debate issues and move towards collaborative decisions.

These four stages could have application across sectors, but they privilege the organizational over the societal dimension. Heath and Palenchar (2009) promote striking a balance between organizational interests and those of the organization's stakeholders, claiming that strategic issues management aims to 'foster a supportive climate between each organisation and those people who can affect its success and are affected by its operations' (2009: 9). While this suggests an approach in which the rights of society, stakeholders and businesses are judged of equal merit, the authors acknowledge that these rights may not align, and that issues management can only reconcile them 'to the extent possible within current market and public policy forces' (2009: 38). The reality is that those market forces are likely to privilege investors' desire for profit over the rights of consumer groups or the workforce. Issues management is brought back from a societal concern to a corporate organization's concern. Similarly Jaques (2006, 2010) claims that issues management is now used across sectors but focuses on whether NGOs are pro or anti-business, vastly oversimplifying the reasons why NGOs seek to monitor emerging issues.

An oppositional dynamic

The roots of issues management in the desire of companies to resist NGO challenges to their policies and practice has a deeper impact than just creating a vacuum in theory for the non-profit PR strategist. They also create issues that NGOs need to manage. Businesses are advised to react to NGO activity in the same way as to a natural disaster: to mitigate damage and get back to business as usual as quickly as possible. Crisis management frameworks that include denial and counterattack (e.g. Hearit 2001) legitimise the attitude that businesses need not engage with the actual challenge within NGO activities. The emotive language in some literature reinforces this. Regester and Larkin (2008) claim that companies are 'used to rational decision making' while NGOs are 'on a crusade' (2008: 29–31). They refer to Chase talking about NGO campaigns' '*appearance* of legitimacy' (my emphasis). This dismissive attitude helps reinforce corporate suspicion of NGOs and a reluctance to reflect on inequitable business policies and practices.

With historical roots as a tool for business to respond to NGO attack, a resulting persistent corporate bias, and a focus on the organizational rather than the societal impacts of issues, issues management models have limited relevance to practitioners in the non-profit sector.

Other approaches to issues management

The origins of issues management lead the literature to foreground either conflict or organizational interests. However, non-profits are not restricted by these defensive origins. For this sector, issues provide a range of opportunities and challenges.

In contrast to the functional school approach of Chase, Regester and Larkin and Jaques, L'Etang (2009) has a less corporate focus. Her critical discussion of issues such as health, poverty and corporate responsibility opens up the possibility of an approach that can be useful for non-profits by foregrounding the societal impact of issues rather than their organizational impact. Also relevant is L'Etang's discussion of risk, which she links closely to issues management, and of Ulrich Beck's concept of the risk society (Beck 1992 cited in L'Etang 2009), which presents risk as the result or side-effect of globalisation and industrialisation. Demetrious (2013) takes Beck's idea further to consider that the core activity of non-profits lies in mitigating damage to planet and people created by the business pursuit of profit. This approach turns on its head the dominant model of issues management, in which NGOs create issues for the corporate subject. Drawing on L'Etang and Demetrious we can instead argue that it is businesses, not NGOs, who create risks or issues, as companies push for increasing globalisation.

L'Etang introduces the notion of power, noting that 'some risks are taken by those in power on behalf of others'. Understanding the use or misuse of power, and how to redress imbalances of power, lies at the heart of many non-profit activities, whether challenging risk-taking powerful businesses (as NGOs do who call to account corporate policies that damage the environment or erode workers' rights), advocating on behalf of those with less power (as charities do who work with the homeless, or survivors of domestic violence), or empowering others to create more social justice in their own lives (as international development organizations do). Power, particularly when misused, or created through hidden routes such as corporate lobbying, is rarely openly acknowledged. Using the concept of power to consider issues management we can see that the conflict so often mentioned in the literature can also be constructed, from an NGO perspective, as challenges to entrenched or misused power.

These writers, from the critical school of PR, create a new way of perceiving issues, by arguing that risk to society is as valid a topic for consideration as risk to a company's reputation. This allows us to move outside narrow corporate-centric definitions of issues management towards a societal approach.

More recently, Sommerfeldt and Xu (2015) have considered how non-profit organizations can approach issues management. Accepting the dominant idea that issues management inevitably includes conflict between activist groups and business, their work focuses on the role of legitimacy in issues management, and the competition between businesses and non-profits to be seen as the *most legitimate* organization with the *most legitimate* proposal for how to treat an issue. Like others, these authors overlook the possibility of issues management existing without conflict. However, their work is useful in several regards. Firstly, it brings some of the attention away from a company's reputation and back onto the issue itself. Secondly, it reinforces the idea that different voices in society can propose solutions for problems. And thirdly, it identifies (drawing on Coombs 1992) that non-profit organizations are vulnerable to accusations of illegitimacy, particularly when critiquing the legitimacy of others.

Managing issues: when society is the priority

One difference in the approach to issues management by different sectors is that businesses tend to focus on issues management from an organizational perspective. Their main concern is the potential risk to the reputation or bottom-line of the business, with societal impacts either overlooked entirely or seen as subsidiary to business interests. Miller and Dinan (2008) go further, saying that public relations exists to privilege the interest of the corporation over that of society.

By contrast, non-profit organizations tend to approach issues management as societal rather than organizational in scope. NGOs welcome public debate around issues as an opportunity to represent the interests of those for whom they advocate, and to discuss potential solutions to societal problems, regardless of the role of the individual NGO in those solutions. Debating different perspectives on an issue is an important aspect of a democratic pluralist society, and of NGOs' role within that. Corporate issues management can be about getting issues *off* the public agenda. NGOs usually want to get an issue *on* the agenda.

Monitoring issues also enables NGOs to identify changes in context. Developments in science, political priorities, societal attitudes and international economics can all impact on health, child welfare, global poverty, animal rights, human rights or environmental protection. These contextual issues can be examined for the new challenges and opportunities they open up for all those working to deliver positive social change in that field.

One useful way to consider issues management from the non-profit perspective is, therefore, as a way to monitor broad societal, political, economic and technological shifts that impact on the non-profit's area of interest – rather than their impact on the NGO itself. Identifying an issue becomes the starting point for researching the societal problem or opportunity inherent in the issue itself. Secondary to that is prioritizing the impact of the issue, again looking at the impact on the societal problem or opportunity, *not* its impact on the non-profit organization. Only then may a non-profit develop an organizational strategy around the issue to improve social justice. Such a strategy may involve enabling individual behaviour change (e.g. encouraging young people to drink responsibly or drive safely), providing service delivery at the point of need (e.g. foodbanks for those on low incomes), advocacy, or lobbying government for legislative or policy change (e.g. to reduce sexual harassment). It could also include engagement with a business, either colla-borative or confrontational (e.g. applauding a corporate's change of policy to encourage others to follow suit, or highlighting a corporate's persistence in pursuing policies that damage the environment).

This range of responses to an emerging societal issue by non-profits is largely overlooked by issues management literature, with its focus on NGO attack on business, but is discussed more fully in campaigning resources for NGOs such as Lamb (2011) and Stachowiak (2013). Stachowiak identifies ten different pathways for change. These include framing issues, developing policy options or solutions and change at the individual level. None explicitly outlines corporate engage-ment, instead discussing the conditions under which non-profits may collaborate with partners (from any sector) or work with power elites (from any sector). Stachowiak (2013: 1) hints at the complex factors that will determine which route an NGO strategy may take: 'Advocates and funders each come to policy work with a set of beliefs and assumptions about how change will happen, and these beliefs shape their thinking about … which tactics to undertake in which situations, and what changes need to be achieved along the way.' This nuance is very different from the binary approach of the corporate-centric literature on issues management, and indeed navigating these nuances is one of the main challenges facing non-profits.

Another difference in the sectoral approach to issues management is that busi-nesses may entrust this role to communications teams. Most NGOs, by contrast, typically include views from advocacy, policy and research, campaigns, public affairs, fundraising and communications departments as well as from service delivery teams on the ground, as the potential impact of the resulting insights go much further than simply organizational reputational risk. Heath and Palenchar (2009: 12) describe issues management as a 'multifunctional discipline', involving business planning, issues monitoring, CSR and dialogic communication. This idea can be extended for the non-profit sector, where issues management necessarily involves a whole-of-organization approach.

A new issues management approach for non-profits

The historical roots of issues management in the desire of business to resist activist criticism creates the need for a new approach which more explicitly reflects the goals of non-profit organizations. This new approach should:

- Reflect non-profits' core activity; delivering progressive social change
- Identify particular issues that challenge NGOs; in addition to those identified in mainstream issues management models

- Acknowledge that non-profit activities include challenging power holders, who may react using a variety of responses including counterattack against the NGO rather than addressing the issue itself.

I suggest that non-profit practitioners undertake issues management in two ways: firstly through applying a societal perspective to issues rather than a solely organizational perspective, and secondly through anticipating and countering attacks on their legitimacy.

Applying a societal perspective to issues monitoring

By participating in a whole-of-organization approach to monitoring the context of key societal issues from obesity to environmental degradation to poverty, the strategic communications professional inside an NGO will work closely alongside campaigning, policy, research, fundraising and public affairs colleagues to identify, understand and prioritise the factors that influence how key societal issues are perceived, experienced and shaped and their impact on society, whether positive or negative. This aspect of issues management inside a non-profit differs from conventional issues management in that its focus is societal and not organizational. At this stage, the issues management team are exploring the evolution of, for example, transport, or food production, without being constrained by the relationship between the issue and their own organization. This aspect is developed more fully on pp. 47–48.

Managing the legitimacy gap

The legitimacy gaps for non-profits have different causes from those experienced by businesses, and can even follow the success of the non-profit in raising awareness about a societal problem. I suggest that the three main causes of a legitimacy gap for non-profits are: success; the failure to meet expected standards; and the campaigning environment.

Success can make the NGO a target

NGOs face growing restrictions on the right to act in the public interest: to comment, advocate, challenge, hold to account, or campaign. In the UK, the Transparency of Lobbying, Non-party Campaigning and Trade Union Administration Act 2014 (United Kingdom 2014) limits the ability of charities to contribute to public debate around issues, particularly in the run-up to a general election (Lamb 2014). Though originally described as an attempt to address concerns about commercial lobbyists (whom we could compare to issues managers inside businesses), the Act applies to a broad range of non-profit activity. The retrospective application of the legislation to the snap general election in June 2017 broadened its impact, with the Special Rapporteur of the United Nations noting his concerns (United Nations

2017: 8), and describing the Act as having had 'a chilling effect on the work of charities during election periods, with many opting for silence on issues they work on'. The UN report noted that the legislation is not equitable, having more impact on civil society than on businesses, and called on the UK government to review the definition of 'regulated activity'.

Internationally, the civil society alliance Civicus (2017) reports growing restrictions on NGOs and activists in countries including Ethiopia, Egypt, Turkey and Poland, from government surveillance, detentions and arrests for peaceful advocacy to legislation that restricts campaigning.

Attacks on non-profits, especially when led by or reported in the media, can challenge their legitimacy by undermining public trust. A 2016 survey by nfpSynergy reported that 70% of journalists covering this sector agreed 'media scrutiny of charities is here to stay for the foreseeable future' (Corfe 2016). These stories often conflate the idea of party political activity – which is outside charities' remit in the UK as defined by the Charity Commission – with activity that is political in the sense that it generates debate about issues which are active in the political arena. This conflation goes largely unchallenged but underpins attacks by critics. Conservative MP Brooks Newmark, then Minister for Civil Society, told charities in 2014 in a speech not to campaign on issues in the political arena, but to 'stick to their knitting'.

Failure to meet the standards expected by trustees, beneficiaries and supporters

NGOs can face condemnation for failing to meet the high ethical standards expected by supporters. This may happen when their campaigns cause offence (for example controversial advertisements by children's charity Barnados attracted complaints), due to accounting and financial failures (such as in the Kids Company) or because of fundraising techniques which breach the public's view of acceptable levels of intrusion (Bentley et al. 2015).

Changes in the campaigning environment and public attitudes to social change

Changes in societal attitudes, and new technology-enabled ways of engaging with politics, can create issues for NGOs, as the expectations of their supporters change. Hypermodern organizations such as Avaaz, 38 Degrees, SumOfUs and Change. Org offer supporters the opportunity to engage in social change communication and lobbying activities without a long-term financial commitment. Supporters can engage on a single issue, at a single point in time. These new organizing models pose a risk to existing NGOs' funding and business models and may threaten their fundraising goals, or at least prompt NGOs to review their mobilising and organizing approaches.

The recent surge of interest in social movements such as Occupy, Nuit Debout and BlackLivesMatter and their success in engaging younger activists in innovative and non hierarchical ways may make NGOs less attractive for the next generation of supporters.

The changing nature of public discourse, reflected in the word 'post-truth', poses the challenge of working with extrinsic values when public discourse is increasingly characterised by intolerance and isolationism. Help Refugees and others in the UK and France, for example, face an uphill struggle to combat the toxic public discourse around refugees.

CASE STUDY 3.1: THE BRITISH RED CROSS AND THE NHS 'HUMANITARIAN CRISIS'

Funding for the National Health Service (NHS) in the UK was one of the key issues in the Vote Leave campaign in the run-up to the referendum in June 2016 on whether the UK would leave the European Union (EU). Campaign claims about the additional funding that would be available for the NHS if the UK left the EU influenced the referendum outcome. In the year after that referendum, the NHS remained a high profile and highly emotive issue in public discourse.

On Friday 6 January 2017, following news stories about overcrowding in hospital accident and emergency (A&E) units, and the deaths of two patients after long waits on trolleys in corridors, the British Red Cross issued a news release calling on government to allocate adequate funds for social care to alleviate this pressure. The statement was made in the context of British Red Cross' provision of a 'support at home' service, and drew on their experience of helping to organize social care for patients leaving hospital. Their statement described growing numbers of people being discharged from hospital without sufficient support, while others who were medically fit to leave hospital were unable to do so because of a lack of social care, exacerbating the delays for those waiting in A&E.

Discussing the statement on Sky News, British Red Cross Chief Executive Mike Adamson described the NHS as facing 'a humanitarian crisis'. The comment quickly attracted attention, triggering denials from the NHS and from Prime Minister Teresa May. Possibly due to the already high profile of the NHS, the British Red Cross statement stayed in the media spotlight, and Mike Adamson was forced to defend his use of the phrase humanitarian crisis. Political attention grew and opposition leader Jeremy Corbyn challenged the Prime Minister at Prime Minister's Questions on 11 January, where she described the British Red Cross' comment as 'irresponsible and overblown'. The focus of the story moved away from the situation inside the NHS to the legitimacy of the charity to comment on the situation in which it was providing services.

The incident was notable for the speed and openness with which the Prime Minister rounded on one of the UK's longest established charities, known more for its service delivery than for controversial campaigning, and attempted to shift the story from one about health and social care to one about the role of charity in commenting on social issues. Rather than engage in a discussion about health policy, the Prime Minister attacked the charity's ability to speak out at all.

Attempts to restrict the ability of non-profits to comment on the social issues within which they operate are growing, and form one of the key attacks on legitimacy that non-profit organizations face.

Sources: British Red Cross, Daily Mirror, Independent, Business Insider, Twitter

Conclusion

Issues management theory developed in the 1970s to help businesses deflect public concern about the societal impact of their operations, concerns that were often raised by non-profit organizations. The anti-activist origins of issues management persist to a greater or lesser extent in the generally corporate-centric approach of issues management models today, with their focus on protecting business reputations.

A strategic PR practitioner inside a non-profit organization may conduct issues management in two ways. PR practitioners work alongside colleagues from policy, campaigning, fundraising, advocacy and service delivery to monitor and analyse issues, not for the potential risk they pose the non-profit organization itself, but for their impact on the people, animals or environments for which the charity advocates. PR practitioners inside a non-profit, like their colleagues in a business, are likely to face a legitimacy gap at some point in their career. However, these issues are quite distinct from those faced by their business counterparts, and include attempts by government and media to stifle their ability to campaign or comment on issues of social justice.

Discussion questions

1. What types of issues might non-profits working in your field need to monitor?
2. What legitimacy gaps have you noticed?
3. How can non-profit practitioners keep the focus on the societal implications of issues?
4. How can non-profits resist being labelled a risk for the private sector?
5. What can private sector practitioners learn from the non-profit approach to issues management?
6. What other dominant theories overlook non-profits or cast them as the 'other'?

References

Bentley, P., Osborne, L. and Faulkner, K. (2015) Shame of charities that prey on the kind-hearted and drove Olive to her death: Organisations who exploited pensioner's kind heart admit to sending begging letters. *Daily Mail.* Available at http://www.dailymail.co.uk/

news/article-3083859/Shame-charities-drove-Olive-death-Organisations-exploited-p
ensioner-s-kind-heart-admit-sending-begging-letters.html [accessed 23 July 2017]

Bienkov, A. (2017) Theresa May attacks the Red Cross for 'irresponsible and overblown' comments on the NHS. *Business Insider*. Available at http://uk.businessinsider.com/ theresa-may-red-cross-pmqs-jeremy-corbyn-humanitarian-crisis-in-nhs-2017-1 [accessed 22 July 2017]

British Red Cross (2017) Red Cross calls on government to allocate funds for health and social care. Available at http://www.redcross.org.uk/About-us/News/2017/January/ Red-Cross-calls-on-government-to-allocate-funds-for-health-and-social-care [accessed 22 July 2017] and https://twitter.com/BritishRedCross [accessed 11 January 2017]

Civicus (2017) *State of Civil Society 2017*. Available at http://www.civicus.org/index.php/sta te-of-civil-society-report-2017 [accessed 11 January 2018]

Coombs, W.T. (1992) The failure of the task force on food assistance: A case study of the role of legitimacy in issue management. *Journal of Public Relations Research*, 4(2), 101–122.

Cornelissen, J. (2011) *Corporate Communication: A Guide to Theory and Practice*, 3rd edn, Sage

Corfe, E. (2016) Media scrutiny of charities is the 'new normal', says nfpSynergy Civil Society News. Available from https://www.civilsociety.co.uk/news/media-scrutiny-of-charitie s-is-the-new-normal—says-nfpsynergy.html#.VufChicgGSM [Accessed 15 March 2016]

Deegan (2001) *Managing Activism: A Guide to Dealing with Activists and Pressure Groups*, Kogan Page/CIPR

Demetrious, K. (2013) *PR, Activism and Social Change*, Routledge

Hearit, K.M. (2001) Corporate Apologia, when an organisation speaks in defense of itself. In Heath, R. (ed.), *Handbook of Public Relations*, Sage, pp. 501–511

Heath, R. and Palenchar, M. (2009) *Strategic Issues Management: Organizations and Public Policy Challenges*, 2nd edn, Sage

Jaques, T. (2006) Activist 'rules' and the convergence with issue management. *Journal of Communication Management*, 10(4): 407–420

Jaques, T. (2010) Embedding Issue Management: from process to policy. In Heath, R. (ed.) *The Sage Handbook of Public Relations*, 2nd edn, Sage, pp. 435–447

Jaques, T. (2014) Issue Management. In Tench, R. and Yeomans, L. (eds), *Exploring PR*, 3rd edn, Harlow: Pearson Education, pp. 300–312

Lamb, B. (2011) *The Good Guide to Campaigning and Influencing*, National Council for Voluntary Organisations (Great Britain)

Lamb, B. (2014) Is charity campaigning under threat from the coalition government? *Voluntary Sector Review*, 5(1): 125–138

L'Etang, J. (2009) *Public Relations Concepts, Practice and Critique*, Sage

Miller, D. and Dinan, W. (2008) *A Century of Spin: How Public Relations Became the Cutting Edge of Corporate Power*, Pluto

Regester, M. and Larkin, J. (2008) *Risk Issues and Crisis Management in Public Relations: A Casebook of Best Practice*, 4th edn, CIPR Kogan Page

Smith, M. (2017) Theresa May admits £350 million pledged to NHS by Brexit campaign isn't going to happen. *Mirror*. Available at http://www.mirror.co.uk/news/politics/theresa-adm its-350-million-pledged-10124021 [accessed 22 July 2017]

Sommerfeldt, E. and Xu, S. (2015) Legitimation strategies in radical activist issues manage-ment. In Waters, R. (ed.), *Public Relations in the Non-Profit Sector: Theory And Practice*, Routledge, pp. 185–203

Stachowiak, S. (2013) *Pathways for Change: 10 Theories to Inform Advocacy and Policy Change Efforts*, Centre for Evaluation Innovation

United Kingdom (2014) *Transparency of Lobbying, Non-Party Campaigning and Trade Union Administration Act 2014*, chap. 4. Available from http://services.parliament.uk/bills/

2013-14/transparencyoflobbyingnonpartycampaigningandtradeunionadministration.html [accessed 23 July 2017]

United Nations (2017) A/HRC/35/28/Add.1 *Report of the Special Rapporteur on the Rights to Freedom of Peaceful Assembly and of Association on his Mission to the United Kingdom of Great Britain and Northern Ireland.* Available from http://www.ohchr.org/EN/HRBodies/ HRC/RegularSessions/Session35/Pages/ListReports.aspx [accessed 23 July 2017]

Wilkinson, R. (2017) British Red Cross CEO defends NHS 'humanitarian crisis' remarks. *Independent.* Available at http://www.independent.co.uk/news/uk/home-news/nhs-bri tish-red-cross-chief-executive-mike-adamson-defends-humanitarian-crisis-remarks-a 7516751.html [accessed 22 July 2017]

PART II
Communicating to build trust

4

BEYOND CLICKS FOR CAUSES

Enabling agile digital communications

Ann Longley and Tove Nordström

Introduction: the daunting pace of change

The non-profit sector plays a vital role in society. However, its survival and effectiveness increasingly depends on its ability to assess, master and deploy digital technologies. Digital technology is driving unprecedented change causing all media to converge (Jenkins 2006) whilst enabling new entrants to establish themselves quickly and with relative ease. Non-profit organizations failing to adapt to digital opportunities and threats may face obsolescence (Bull et al. 2015), whilst non-profit employees with easily replicable skills may increasingly become redundant. By 2025, 25 per cent of jobs could be lost to robots and automation (Thibodeau 2014). Strategic use of digital platforms and tools can help non-profits engage and reach their audiences, help diversify income streams and gain much needed efficiencies. With non-profit income in the UK under pressure since 2009 (NCVO 2015), their use is about future proofing, not just communications, but the organization as a whole.

Due to the complex, fast-moving nature of the digital landscape and the uncertainty it brings, non-profits need to change their cultures to keep pace. They need digitally mature cultures putting technical and 'customer' considerations upfront, ensuring they remain relevant by being nimble enough to exploit suitable digital technologies for strategic communications and other core purposes. Organizational-wide transformation is needed to embed this cultural shift. Communications professionals have an important role to play in the change process as non-profits must adopt digitally enriched internal and external communications to thrive in the digital age.

To respond to tech-fuelled 21st century societal changes and to support the development of digitally mature cultures, a new digital communications model for the non-profit sector is needed. The **Agile Digital Communications Approach (ADCA)** is introduced here as a means for non-profits to be sustainable now and in the future. It has been created to help non-profits keep up with ever-evolving technology, use data to become more efficient, and prove their delivery of results. The model stretches beyond catalyzing 'clicktivism', the phenomenon whereby the public shows support for causes with 'clicks' but no other actions (Howard 2014), to address how non-profits use digital communications techniques and channels to raise awareness, build communities of advocates, deliver services, and raise funds. This conceptual model is inspired by the **agile** movement, a philosophy and set of principles for software development putting customer needs at its heart. It espouses collaborating with customers and empowering capable teams using face to face communication (*Agile Manifesto* 2001). Agile principles are so apt, they have inspired business leaders to advocate creating agile enterprises capable of adapting to fast changing market conditions (McKinsey 2017). They are equally relevant for non-profits who are also impacted by these changes.

The importance of digital strategy

Non-profits today need digital capabilities in place to ensure they deliver their missions. A digital strategy is needed, but it should not be a separate entity. It should be fully integrated into organizational masterplans and operating models demonstrating how digital will support and deliver strategy seamlessly across all functions including communications. The majority of UK non-profits believe digital tools and technology will change the sector significantly, yet half have no digital strategy (Amar and Evans 2017). With many non-profits boards failing to grasp the importance and magnitude of the challenge, the issue has become one of governance (Amar 2016). Digital skills are low or in need of improvement on 71 per cent of boards (Amar and Evans 2017). They worry about missing out on opportunities for digital fundraising, giving competitors an advantage, or even becoming irrelevant. 47 per cent think their non-profit is not agile enough and recognize their culture needs changing (Amar and Evans 2017).

Digitally enriched fundraising

With lack of resources, skills and funding being the biggest barriers to getting more from digital, many non-profits are falling behind. This situation is exacerbated by competition from digitally savvy organizations encroaching on the traditional gift-giving territory: technology-led companies, high-profile individuals and others crowdfunding directly for causes. Competitors may increase their share of donations through smart use of digital technology; 61 per cent of UK non-profits rate their digital fundraising skills as fair to low and a majority state their IT infrastructure needs improving (Amar and Evans, 2017). Managing data security and privacy is vital as supporters may not be willing to give regularly to organizations viewed as vulnerable to cyberattacks. Despite these concerns, the majority of non-profits believe developing digital skills would help increase fundraising, grow their networks, and deliver their strategy more effectively (ibid.).

Brave leadership is needed

To become digitally mature, non-profits need to invest in transformation, focusing on people and culture as much as technology. Courageous leadership from CEOs is essential if digital is to take root and become intrinsic to all functions. Breaking down departmental boundaries to ensure cross-team collaboration is a key outcome of successful transformation. Organizational changes, including the ability to co-create campaigns or services with colleagues in other departments, may be resisted due to fear or confusion about expectations, and adherence to outmoded structures. Whilst resistance to change is inevitable, it can and must be worked though.

Learning from others

In spite of cultural differences, non-profits can learn from organizations who put digital first. Forward-thinking non-profits are building agility and efficiency into their DNA with the use of high-growth 'start-up' business practices and design thinking which can also be applied to solving social problems (Yoo 2016). Agile methods have been applied to communications (van Ruler 2014) with *The Reflective Communications Scrum* demonstrating their relevance and adaptability. Equally, *The Lean Startup's* entrepreneurial practices (Ries 2011) which strive to maximize progress with minimal resources when developing new products are also highly relevant to the sector (Simcock 2016).

Attaining digital maturity

If non-profit organizations are to be able to become digitally mature, they need new structures and ways of working as well as new skill sets. When introducing lean and agile practices into non-profits, consider adapting the terminology to improve the likelihood of its acceptance by colleagues who may be sceptical about its relevance. Capacity building and clear behavioural expectations (for instance, for collaboration) are critical. Empowering skilled people to push boundaries, and learn through doing, whilst analysing relevant data, is paramount. All of the above must be communicated effectively through internal communications and proactive employee engagement programmes. Collaborative digital tools can play a supporting role, but face-to-face communications must take precedence.

Senior managers must recognize that digital is a powerful enabler of all aspects of organizational strategy and learn to use it to achieve strategic goals. They also need to recognize that disruptive innovation may threaten business as usual (International Civil Society Centre 2013; Christiansen et al. 2015) and take steps to mitigate risks. Communication leaders need strategic oversight to ensure their organizations' reputations are protected, and operational involvement, so stakeholders are engaged effectively with communications.

Digital communications challenges and opportunities

The Internet has transformed and revolutionized communications irrevocably, triggering the need for a new approach. Traditional media channels still deliver value, but digital media fragments and augments it. A new generation of stakeholders consume media in radically different ways (Tapscott 2009). Unlike passive audiences of the past, stakeholders now actively shape and convey brand messages creating their own content. Internet access via mobile has exceeded desktop access globally (Stat Counter 2016), and consequently, non-profits can now be present in almost everyone's pockets (GSMA 2017). A donation is just one click away from well-placed content, underscoring the need for responsive design (Marcotte 2010).

New channels and features

The Internet has catalyzed a host of new channels including social networking sites, most notably Facebook, functionality (like search), formats including blogs, forums and email, and tools such as apps, voice activated assistants and chatbots. They all connect the public, whilst offering non-profit organizations increased possibilities for transparency and new ways of creating social value and impact. Crucially, websites, social networking sites, messaging services and apps give organizations the ability to publish content directly and build unmediated relationships with their stakeholders. New functionality and features are constantly added than can benefit communications efforts (Phillips and Young 2009). Facebook and other major players like Apple are supporting non-profits by rolling out frictionless donation mechanisms on their platforms (Zillman 2015) making them attractive partners. The low access cost is a major attraction for non-profits (Curtis et al. 2010).

Listening and responding

The Internet also enables listening and responding to stakeholders in real time (Coombs and Holladay 2010), which is important as discussions about non-profits and the causes they address occur online (Brown 2009). Non-profits can gain insight and build trust by joining relevant conversations (Scoble and Israel 2006). For Cancer Research UK, listening online highlighted a significant fundraising opportunity.

CASE STUDY 4.1: CANCER RESEARCH UK'S #NOMAKEUPSELFIE

Cancer Research UK (CRUK) made internet history when it raised £8m in six days on the back of an Internet trend which became associated with its brand (Press Association 2014). Above all, it shows the importance of scanning the online environment for opportunities, the power and potential for seeding and growing ideas online, and the need for organizational agility to respond to such opportunities quickly.

#NoMakeUpSelfies (NMUS) began appearing online organically around 2012 relating to discussions about the pressure on women to maintain their appearance. In 2014, a young mum created a page on Facebook linking the trend to cancer awareness. Women were encouraged to post NMUS and make a donation to CRUK. The message struck a chord and the call to action began spreading online on a peer-to-peer basis.

People started asking CRUK if it was involved. CRUK quickly set up a mobile donation channel advising the public to 'Text Beat to donate £3'. Employees responded to public comments online about how the money would be used with handwritten signs. They thanked the public at every milestone as the organic campaign grew. Celebrities got involved sharing their own NMUS and the text to donate code and UK media started picking up the campaign. CRUK then supported the activity with paid social media to further increase reach and maximize fundraising. The campaign helped increase the size of CRUK's social communities significantly and created a huge spike in website visits and donations. The success was based on CRUK's fast, authentic and personal response (Digital Training Academy 2014) to a non-planned campaign. It was a grass-roots initiative that CRUK was nimble enough to embrace.

Two-way communications and beyond

Trusting relationships require transparency (Welch 2006), subsequently generating commitment and collaboration. These aspects are crucial if non-profits are to receive long-term public support (Edwards 2006). Lack of transparency can damage credibility and stakeholder relationships (Sweetser 2010). Despite an increased interest in the use of social media relating to transparency, Gandía (2011) argues that many non-profits are missing out on this opportunity.

In 1984, Grunig and Hunt recommended the two-way symmetric model of communication, advocating mutual understanding and dialogue as the one to aspire towards in terms of best practice and ethics. In 2009, Grunig went on to highlight the significance social media could have on two-way communication bestowing public relations with a more interactive, global, strategic, and socially responsible approach. Whilst two-way communication with stakeholders can help create an open transparent organization, this dynamic also makes it more difficult to hide public concerns. Phillips and Young (2009: 157) argue that 'your brand is no stronger than your reputation and will increasingly depend on what comes up when you are Googled'. In this context, the ability to build a strong brand online generating advocacy from stakeholders, such as donors and volunteers, is crucial. Word of mouth is proven to be more effective than advertising (Nielsen 2015), so inspiring the public to participate and share a non-profit's messages can be highly effective. However, although desirable, this outcome is impossible to guarantee as communications now take place as 'a multi-way diachronic process of ongoing construction of meaning in which one cannot foresee who is – or will be – involved, in what way, and what the results will be' (van Ruler, 2014).

Stakeholder diversity

Audiences that may not initially be seen as key stakeholders can become important when they engage in discussions that affect the organization's primary stakeholders and their interests (Jensen 2001). Ihlen et al. (2009: 142) observe those who 'do not seem like stakeholders at the present, might choose to take an interest in a company at a later stage'. Social media should therefore be seen to encourage a three-way model of communication allowing third parties to share and receive messages on a peer-to-peer basis (Ferber et al. 2007). To maximize their impact, non-profits can now bolster their communications by embracing the full potential of social communications to enable the spread of content directly via third parties, and on a peer-to-peer basis (Jenkins et al. 2013).

Opening up communications

Blogs and podcasts can be cost-effective ways to reach new audiences (Ingenhoff and Koelling 2009). They also help organizations come across as more human (Scoble and Israel 2006) as they are delivered directly. For 'humanization' to occur, it is essential to maintain a high level of authenticity with real people discussing real issues (Kanter and Fine 2010). That means empowering employees and other stakeholders to create content and embrace the art of listening. Social media is a perfect platform to observe what competitors are doing as well as learn what kind of content stakeholders find interesting and what channels they use. People's ideas, behaviours and questions can subsequently be used to engage in conversations, enrich content and inform new services. Kanter and Fine (2010: 10) argue that conversations are vital to non-profits since 'conversations activate the natural creativity and passion that people bring to causes they care about'. These possibilities are supercharged by live video streaming now available on most major social networks.

Similarly, Jenkins (2006) emphasized the importance of participatory culture and spreadable media. Grassroots participatory approaches enabled by social media like the NMUS are just as important for the future of non-profit communications as top down ones have been in the past. They are important as, in addition to raising awareness, they can encourage people to take action (Lovejoy and Saxon 2012).

The digital revolution brings with it innovative technologies, tools and tactics that help non-profits to achieve their communications and fundraising objectives whilst becoming more efficient, transparent and accountable. Emerging mediums like virtual and augmented reality build empathy through highly immersive brand experiences that help raise funds (Petronzio 2017; Overly 2016). The UN's 'Clouds Over Sidra' Virtual Reality film engaged the audience in life as a Syrian refugee, raising \$3.8m and surpassing its \$2.2m target. Marketing automation and artificial intelligence supercharge some public relations tasks and so should be integrated into non-profits' communications workflow to aid efficiency. Technologies such as contactless payments, mobile wallets and blockchain are transforming financial workflows, from fundraising to dispersal (Allison 2017) enabling a greater degree of transparency disrupting traditional operations.

CASE STUDY 4.2: ST MUNGO'S USE OF BLOCKCHAIN

St Mungo's, a UK charity tackling homelessness, is working with social tech start up Alice.si using smart contracts on the Ethereum public blockchain to give donors visibility of the impact of their donations. St Mungo's is using the tech for an innovative trial appeal helping 15 homeless people rebuild their lives (Allison 2017). Using blockchain, donations are, in effect, 'frozen' until St Mungo's can demonstrate they have achieved their aims.

The technology makes the performance of the projects public and auditable. Funds are disbursed according to the completion of pre-set goals. If the goals are not achieved, the donors get their money back. Specific goals include helping the homeless individuals find and then stay in a new home, with individual support provided for up to six months after they move in to help them transition. Other goals entail treatment for substance misuse or mental health issues if needed.

To avoid the volatility of cryptocurrencies dispersed via blockchain, public donations are made in pounds sterling using debit or credit cards. The trial is being run in partnership with the Greater London Authority and the Financial Conduct Authority, within its sandbox programme, with additional support from the Nominet Trust.

This project is noteworthy due to the transformative benefits of using blockchain to rebuild public trust. The approach also allows St Mungo's to give people the personalised support they need to rebuild their lives. Although the outcome of this trial is as yet unclear, it is included here due to its potential to disrupt traditional operating models. It shows how experimentation with digital tech may lead to radically new ways of working, generating completely new communications' narratives and conversations with the public.

The Charity Aid Foundation (CAF) has been exploring the potential of blockchain through a number of papers including 'Losing the middle but keeping the heart: Blockchain, DAOs and the future decentralisation of charity'. It explores how new organizational forms such as Distributed or Decentralized Autonomous Organizations (DAO) made possible by blockchain may help improve trust (Davies 2017) through transparency. The St Mungo's experiment and CAF's thought leadership demonstrates how radically technology is shaking up the status-quo.

Unlocking Agile Digital Communications

To fully embrace digital opportunities in today's always-on digital communications environment requires a flexible and evolving approach to communications planning and execution. It must nimbly grasp digital opportunities and minimize risks as a part of daily practice. The **Agile Digital Communications Approach (ADCA)** presented here is not linear or frozen in time. It is dynamically powered by a continuous feedback loop helping non-profits select the right approaches and become more targeted and effective with their communication in real time. It is a conceptual model derived from a non-profit's purpose outlining clear actions and outcomes. Inputs include strong strategic leadership and creativity based on sound insights as they can lead to transformative brand experiences and organizational sustainability especially if non-profits can prove their social impact. Harnessing digital data, securing traditional coverage and leveraging media and other partnerships makes great sense for any organization with limited resources.

The **ADCA** helps non-profits build trust, advocacy and ultimately sustainability by providing life-changing activity based on the convergence of common interests defined through active stakeholder engagement. The aim and result should be shared transformative (i.e. life-changing or planet preserving) brand experiences, demonstrably helping beneficiaries, igniting donor advocacy, whilst generating public trust and media interest. By encouraging social sharing throughout an extensive digital communications ecosystem comprised of the contacts of all

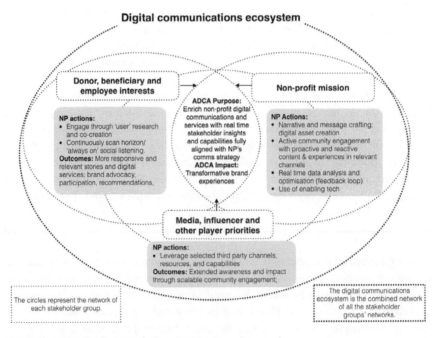

FIGURE 4.1 The Agile Digital Communications Approach
Source: Longley and Nordström

stakeholders (donors, beneficiaries, employees, media, and corporate partners), non-profits can exponentially maximize their impact and reach.

Using the ADCA

To create a sustainable non-profit today requires an understanding and appreciation of how stakeholders' lives increasingly rely on digital communications, social networks and utilities (e.g. health trackers, virtual assistants, alerts, ecommerce) and how digital data can provide sophisticated, even predictive, insights and solutions. This understanding must be underpinned and supported by an operating model that uses digital and other data to spark actionable insights leading to engaging and transformative experiences. As with any approach, it begins by setting clear objectives supported by highly collaborative ways of working. It reflects a fast moving world where non-profits need to embrace emerging best practices and digital tech to achieve their missions.

ADCA purpose: creating transformative brand experiences

The ultimate output of the ADCA is a unified brand experience fully aligned with a non-profit's communications strategy created on the back of sound insights delivering measurable outcomes. It is based on the premise that the mission of the non-profit organization will be met if converged with the needs and interests of primary stakeholders plus the media and other players, in particular, corporate partners. As non-profits exist to create social or environmental benefits, to get results their activity must demonstrate how it will do so in a credible and timely manner. Stakeholders can now be part of the story, helping non-profits decide what messages to highlight or services to offer. In the digital age, reporting back can also be a way to generate further interest and impact as St Mungo's blockchain project shows.

Achieve non-profit mission with content, digital channels, data and enabling tech

Digital clearly has a central role to play in communications today. The most engaging brand experiences today are multi-channel and yet seamlessly joined up. Traditional media outlets are no longer exclusive mediators of direct relationships with the public, and social media has made much dialogue public. In the networked age, a website is vital, but insufficient on its own. A distributed presence on social media optimizes and amplifies a non-profit's message and mission. Facebook will soon have two billion active users across the world, 600 million use Instagram, and 317 million users are on Twitter (Allen 2017). Using such channels to build a strong eco-system and network of supporters is the aim as advocates can and will help spread messages and drive their own initiatives to raise awareness and funds as NMUS has shown.

With new channels and influencers constantly emerging, rigor is needed to decide which ones to use. Whilst access to some may be free, the cost to operate them may be considerable. Channel decisions should be made based on objectives and use by target audience. The cost to use the channel should be less than the expected return at least in the long term. It is important to filter and prioritize digital opportunities given resource scarcity, however scope for experimentation (i.e. testing and learning) is equally important in the face of disruption. By carefully experimenting with new communications and transactional approaches as St Mungo's have done, non-profits can learn through doing, and *in doing* so enhance overall performance and reputation setting new standards for the sector.

It is essential to provide engaging and transformative brand experiences on digital channels by creating, curating, publishing and broadcasting relevant content. Whilst press releases still have some use, publishing stories and visual assets via selected digital media channels drives greater visibility and engagement online. A messaging hierarchy and publishing schedule based on relevant content pillars (reflecting the non-profit's mission and stakeholder needs) provides the foundation for a winning content strategy. It should trigger dynamic conversations centred around the non-profit and the issues it tackles. Proactive as well as reactive content is essential for community building. Frequently updated content helps attract website visitors and can boost visibility in search. Visual content performs best as the brain processes images faster than words. Additionally, organizations can leverage user-generated content as Cancer Research UK did with the NMUS. To respond effectively requires the right internal set up with community managers potentially extending their office hours using marketing automation, and working closely with colleagues in other departments.

Digital technology can also be used to deliver new services to support the very conditions non-profits seek to address. For example, apps and utilities using AI show promise in social care. Community features and gamification can help non-profits attract new audiences, demonstrate measureable impacts, fill service gaps, and cut through clutter. Online communities are particularly helpful for supporting people suffering from wide-ranging health conditions. The key to delivering authentic and engaging experiences is to ensure solutions are based on real needs and insights underpinned by ethical considerations. Scanning the environment for digital technology that can help non-profits achieve their objectives is a key component of the ADCA model.

Harnessing empirical data to evaluate, optimize and report back is also an important part of it. Digital channels provide myriad metrics. To make them meaningful, they need to be aligned with overarching communications and marketing objectives. Digital data sources that can be used to plan and evaluate communications activities are diverse and include, but are not limited to website traffic and referrer data, donations, engagement metrics from social networking sites, social media mentions, and video views. Digital data can help non-profits prepare for critical situations, retarget prospective donors, and provide instant feedback to optimize programmes. It is important to begin with clear objectives, analyse the data for actionable insights, then design, evaluate and optimize brand experiences accordingly.

Leveraging donor, beneficiary and employee interests

Non-profit communications must also consider the behaviour, habits and interests of connected stakeholders including donors, beneficiaries and employees who are using digital media for a variety of reasons. Leveraging stakeholder insights when planning communications and brand experiences (which here include social media campaigns, community fora, websites, apps, videos or other digital products and services) will increase the likelihood they will share non-profit assets with their networks and make donations. Traditional approaches like surveys or market research reports are helpful to define relevant macro-level trends, but they are insufficient on their own. Research can now be done in a variety of digitally enabled ways ranging from social listening to user testing, and co-creation.

Uncovering actionable stakeholder insights is no longer an annual activity or quarterly event. In an always-on communications world, it is necessary to be *always-on* to monitor what is being said about your brand online, to manage reputation instantly, as well as inform engagement opportunities. Non-profits can now assess and strengthen the impact of communications campaigns in real time by reviewing performance data and by listening and responding to stakeholder comments. For most non-profits, it will be hard to sustain a brand without a continuous presence.

Whilst traditional planning cycles are still needed, scanning the online environment for relevant trends and topics associated with your organization on a daily basis is not only possible but advisable. It is important to pick up negative signals to decide what if any action to take as well as identify popular topics, influencers and hashtags to legitimately piggyback on to promote causes and key messages as demonstrated by NMUS.

Engage media, influencers and other players by addressing their priorities and utilizing their assets

Traditional media coverage continues to be important with the added benefit of big followings on their social media accounts. Pursuing social mentions on them, alongside base coverage on websites and in print is advisable. The significant and authoritative digital presence of top media outlets can help significantly boost and endorse non-profit campaigns. Partnerships with socially connected influencers are also worth pursuing. Although time consuming and difficult to manage, influencer engagement can deliver advantages, including access to younger audiences. Many high-profile influencers and celebrities charge high rates for social posts. It is important to build strong relationships with those who are warm to non-profit causes as they are more likely to work collaboratively without any charge ensuring mutually beneficial outcomes are achieved. Taking this approach means the resulting content will be more credible and authentic than it would be if the influencer's posts were sponsored. Jack Harries' Climate Change videos co-created with WWF are exemplary (Harries 2015).

Content creation, promotion and PR are important to consider when negotiating corporate partnerships. Corporates have their own audiences, technology and human resources to contribute. Finally, non-profit and corporate partner employees can also make great brand advocates who help 'humanize' brand messages by sharing them with their own connections. This approach can work at all levels of the organization from the CEO to frontline staff and, under the right conditions, even beneficiaries.

In closing, the **Agile Digital Communications Approach** is a springboard to evolve digital communications in non-profits. To transform the organization, one should connect with sector initiatives like the NPC's Digital Transformation Programme and secure assistance from a transformation specialist. To achieve their missions in the digital age, the sector may well need to be re-invented.

Discussion questions

1.   What do we mean by digital communications?
2.   Why should non-profits embrace digital communications?
3.   What kinds of external digital communications tactics should non-profits consider?
4.   What is the role of internal communications in developing digitally mature cultures?
5.   How can non-profits become more digitally savvy?
6.   Who is responsible for digital transformation in a non-profit organization?
7.   What new communications possibilities are now possible?
8.   What is the role of communications professionals in digital transformation?

References

Agile Manifesto (2001) Available from: http://agilemanifesto.org/authors.html

Allen, R. (2017) Top Social Network sites by number of active users 2017. *Smart Insights.* [Online] Available from: http://www.smartinsights.com/social-media-marketing/social-media-strategy/new-global-social-media-research/attachment/top-social-network-sites-by-number-of-active-users-2017/

Allison, I. (2017, 12 May) Ethereum is helping London's homeless with St Mungo's and smart contracts. *IBT Times.* [Online] Available from: http://www.ibtimes.co.uk/ethereum-helping-londons-homeless-st-mungos-smart-contracts-1620724

Amar, Z. (2016) Charity boards are failing to adapt to the digital age – this has to change. *The Guardian.* [Online] Available from: https://www.theguardian.com/voluntary-sector-network/2016/apr/11/charity-governance-digital-technology-trustees

Amar, Z. & Evans, D. (2017) *Charity Digital Skills Report 2017.* [Online] Available from: http://report.skillsplatform.org/charitydigitalreport-overview/

Brown, R. (2009) *Public Relations and the Social Web: How to Use Social Media and Web 2.0 in Communications.* London: Kogan Page Limited.

Bull, D., Lumley, T., Sabri, F. & Bowler, R. (2015, December) *Tech for Common Good: The Case for a Collective Approach to Digital Transformation in the Social Sector.* London: NPC. [Online] Available from: http://www.thinknpc.org/publications/tech-for-common-good/

Christiansen, C.M., Raynor, M.E. & McDonald, R. (2015, December) *What is Disruptive Innovation?* Boston: Harvard Business Review.

Coombs, W.T. & Holladay, S.J. (2010) *PR Strategy and Application: Managing Influence.* UK: Wiley-Blackwell.

Curtis, L. et al. (2010) Adoption of social media for public relations by non-profit organizations. *Public Relations Review,* 36: 90–92.

Davies, R. (2017, May), *Losing the Middle but Keeping the Heart: Blockchain, DAOs and the Future Decentralisation of Charity*, London: Charity Aid Foundation (CAF). [Online] Available from: https://www.cafonline.org/docs/default-source/about-us-policy-and-campaigns/losing-the-middle-keeping-the-heart–blockchain-daos-and-future-of-charity.pdf

Digital Training Academy (2014) 'No Make-up selfie' raises £8m for Cancer Research in a week. *Digital Training Academy.* [Online] Available from: http://www.digitaltrainingacademy.com/casestudies/2014/03/no_make_up_selfie_raises_8m_for_cancer_research_in_a_week.php

Edwards, L. (2006) Public relations theories – an applied overview: systems theories. In Tench, T. & Yeomans, L., *Exploring Public Relations* (pp. 142–165). Essex: Pearson Education Limited.

Ferber, P., Foltz, F. & Pugliese, R. (2007) Cyberdemocracy and online politics: a new model of interactivity. *Bulletin of Science, Technology & Society*, 27(5): 391–400.

Gandía, J.L. (2011) Internet disclosure by nonprofit organizations: empirical evidence of nongovernmental organizations for development in Spain. *Nonprofit and Voluntary Sector Quarterly*, 40(1): 57–78.

Grunig, J.E. (2009) Paradigms of global public relations in an age of digitalisation. *Prism*, 6(2).

Grunig, J.E. & Hunt, T. (1984) *Managing Public Relations.* USA: Wadsworth/Thomson Learning.

GSMA (2017) *The Mobile Economy 2017.* [Online] Available from: https://www.gsma.com/mobileeconomy/#

Harries, J. (2015) *Our Changing Climate.* [Online] Available from: https://www.youtube.com/watch?v=gE7vkCz39eg

House of Commons (2016) The 2015 charity fundraising controversy: lessons for trustees, the Charity Commission, and regulators. [Online] Available from: https://www.publications.parliament.uk/pa/cm201516/cmselect/cmpubadm/431/431.pdf

Howard, E. (2014, 24 September) How 'clicktivism' has changed the face of political campaigns. *The Guardian.* [Online] Available from: https://www.theguardian.com/society/2014/sep/24/clicktivism-changed-political-campaigns-38-degrees-change

International Civil Society Centre (2013) *Riding the Waves: A Proposal for Boards and CEOs on How to Prepare their Organisations for Disruptive Change.* International Civil Society Centre. [Online] Available from: https://icscentre.org/downloads/RidingTheWave_web_spreads.pdf

Ihlen, Ø., van Ruler, B. & Fredriksson, M. (eds) (2009) *Public Relations and Social Theory: Key Figures and Concepts.* New York: Routledge.

Ingenhoff, D. & Koelling, A.M. (2009) The potential of Web sites as a relationship building tool for charitable fundraising NPOs. *Public Relations Review*, 35: 66–73.

Jenkins, H. (2006) *Convergence Culture: Where Old and New Media Collide*, New York: New York University Press.

Jenkins, H., Green, J. & Ford, S. (2013) *Spreadable Media: Creating Value and Meaning in a Networked Culture (Postmillennial Pop).* New York: New York University Press.

Jensen, I. (2001) Public relations and emerging functions of the public sphere: An analytical framework. *Journal of Communication Management*, 6(2): 133–147.

Kanter, B. & Fine, A.H. (2010) *The Networked Nonprofit.* San Fransisco, CA: John Wiley & Sons, Inc.

Lovejoy, K. & SaxonG.D. (2012) Information, community and action: how non-profit organisations use social media. *Journal of Computer-Mediated Communication.*

Marcotte, E. (2010, 25 May) Responsive Web Design. *A List Apart.* [Online] Available from: https://alistapart.com/article/responsive-web-design

McKinsey (2017, August) How to go agile enterprise-wide: An interview with Scott Richardson. McKinsey&Company. [Online] Available from: http://www.mckinsey.com/

business-functions/digital-mckinsey/our-insights/how-to-go-agile-enterprise-wide-an-interview-with-scott-richardson?

Nielsen (2015) Recommendations from friends remain the most credible form of advertising among consumes; branded website are the second highest-rated form. [Online] Available from: http://www.nielsen.com/ca/en/press-room/2015/recommendations-from-friends-remain-most-credible-form-of-advertising.html

NCVO (2015) *A Financial Sustainability Review, 2015.* [Online] Available from: https://www.ncvo.org.uk/images/documents/policy_and_research/funding/financial-sustainability-review-of-the-voluntary-sector-july-2015.pdf

Overly, S. (2016, 12 October) How non-profits use virtual reality to solve real-world issues. *Washington Post.* [Online] Available from: https://www.washingtonpost.com/news/innovations/wp/2016/10/12/how-nonprofits-use-virtual-reality-to-tackle-real-world-issues/?utm_term=.a24ccbf2c7d8

Petronzio, M. (2017, 3 March) VR film series shows how you can help non profits transforming young lives. *Mashable.* [Online] Available from: http://mashable.com/2017/03/03/epic-foundation-virtual-reality-films-vr/#x2pwrAX.4uqI

Phillips, D. & Young, P. (2009) *Online Public Relations: A Practical Guide to Developing an Online Strategy in the World of Social Media.* 2nd edn. London: Kogan Page Limited.

Press Association (2014, 25 March) No-makeup selfies raise £8m for Cancer Research UK in six days. *The Guardian.* [Online] Available from: https://www.theguardian.com/society/2014/mar/25/no-makeup-selfies-cancer-charity

Ries, E. (2011) *The Lean Startup.* New York: Crown Publishing Group.

Scoble, R. & Israel, S. (2006) *Naked Conversations: How Blogs are Changing the Way Businesses Talk with Customers.* Hoboken, N.J.: John Wiley & Sons, Inc.

Simcock, J. (2016, 19 April) How agile working can save costs and increase performance. *Third Sector.* [Online] Available from: http://www.thirdsector.co.uk/agile-working-save-costs-increase-performance/digital/article/1391787

Stat Counter (2016, 1 November) Mobile and tablet internet usage exceeds desktop for first time worldwide. *Statcounter.* [Online] Available from: http://gs.statcounter.com/press/mobile-and-tablet-internet-usage-exceeds-desktop-for-first-time-worldwide

Sweetser, K.D. (2010) A losing strategy: the impact of nondisclosure in social media on relationships. *Journal of Public Relations Research,* 22(3): 288–312.

Tapscott, D. (2009) *Grown Up Digital: How the Net Generation is Changing Your World.* New York: McGraw-Hill.

Thibodeau, P. (2014, 6 October) One in three jobs will be taken by software or robots by 2025. *The Telegraph.* [Online] Available from: http://www.telegraph.co.uk/technology/2016/11/01/mobile-web-usage-overtakes-desktop-for-first-time/

van Ruler, B. (2014), Agile public relations planning: the reflective communication scrum. *Public Relations Review,* 4: 187–194.

Welch, M. (2006) Rethinking relationship management: exploring the dimension of trust. *Journal of Communication Management,* 10(2): 138–155.

Yoo, Youngjin (2016, 17 August) The problem with innovation. *Beyond.* [Online] Available from: https://beyond.case.edu/articles/wKIZpb2e/the-problem-with-innovation

Zillman, C. (2015) With new 'donate' button, Facebook vies to become hub for charitable giving. *Fortune.* [Online] Available from: http://fortune.com/2015/11/18/facebook-donate/

5

THE EMERGENCE AND GROWTH OF STRATEGIC PARTNERSHIPS BETWEEN NGOS AND CORPORATES

Balancing risks and leveraging communications

Kevin Read and Caroline Diehl

From Adam Smith ([1786] 1843) onwards there has been a view that the market, however visibly, or otherwise, serves society. Corporate philanthropy, often rooted in economic success associated with industrialization from the late 18th century onwards, established channels for the redistribution of wealth and a plethora of causes, often linked to social reform. Indeed, this tradition goes back even to the philanthropy of the medieval guilds. Yet, other than the ground-breaking philanthropy of the Victorian Quakers firms (Brejning 2013) it is not until the 1920s (Heald 1970), that companies begin to recognize explicitly their obligations to wider society, and build this activity into their corporate and public relations. In post-war society this outlook grew, leading to the emergence of social action programmes pioneered by business leaders.

The idea that economic and social value could co-exist, developed by Michael Porter and Mark Kramer (2002) at the beginning of the new millennium, is countered by free market economist Milton Friedman (2007), who argues that business had no obligation to support social causes or NGOs. Porter and Kramer's (2002) social value framework has accelerated the willingness of NGOs to seek longer-term partnerships with corporates. Growing numbers of NGOs now see the added value of moving beyond a fundraising focus.

The myriad challenges of these new types of partnership (Pattberg 2005; Austin and Seitanidi 2012) are examined. Steady partnership growth means there is now more focus on how these new types of relationship can be delivered and measured.

The nature, scale and complexity of NGO–corporate partnerships continue to grow, with initiatives often based around a single cause or campaign. The United Nations with their Sustainability Goals explicitly supports the concept of responsible business and in their 21st century NGO report (2003) they suggest NGOs will become more flexible, pragmatic and business like.

This chapter will explore how the concept of social value evolved and the communication and practical challenges arising from new partnerships. It will also discuss the distinct steps that corporate partnerships tend to go through. Critical 'Fit to Partner' tests will be discussed. The reasons for alliances failing will be explored and a new partnership classification will be provided.

Establishing social and collaborative value

Porter and Kramer (2002: 68) believe 'There is no inherent contradiction between improving competitive context and making a sincere commitment to bettering society'. They argue that it is acceptable to make tangible returns on good will causes. In contrast, free market economist Friedman (2007) argues that businesses have no role whatsoever in supporting society or the work of charities.

Tougher economic circumstances, increasing pressure to become more business-like and efficient, the relentless need to fundraise and the rapid growth of the charity sector may have all contributed to an NGO re-think on partnerships.

The best NGO–corporate partnerships align brand values and deliver mutual benefit. Pattberg (2005) examines how NGOs have been moving beyond arms-length fundraising to co-operative partnerships. He highlights the challenges NGOs need to tackle with lower levels of state support. He suggests that whilst businesses can cause problems for society, they can also help deliver solutions to solve them.

Some NGOs have now adopted a neoliberal agenda; accepting that market-based approaches have a distinct role in helping to tackle NGO causes. Jessica Dempsey and Daniel Suaraz (2016: 667) explain that among the conservationist community there is an emerging consensus that NGOs, 'must now court, rather than confront, entrenched power structures, established regimes of capital accu-mulation, and private capital itself'. Ben Schiller (2005: 3) observes, 'NGOs are becoming more practical, flexible, less dogmatic and more eager to seek solutions from the business sphere'.

Austin and Seitanidi (2012) show that new balances between social and eco-nomic value are becoming more common, and that there is a growing focus on co-created value. They explain that a business can have 'Policies and operating practices that enhance the competitiveness of a company while simultaneously advancing the economic and social conditions in the communities in which it operates' (Austin and Seitanidi 2012: 6).

Theoretical frameworks can help explain the shift toward greater levels of collaboration, and at times, complexity. Systems theorist, Niklas Luhmann (1995), believes that as an organization experiences a more and more complex environment it will create more complexity for itself. Anselm Schneider, Christopher Wickert and Emilio Marti (2017: 186) add that 'To create collaborative complexity, organizations may, for instance, form strategic alliances or set up initiatives to create new industry norms and standards.'

NGO–corporate alignment experts, Amy Shumate and Michelle O'Connor (2010) argue that the establishment of value rests heavily on the ability to com-municate and convince stakeholders of the legitimacy and character of the alliance. Schumate and O'Connor (2010: 8) also suggest that successful communication can help liberate new sources of funding and that 'The communication of the existence and character of the cross-sector relationship to stakeholders, rather than the resources exchanged within the relationship, is of primary importance.'

The partnership critique

Extensive concerns (Seitanidi and Ryan 2007; Adams 2017) have been expressed about corporates developing closer relations (Muthuri 2008) with charities (Shumate et al. 2017; Rivera-Santos, Rufin and Wassmer 2017). A major issue is the differing cultures and values of NGOs and corporates. It is argued their respective reasons for existence are so fundamentally different that a partnership cannot be sustained without leading to organizational and behavioural changes at both governance and delivery levels.

When partnerships are established, whether for a fixed or longer span of time, there is a major issue of who is empowered to run the project, with what authority, and importantly, who are they accountable to. Conflicts between partners around governance issues regularly occur and compromises in this area can run the risk of diluting, especially for the NGO, established principles and practices.

When partnerships are primarily based on securing funding rather than representing a genuine collaborative partnership, the NGO can become the subordinate partner. Kathleen Kelly (1993) has observed traditional fundraising is based around resources being brought in for generic causes rather than specific projects.

Brand values, PR and messaging around partnerships can become a source of conflict and lead to a loss of control of communications. Care needs to be taken that charitable values are not used to endorse a commercial product, in direct contradiction to Charity Commission (2017a) requirements. Recent growth in charity commercial partnerships has caused the Charity Commission (2017b) to issue strong warnings and guidance to charity trustees considering commercial partnerships and agreements. 'The commission therefore expects that trustees review any current arrangements to satisfy themselves they remain in the charity's best interest' (Charity Commission 2017b).

Tensions and disagreements regularly occur within partnerships. Strong, high funding corporates may pressurize directly, or otherwise, to ensure that projects continue to fit with their agenda. Difficult choices can arise for the NGO if essential resources or know-how are making a difference but the manner of the delivery represents a difficult cultural or value conflict, and where the corporate is using the NGO's values to endorse products and services, or even behaviours.

Funds provided by corporates will often be donated on the basis that they are set against a specific objective and consequently the corporate may seek influence over the programme delivery and request public recognition for their involvement (Kelly 1993).

Co-optation, that is the taking-on of the corporate partner's outlook and values, can also be a major issue as NGOs can find themselves compromising their campaigns and principles (Baur and Schmitz 2012; Schiller 2005). This area is further complicated by NGOs introducing new methods to educate and raise funds such as sponsorship arrangements and direct links with celebrities. Such approaches can cause challenges with NGO employees and volunteers who can struggle to work with corporates that see and understand the world in different ways from themselves. Schiller (2005: part 1) explains, 'NGOs having for years campaigned against companies, find it difficult now to trust their motives'.

Other critics (Adams 2017; Kasland 2016) have suggested that in most partnerships it is the corporate rather than the NGO that is the winner. Adams believes that 'Relationships between corporations and conservation organizations are in no sense equitable. Businesses are able to carry forward their work with only marginal changes to corporate strategies' (2017: 252).

The concept of **confrontational activism**, identified by Ron Aminzade and Doug McAdam (2002), highlights the direct and vocal campaigning approach that many NGOs take to shift corporate behaviour. Shaker Neubaum and Donald Zahra (2006) suggest this style of campaigning has diminished with the growing number of partnerships. Furthermore, corporations may gain special access to discuss sensitive issues or may apply pressure for an NGO to take a lighter or more neutral stance on issues that might be business critical.

Many NGOs have clear agendas and priorities. The offer of a corporate partnership may lead to a natural re-ordering of priorities or for agendas to be adjusted. These are difficult choices and have to be looked at on an individual basis. Caution here might help explain why many partnerships are established on a short-term basis, guarding against the criticism that a long-term agenda has been challenged, or even changed, by the corporate redefining direction.

The evolution of collaboration

Austin (2000) identifies four distinct phases for partnership collaboration. The initial philanthropic stage concentrates on resources being provided but with no expectation that collaborative value will arise. Secondly, transactional arrangements, also referred to as magnified philanthropy, occur where the basis of collaboration is cause-related, often with employee participation, typically on a volunteering basis. This can evolve into the third stage, integrative collaboration. This involves the corporate deepening its commitment and adopting new thinking and institutional behaviour. The relationship becomes essential to the corporate with a focus on trust, learning, shared knowledge and transparent communications with the NGO partner. The final phase of the 'Collaboration Continuum' (Austin 2000) describes transformational partnerships. Collaboration is focused on societal problems, the relationship is more complex and the likelihood of significant innovation is higher.

NGOs and corporates need to develop strong and specific processes that promote efficiency and a strong cultural fit throughout a partnership. Whether the initial approach comes from an NGO or corporate there will always be the need to identify common ways of implementing and scrutinizing the execution of campaigns. The corporate needs to establish and sustain the support of its business.

True partnership occurs (Schiller 2005) when both parties contribute skills, expertise and resources, and share the risk.

Role of the broker

The proliferation of partnership means there is an increasingly important role for intermediaries to help bring together corporates and NGOs. One challenge is that larger corporates often want to work with larger charities that are well established and respected. It is the bigger NGOs that dominate the partnership landscape. However, a broker role, managed by NGOs and PR and marketing consultancies can help. The Media Trust[1], over 20 years, has helped match the skills of professional volunteers from corporates in the creative industries with smaller or specialist charities.

Strong partnerships require the continual supply of intelligence, good sourcing and professional matching. The emergence of intermediaries greatly helps, especially when they can bring the added advantage of overseeing projects, helping to measure their success and guiding both parties through a programme, including advising on key communications and PR elements, at all stages of the partnership, from planning and launch through to completion and exit.

'Fit to Partner Test'

Many partnerships are for a fixed length of time, typically 3–5 years, with a mid-term review. In working through the core criteria for a partnership there is the need for patience, diligence and enthusiasm. Jan Jonker and Andre Nijhoff (2006) and John Peloza and Loren Falkenberg (2009) identify various matching criteria and authors. In this chapter we build on this to develop a five stage 'Fit to Partner Test' to help NGOs and corporates decide on partnership fits.

FIT TO PARTNER TEST

1 Need and understanding

NGOs and corporates should first identify why the partnership is needed and whether mutual understanding can be established and sustained. Both parties need to explore and respect each other's vision and values. Commitment from both senior teams is vital. Both parties must acknowledge the potential social and commercial value. The integrity and independence of both parties needs to be sustained.

2 Cultural fit

There is a need to establish whether there can be a strong cultural and working fit. Agreements need to be established around common working practices, the style of working and how learning can be shared, and where relevant, knowledge transferred in both directions. This is especially important among sub-groups working

---

together on delivery. Consideration should be given to the personalities associated with the partnership, such as the faces, known or unknown, of the corporate's advertising campaigns, or the leadership team and board, alongside the charity's celebrity supporters, or royal patrons, or more disadvantaged beneficiaries.

3 Scope and benefits

The tangible benefits, outputs, timings and outcomes of the partnership need to be understood. Financial dealings, including tax arrangements, need to be transparent. Resourcing must be mutually agreed for the whole period of the partnership. Potential access to new stakeholders, for either party, must be mapped out and mutually agreed, including clarity on data acquisition.

4 Reputational risks

Reputational impact, for both parties, needs to be considered, alongside an in-depth analysis of brand fit with stakeholders. The right levels of governance, and accountability, need to be put into place by both parties. Charity Commission regulations need to be adhered to, and consideration given to any other regulatory areas.

5 Commitment on communications

A final decision needs to be taken about whether and how details of, and progress on, the project can be confidently and transparently communicated to internal and external audiences. Throughout a partnership there will be the need to explain, educate, illustrate and evidence the benefits arising. Both parties therefore need to be committed to effective communications, both internally and externally. Advance planning for the communications journey across the length of the proposed partnership, both proactive and reactive, is imperative, and should be mapped out before the partnership is committed to.

There may be an imbalance between how a corporate, rather than an NGO, uses these tests because, as Noel Hyndman (2017) states, a charity's work will be consistently subject to higher levels of scrutiny when it comes to accountability, legitimacy and transparency. NGOs face 'higher ethical standards than ... expected from business' (Hyndman 2017: 5). In this chapter we also note the increased scrutiny by the media of charity activity, including charity–corporate partnerships.

Categorizing and communication benefits

The level and type of benefits arising from partnerships have also come under scrutiny. Many are explicit and identified by reference to project scopes. Others, such as the impact a partnership might have on areas such as diversity practice, or on staff retention, are less clear.

Potential partners can assess whether their relationship is likely to stimulate innovation, exchange of expertise, the sharing of technology or the provision of access to new networks. When assessing benefits both partners need to look at the likelihood of them arising and accept that the gains may not be symmetrical.

Organizationally it is possible to predict whether benefits will flow from new human interactions, working collaboratively, new levels of trust and shared learning. However, tensions may occur and there might be a reluctance to share and collaborate. The costs in additional time and management must be factored in, and balanced against the opportunity costs of positive staff, volunteer and customer engagement, alongside other financial and brand benefits.

Internal communications across both the corporate's staff and suppliers, and the charity's staff and volunteers, must be carefully planned, costed, monitored and reviewed, on an ongoing basis. In a world led by word of mouth and social media, the partners' internal stakeholders will be the most important brand champions, on a level with customers, beneficiaries and high-level stakeholders.

On the macro level NGOs with partnerships increasingly acknowledge that corporations can be part of a solution to a problem they may have once contributed to. Deeper mutual understanding can lead to the opening of new market opportunities and other collaborations.

For many corporates collaborations form part of wider corporate responsibility initiatives. As Aimei Yang and Wenlin Liu (2016: 2) argue, 'Cross-sector alliances among multinational corporations and international non-governmental organizations (INGOs) are a form of international corporate social responsibility.'

Another reason why corporates are keen to establish partnerships with NGOs is highlighted by Dirk Matten and Jeremy Moon (2008). They illustrate that in some societies giving back is highly regarded. Failure to meet this expectation can cause corporations to face criticism, or in an extreme case, social condemnation.

Barriers and causes of failure

There is a diverse set of reasons why partnerships do not succeed. Ida Berger, Peggy Cunningham and Minette Drumwright (2004) characterize these failings as 'a series of misses'. Either occurring separately, or in combination, they highlight straightforward misunderstandings, the misalignment of costs and benefits, the mismatch of power and the misfortune of time. They also refer to partner mismatches and mistrust.

With collaboration, a range of other potential problems can arise that might lead to the severing of partnerships, which in turn can lead to negative and damaging PR for both sides. It is a major worry to an NGO if the corporate partner is accused of behaving in an unethical or insensitive manner.

Equally, the corporate partner can be damaged by association with unprofessional or unethical behaviour in the NGO. For example, Age UK's partnership with E.ON to promote their pensions led to long-running and mutually damaging PR. *The Daily Mail* (2016) suggested 'Energy firm E.ON paid £6m to Age UK in return for the charity promoting expensive tariffs to pensioners'.

Partnerships are entered into with the best of intentions. However, when underway, expected behaviours may not occur or the corporate or the NGO partner may be distracted with other pressing matters. The anticipated fit may prove too narrow, or potentially ill-fitting.

As with commercial partnerships it is sometimes the lack of results that lead to project foreclosure. The same can apply to NGO–corporate collaborations. Unexpected personality clashes or an inability to adapt to processes and systems, or a weak response from customers and staff, or negative PR, can all lead to the early ending of projects. The risks around ending reinforces the need for in-depth and rigorous forward planning around PR, brand values, messaging and marketing, for internal and external stakeholders.

Partnerships: towards a classification

In the last decade, the range, scale and commonality, of NGO–corporate partnerships have grown significantly. These arrangements tend be on a project or short-term or fixed-term basis, but are regularly occurring at a local, national and trans-national basis, often with a diverse range of stakeholders. To assist with the future study of the emergence and success, and promotion, or otherwise, of these collaborations, the authors of this chapter propose a new taxonomy.

A six-part system classification drawing on UK and international examples of corporate and NGO partnerships has been developed.

a. Domestic: employee, volunteering and fundraising focused

There are multiple examples of well-established partnerships in the UK, many focused on public fundraising. Such partnerships are often closely linked with employee volunteering and this organized activity can often link to an organization's Corporate Social Responsibility (CSR) activity.

Employees often play a major role in selecting charities they would like to support. Some employers are prepared to match fund. Following the establishment of a partnership there is typically a combination of national activity, generated by the partners' head offices, and local activity through local branches, local stores, and local charity outlets. Activity can range from local fundraising events to donating a percentage of customer spending. These approaches drive a powerful mix of local to national PR, and create opportunities for communication with a wide mix of stakeholders, from customers to politicians, to volunteers and donors.

Social media is often a key element of the partnership, including the opportunity for mass generation of content by locally engaged customers and volunteers; often a key requirement of the partnership. Efforts are regularly being made to broaden out the scope of these partnerships, and deepen brand association.

SHELTER

The amounts raised can be substantial, for example, British Gas has raised more than £1m for Shelter. KPMG raised £600k in two years and extended their support by providing pro bono retail, financial and HR advice. CBRE, one of Shelter's most recent partners committed to fundraising targets but also wanted to provide pro bono knowledge and expertise.

b. Domestic: innovation focused

Many domestic charities are looking for new ways to capture the imagination of volunteers and the public. Such activities can be one-off.

NSPCC

An innovative partnership occurred at Christmas 2016 when the New West End agreed a partnership around the Oxford Street Christmas Lights. On 6 November, Oxford Street was transformed into a traffic-free playground of fabulous fun for families. This Little Stars campaign encouraged £5 donations which gave the right to name an Oxford Street light after someone special.

c. Media-channel led, cause-based partnerships

An alternative approach has been for media channels to lead or co-ordinate with NGOs major awareness raising and fundraising initiatives. Building on the long UK track record of media generated Telethons and local fundraising events, Band Aid in 1984 become the first in a new generation of broadcast-led fundraising vehicles.

Media corporate partnerships with NGOs across local, regional and national channels have led the way in giving high profile opportunities for fundraising, ranging from ITV's Text Santa, where different charities are selected each year to benefit from profile and fundraising, through to local radio and local newspaper fundraising initiatives. London's *Evening Standard* Dispossessed Fund has chosen to partner with highly difficult and often unpopular causes, and raised significant funds for a wide range of small and very needy charities, through in-depth partnerships and understanding of their causes.

The immense value for a charity and for the media company's staff and audiences makes these partnerships a high priority for charities, and a driver for media companies, resulting in increased profile, support for target beneficiaries, and a new source of 'unrestricted' income.

COMIC RELIEF

Since 1999, Sainsbury's has raised more than £100m for Comic Relief, through the charity's corporate partnership with the BBC. The core focal point is Red Nose Day when funds are raised to help support people living tough lives in the UK and some of the world's poorest communities. The retailer uses extensively their know-how to promote red noses in store as well as other related 'goodies', but crucially gains a unique profile via the BBC. Many in-store grocery products are also connected with further fundraising, and employees arrange their own fundraising activities. Specific causes are not identified and Sainsbury's is one of ten official Comic Relief partners.

---

d. Corporate membership: long-term human, skill and financial contribution

Another approach involves establishing a membership model. In return for regular donations or membership fees, corporates become corporate members of a charity. Benefits arising can be diverse, ranging from regular brand checks, being directly associated with an initiative or being offered a seat on the charity's board. Monies raised are not for specific purposes and can be set against a range of tasks. Corporate members often place staff engagement at the heart of their partnership involvement. Knowledge exchange, development and learning all feature as benefits. Membership is often linked to public affairs, corporate PR and internal communications.

THE MEDIA TRUST

The UK's Media Trust was established in 1994 with a core objective to recruit corporate members from the media and communications world. In 2017 these included 45 major brands including the BBC, Channel 4, Facebook, Google, ITV, Sky, Weber Shandwick and WPP. Corporate members host workshops and training, donate airtime, media space and bandwidth, and give a voice to a range of charity and community stories and voices. A key corporate benefit is the range of engagement, development and networking opportunities for their staff, ranging from creative volunteering, as individuals or in teams, to fundraising challenges. The model allows for a wide variety of charity and community causes to receive help and assistance with their communications.

---

e. International collaboration – single cause

Large charities, including some INGOs,[2] often look for partnerships with prominent corporates. Co-operation depends on finding a cause, or a scope of work, that works for both parties. The partnerships often are for limited periods, although if successful they can be extended. Broad causes can allow for both parties to be flexible around delivery, varying skills and knowledge transfer, and changing, if necessary, fields of operation. Fundraising can still be undertaken by employees. The collaborations can be multi-party, especially among NGOs. Internal and wider stakeholder communication is widespread.

GSK (GLAXOSMITHKLINE) AND SAVE THE CHILDREN

In May 2013, GSK and Save the Children launched a five-year partnership, with the stated ambition to help save a million children's lives. The campaign focused on four key areas: improving access to basic healthcare, training and equipping healthcare workers, developing child friendly medicines and working on national and local levels for stronger healthcare policies. The mid-term report illustrated the depth and success of the partnership, highlighting its work in the Democratic Republic and Kenya. Some 125,000 children were treated for malaria, pneumonia and diarrhoea, nearly 11,000 health workers trained, products (specifically chlorhexidine) were reformulated and more than 100,000 children were assisted during and after emergencies. In 2015 the partnership extended to 37 countries and GSK's employees raised by the end of 2015 nearly £2m. Their donations were match funded by the corporation (GSK and Save The Children Partnership Report 2015).

---

f. International multi-agency collaboration (NGO and commercial)

Another emerging partnership type is a multi-agency arrangement that seeks to tackle NGO concerns and commercial needs. This often involves international trade bodies and other international agencies as well as expert NGOs on the ground with delivery experience. The partnership can be linked to wide causes and is usually of a fixed period. Success can lead to extensions. Fundraising and corporate donations can form part of these programmes, which are increasingly common among conservation, and sustainability, focused NGOs.

DIAGEO AND WATER AID

Water Aid first started working with Diageo in 2006, and became their official charity partner in 2011. Since the partnership commenced Diageo has donated more than £1m. Between 2011 and 2016 a five-year agreement was put in place to concentrate on water stewardship around the issues of usage, waste and replenishment. The focus was also on marginalized communities, such as those in the East Africa Rift Valley. By 2015 safe water was being provided to 10 million people. Such achievements were made possible by partnerships that also included working as part of the UN Global Compact CEO Water Mandate, the CDP Water programme, and among others with Beverage Industry Environmental Round-table. Initial success led to new targets for 2020 (Diageo Water Blueprint 2015).

Conclusion

NGO leaders need to look at the possibility of corporate partnerships. However, it is not a journey to be taken lightly. Fitness tests (like the 'Fit To Partner Test' introduced in this chapter) need to be applied to check for the impact on brand, culture and working practices. Clarity on the desired outcomes is vital, as is the need to ensure employees, existing funders and volunteers are comfortable with the partnership. The vision and values of a charity must not be diluted, and regulatory requirements must be complied with.

Leaders need to be prepared to be open and transparent in communications about collaborations but prepared to discontinue if circumstances warrant. As with all communications, the partnership will generate social media comment and content that brings both risks and fantastic opportunities for brand enhancement, data capture and new customers, donors and volunteers. There are many successful collaborations that have led to tangible results and clear shifts in understanding and attitudes. Others have helped widen access to important stakeholder groups, and some continue to play a vital role in closing funding gaps. A new way of categorizing the NGO–corporates partnerships is supplied in this chapter, and this will hopefully stimulate further research.

What is clear is that collaboration, both creative and complex (Schneider et al. 2017), is here to stay for the foreseeable future, and to be at the heart of driving high profile and high impact communications opportunities.

Discussion questions

1. What are some of the benefits of non-profit and corporate partnerships?
2. Identify an NGO–corporate partnership of your choice and assess it using the 'Fit To Partner Test'.
3. How can PR and communications be used to explain, develop and promote NGO partnerships with corporates?
4. What are the communications risks and opportunities that need to be considered before entering into, and announcing, new partnerships?
5. When in an NGO–corporate partnership, how should a communications team from an NGO work with a communications team from a corporate?
6. Identify an NGO–corporate partnership that has not worked well in communication terms. What could have been done better?
7. Identify an NGO–corporate partnership that worked well in communication terms? Identify some of the success factors.

Notes

1 Founded by Caroline Diehl; see www.mediatrust.org/about-us
2 International non-governmental organizations.

References

Adams, W.M., 2017. Sleeping with the enemy? Biodiversity conservation, corporations and the green economy. *Journal of Political Ecology*, 24: 243–257.

Aminzade, R. and McAdam, D., 2002. Emotions and contentious politics. *Mobilization: an international quarterly*, 7(2): 107–109.

Austin, J.E., 2000. Strategic collaboration between nonprofits and business. *Nonprofit and Voluntary Sector Quarterly*, 29 (suppl 1): 69–97.

Austin, J.E. and Seitanidi, M.M., 2012. Collaborative value creation: A review of partnering between nonprofits and businesses: Part I. Value creation spectrum and collaboration stages. *Nonprofit and Voluntary Sector Quarterly*, 41(5): 726–758.

Baur, D. and Schmitz, H.P., 2012. Corporations and NGOs: When accountability leads to co-optation. *Journal of Business Ethics*, 106(1): 9–21.

Berger, I.E., Cunningham, P.H. and Drumwright, M.E., 2004. Social alliances: Company/nonprofit collaboration. *California Management Review*, 47(1): 58–90.

Brejning, M.J., 2013. *Corporate Social Responsibility and the Welfare State: The Historical and Contemporary Role of CSR in the Mixed Economy of Welfare*. Ashgate Publishing, Ltd.

Charity Commission, 2017a. Publications and information. Available at https://www.gov.uk/government/organisations/charity-commission/about/publication-scheme (accessed 10 July 2017)

Charity Commission, 2017b. Commercial activities alert. Available at https://www.gov.uk/government/news/commission-issues-alert-to-charities-engaged-in-commercial-activities (accessed 10 July 2017)

Daily Mail. Energy firm E.ON 'paid £6m to Age UK in return for the charity promoting expensive tariffs to pensioners'. 4th February, 2016. Available at http://www.dailymail.co.uk/news/article-3431006/Energy-firm-E-paid-6m-Age-UK-return-charity-promotin g-expensive-tariffs-pensioners.html (accessed 10 July 2017).

Dempsey, J. and Suarez, D.C., 2016. Arrested development? The promises and paradoxes of 'Selling nature to save it'. *Annals of the American Association of Geographers*, 106(3): 653–671.

Diageo Water Blueprint, 2015. Available at https://www.diageo.com/pr1346/aws/media/3791/diageo_water_blueprint_april_2015.pdf (accessed 10 July 2017).

Evening Standard Dispossessed Fund, 8th August, 2016. Good causes are handed £1m to help London's vulnerable. Available at http://dispossessedfund.org.uk/news/2016/08/good-ca uses-are-handed-£1m-to-help-londons-vulnerable.aspx (accessed 10 July 2017).

Friedman, M., 2007. The social responsibility of business is to increase its profits. In *Corporate Ethics and Corporate Governance* (pp. 173–178). Berlin Heidelberg: Springer.

Heald, M., 1970. *The Social Responsibilities of Business: Company and Community 1900–1960*. Transaction Publishers.

Hyndman, N., 2017. Editorial: The charity sector—changing times, changing challenges. *Public Money & Management*, 37(3): 149–153.

Jonker, J. and Nijhof, A., 2006. Looking through the eyes of others: Assessing mutual expectations and experiences in order to shape dialogue and collaboration between business and NGOs with respect to CSR. *Corporate Governance: An International Review*, 14(5): 456–466

GSK and Save the Children Partnership Report, 2015. Available at https://www.gsk.com/m edia/2756/save-the-children-partnership-progress-brochure.pdf (accessed 6 February 2018).

ITV Text Santa, 2017. Available at http://www.itv.com/textsanta (accessed 20 July 2017).

Kasland, G., 2016. *From Philanthropy to Creating Shared Value: A Literature Review on Business–NGO Partnerships* (Master's thesis).

Kelly, K.S., 1993. Fundraising encroachment on public relations: A clear and present danger to effective trustee leadership. *Nonprofit Management and Leadership*, 4(1): 47–68.

Luhmann, N., 1995. *Social Systems*. Stanford University Press.

Matten, D. and Moon, J., 2008. 'Implicit' and 'explicit' CSR: A conceptual framework for a comparative understanding of corporate social responsibility. *Academy of Management Review*, 33(2): 404–424.

Muthuri, J.N., 2008. Participation and accountability in corporate community involvement programmes: a research agenda. *Community Development Journal*, 43(2): 177–193.

Neubaum, D.O. and Zahra, S.A., 2006. Institutional ownership and corporate social performance: The moderating effects of investment horizon, activism, and coordination. *Journal of Management*, 32(1): 108–131.

Pattberg, P., 2005. The institutionalization of private governance: How business and nonprofit organizations agree on transnational rules. *Governance*, 18(4): 589–610.

Peloza, J. and Falkenberg, L., 2009. The role of collaboration in achieving corporate social responsibility objectives. *California Management Review*, 51(3): 95–113.

Porter, M.E. and Kramer, M.R., 2002. The competitive advantage of corporate philanthropy. *Harvard Business Review*, 80(12): 56–68.

Project Sunrise, Final Report, 2015. Foreword by J. Tait. Oxfam and Unilever.

Rivera-Santos, M., Rufin, C. and Wassmer, U., 2017. Alliances between firms and nonprofits: A multiple and behavioral agency approach. *Journal of Management Studies*.

Schiller, B., 2005. *Ethical Corporation Report Business-NGO Partnerships*. London: Ethical Corporation. 2-16.

Schneider, A., Wickert, C. and Marti, E., 2017. Reducing complexity by creating complexity: a systems theory perspective on how organizations respond to their environments. *Journal of Management Studies*, 54(2): 182–208.

Seitanidi, M.M. and Ryan, A., 2007. A critical review of forms of corporate community involvement: from philanthropy to partnerships. *International Journal of Nonprofit and Voluntary Sector Marketing*, 12(3): 247–266.

Shumate, M. and O'Connor, A., 2010. The symbiotic sustainability model: Conceptualizing NGO–corporate alliance communication. *Journal of Communication*, 60(3): 577–609.

Shumate, M., Atouba, Y., Cooper, K.R. and Pilny, A., 2017. Interorganizational communication. *The International Encyclopedia of Organizational Communication*.

Smith, A. 1843. *An Inquiry into the Nature and Causes of the Wealth of Nations with a Life of the Author: Also, a View of the Doctrine of Smith, Compared with That of the French Economists: With a Method of Facilitating the Study of His Works, from the French of M. Jariner*. Edinburgh: Thomas Nelson.

United Nations, n.d. Sustainable Development Goals: 17 goals to transform our world. Available at http://www.un.org/sustainabledevelopment/sustainable-development-goals/ (accessed 20 July 2017).

United Nations, 2003. *The 21st Century NGO Report*. Sustainability, Global Compact and UNEP. Available at http://sustainability.com/our-work/reports/the-21st-century-ngo/ (accessed 6 February 2018).

Yang, A. and Liu, W., 2016. Corporate environmental responsibility and global online cross-sector alliance network: a cross-national study. *Environmental Communication*: 1–16.

6

NON-PROFIT BRANDING THROUGH MARKETING AND PR

Ian Bruce, Colin Byrne and Hannah Myers

Introduction

Branding helps non-profit organizations to stand out distinctively in highly competitive environments. In the UK there are over half a million voluntary organizations. Whilst non-profits often work collaboratively with **other players** – organizations from a variety of sectors that work in their fields (Bruce 2011) – they also need stakeholders to be aware of their particular benefits to society. This is to attract active support for, and engagement with, their services and/or campaigning aims.

PR practitioners have brand responsibilities (CIPR 2016). Two authors of this chapter have experience as trustees and founders of non-profit organizations (NPOs). They have both been chief executives: one in a large NGO and the other in a global PR consultancy. In this chapter, the authors share their experience of the branding process, drawing on marketing tools and tactics which public relations professionals can use. They begin by exploring the interactions between non-profit PR, brand management, and marketing. Then they suggest a non-profit branding model that can be a resource for a variety of non-profits. The authors identify some of the challenges facing non-profit PR, and consider what non-profits might learn from PR and advertising agencies.

Definition and importance of branding to non-profit organizations

Definition of brand

Many non-profits are rightly proud of their **brand** and **brand heritage**. The non-profit sector has brands that have been around for well over a hundred years, and the value of their **brand equity** is high. However, they occasionally may underestimate the complexities of their **brand attributes** and view a 'brand' as just a logo or a strapline. The logo or strapline is not a brand but merely part of the branding process. It is the visual, symbolic expression of a brand. A contemporary definition of brand comes from *Forbes*: 'your brand is what your prospect', or your potential supporter, donor, or customer, 'thinks of when they hear your brand name' (McLaughlin 2011). According to Pallotta (2011) in *Harvard Business Review*, a brand: 'is much more than a name or a logo. Brand is everything, and everything is brand. Brand is your strategy…your calls to action…your customer service…the way you speak…your people…your facilities…your logo and visuals…the whole array of your communications tools.'

Essentially, brand is the sum of perceptions of an organization's attributes, benefits, and values – the organization's very personality (Aaker 2010; Bruce 2011) and what stakeholders think of it.

The importance of branding to non-profit organizations

The authors believe that branding is especially important for non-profits, although this view is not universally accepted in the sector. Brands help create reputations that are essential for non-profit legitimacy. Non-profits rely on their reputations to have authority and trust to carry out their missions. As Garsten (2017) notes, non-profits benefit from a strong, recognisable brand because it functions as a fundraising support tool (Kylander and Stone 2012), long-term driver of social goals and campaigns (Hilton 2004; Kylander and Stone 2012), source of authority to be a 'social arbiter' (Hilton 2004), and as a way to strengthen 'internal identity, cohesion, and capacity' (Kylander and Stone 2012: 37). However, there is still some scepticism about value of branding (Kylander and Stone 2012; Hilton 2004).

Sceptics' fears include worries that branding is inappropriately commercial (motivated by financial gain that would distract from the non-profit's essential purpose of providing services); and that brand management can lead to senior management imposing conformity and removing opportunity for wider participation in strategic planning (Kylander and Stone 2012). However, the authors of this chapter assert that branding is especially important in non-profits, especially ones that lack large PR and advertising budgets. This is because brands create recognisable images in the public's mind on which the public relies to make judgements about the individual non-profits. Some brands, like Oxfam or local hospices, have a visible brand on the high street. Others, like ActionAid, do not have such an advantage.

Re-branding considerations

Some non-profit brands update their brand to reflect changes they are trying to create in social attitudes. For instance, in 1994 when 'The Spastics Society' became 'Scope' in the UK, this helped the brand image by moving away from the use of a pejorative name for those with cerebral palsy (Rose 2014). Sometimes non-profits with established brands can think about rebranding in response to other players. There may be surprise in the sector with the advent of a shiny, new, and innovative challenger brand (for instance, Bono launching RED, the HIV/AIDS charity). Sometimes brand managers fret about what others think of as strong brand heritage, a traditional positive for non-profits. For example, Oxfam, a major UK development sector's leading brand, worried during the 2010s that their brand was over-associated with Wilsonian idealism (an outdated idea that foreign policy should match domestic philosophy and that good intentions should not be criticized. More practically, their supporters were getting old and dying off).

Some charities think that changing their names will solve their image problems or their lack of public awareness and recognition. Before changing names, non-profits are advised to check their brand equity: how many people have heard of it and think it does a good job? This research can be done fairly easily through a prompted awareness (which asks if a respondent recognizes a brand) omnibus survey. If an organization has a prompted awareness level above 30–40% and a reasonable quality rating, think very hard before changing the organization's name.

If a non-profit does decide to change, Berry and Parasuraman's (1991) research uncovered four criteria needed to help choose a name. A name needs to be:

- **Distinctive** – from your competitors
- **Relevant** – hints strongly at the subject or benefit
- **Memorable** – easily used and recalled
- **Flexible** – allows some wiggle room if and when strategy changes

As aforementioned, the Spastics' Society needed to change its name, but chose Scope, which is flexible but not particularly relevant. Guide Dogs for the Blind's name fits the first three criteria excellently but lacks flexibility. Age Concern was a brilliant name choice to relaunch the National Old People's Welfare Council, but it was not sufficiently distinctive from Help the Aged. Age Concern and Help the Aged merged in 2009 to become Age UK, which fits all the criteria and transfers much of the brand equity of the previous two charity names. The importance of the non-profit brand name and a well nurtured brand is massive, especially when non-profits run the risk of confusion amongst donors if their ends are too similar. For example, when WWF and Greenpeace come to mind, two very different environmental non-profits appear because their brand development has been purposefully unique, though they are both environmental non-profits.

Having discussed some of the most important marketing tools to help make PR and communications effective, how do they all fit together?

Brand-building's roots in marketing

Branding stems from marketing. The use of market research, targeting, and positioning is a process known as **branding**. Marketing has become important in non-profit organizations in most developed countries and has a long history (Kotler and Levy 1969; Rados 1981; Lovelock and Weinberg 1984; Bruce 1994; Sargeant 1999; Wymer, Knowles, and Gomes 2006; Bruce et al. 2016). Marketing involves putting the customer at the heart of the organization. An important variant of marketing is relationship marketing: building long-term relationships with customers with the expectation of repeat purchase.

The concept of the 'customer' is more complicated in non-profits than in most for-profits. This is because the person consuming is often not the person paying. For example, the **beneficiary** consuming the offering (such as someone receiving medical assistance from Doctors Without Borders) does not pay for the service. However, the service costs money that comes from donors. Both the beneficiaries and the donors have needs and wishes which must be met – therefore, both are 'customers'. Non-profits seldom use the term customer, instead using terms more appropriate for their setting, such as audience, stakeholders, publics, or target groups.

In the service delivery field, an important idea is co-creation with customers (Gummesson 2002; Sargeant and Lee 2004; Gainer and Padanyi 2005; Grönroos 2008). This idea posits that a brand's value is created both by the consumer and the supplier of a good or service. Co-creation puts the customer at the center of the non-profit. Since brand rehabilitation only works when it is co-created and influenced by both the brand professional and the target audience.

To best work towards co-creating mutual value with stakeholders, like beneficiaries and donors, segmentation (dividing your potential audience into groups with similar needs and wishes) and targeting (deciding which segments are most viable in your organization) techniques are helpful. When segmenting, it is useful to consider factors like geo-demographics (location, gender, age, education and income); psychographics (values and beliefs); and behaviour (for instance, lack of, irregular, or regular patterns of behaviour). This is further discussed in the branding model later in this chapter.

Market research is another critical resource in non-profit PR. Market research reveals target groups' needs and wishes, and perceptions of non-profits. It is the tool helping understand the non-profit's **positioning**. A classic definition of positioning is given by Harrison (1987: 7): 'the sum of those attributes normally ascribed to it by the consumers – its standing, its quality, the type of people who use it, its strengths, its weaknesses, and any other unusual or memorable characteristics it may possess'.

CASE STUDY 6.1: ROYAL NATIONAL INSTITUTE OF BLIND PEOPLE (RNIB)[1]

The Royal National Institute of Blind People (RNIB) is a non-profit that helps blind and partially sighted people. Market research in 1984 and 1985 showed that a key audience, female donors aged 40 to 70 years old, thought RNIB looked after people well but that the organization was a bit old fashioned. For five years RNIB modernized itself and crafted messages to counteract this negative view. Though the organization initially felt it had been successful, subsequent market research showed little improvement, because the key target group did not believe the messages.

The solution was to extensively feature stories not from its caring social work activities but from the many examples of the modern high-tech computerized equipment it supplied to blind people. These concrete, graphic examples did the trick. RNIB's public relations actions changed its brand image in the eyes of the target group.

Market research helps understand a non-profit's positioning. In the commercial sphere **competitor analysis** helps an organization to identify its brand attributes. A term developed for the non-profit sector is **other player analysis** (Bruce 2011). This refers to other organizations which work in the same field as non-profits. Such organizations may include other non-profits, commercial organizations with social goals, or public sector bodies.

A term in the framework below that is unusual in marketing parlance is 'philosophy', which is relevant to PR strategy development. For example, a non-profit with a philosophy of empowerment of beneficiaries (which involves an element of risk) will have a very different narrative than if their philosophy was one of care (which requires a focus on safety).

CHARITY MARKETING FRAMEWORK. Bruce 1997 and 2005 reframing Borden 1964, and Booms and Bitner 1981. Copyright Ian Bruce

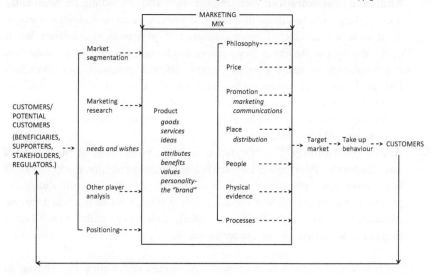

FIGURE 6.1 Marketing Framework for Non-profits
Source: Bruce 1997

Non-profit branding model

To develop an organization's brand, there are five core steps to take (Weber Shandwick Branding Team 2017). Some of them are related to corporate strategy development and so need support at the highest level in the organization.

1. **Vision:** Start with the 'why' and identify your organization's vision, or the higher order purpose. This is the foundation for the brand. For instance, Cancer Research UK's vision is 'to bring forward the day when all cancers are cured' (Cancer Research UK 2017).

2. **Mission:** Move onto the 'how' and articulate the organization's mission. This is the tangible way of carrying out your vision. Following the above example, Cancer Research UK's mission is 'accelerate progress to see three-quarters of people with cancer surviving the disease by 2034' (Cancer Research UK 2016).

3. **Values and personality**: Once you know why you exist and what you are doing you need to articulate your core values and brand personality. Your core values define the core attributes of the organization and should match to tonal values to help ensure your personality reflects what you stand for. For example 'our core value is hopeful, therefore we sound optimistic'. You can use a brand archetypes model (Mark and Pearson 2001) to help develop your organization's personality. This is where audiences can start understanding you on a human, personal level. Cancer Research UK's core values are 'ground breaking, the authoritative voice on cancer, and passionate' (Cancer Research UK 2009). Their personality is centered on teamwork, ambitious research, and passion for their cause.

4. **Audience segmentation:** Determine whom you are talking to. Segmentation can be conducted through qualitative interviews and quantitative surveys. Your audience can include your donors, staff, and your beneficiaries, but it could also be people like policy makers, academics, or relevant professionals. It is important to know how to engage different groups. Cancer Research UK speaks to many groups since cancer affects people of all ages, sexes, and colors and they need to work with lots of different stakeholders to bring about the day when it will be cured. It does not try to appeal to everyone with its brand in the same ways.

5. **Active positioning:** The last step is to place your brand in the minds of your audience. Positioning is your unique location in the marketplace. It helps distinguish you from your competitors and creates your distinctive profile. For example, Cancer Research UK is unique for its national focus on conducting research into all types of cancer, which exemplifies how it brings forward a day when all cancers are cured.

These five steps can be done somewhat simultaneously as they all build up to your brand. They all contribute equally to your organization's personality and will give you the legitimacy to achieve your goals.

CASE STUDY 6.2: MISSION DEVELOPMENT SUPPORTS BRAND DEVELOPMENT AT ACTIONAID

ActionAid has existed in the UK for over 40 years. As an international development charity it operates in a high profile, sensitive, and very competitive space.

In 2013, its brand awareness ranked lower on the Charity Brand Index than NGOs like Oxfam and Save the Children (Third Sector Research 2013). NGOs like ActionAid are often perceived as attempting to 'boil the ocean' – undertaking 'an impossible task or project' or making 'a task or project unnecessarily difficult' (Investopedia 2017) in terms of the range of short-term disasters and long-term challenges they and international governments are trying to handle. All this is at a time when public trust that international aid will lead to lasting change has never been lower.

Following ActionAid's feminist and progressive values (ActionAid 2017), its mission is being fine-tuned to focus singularly on the empowerment of women and girls in the developing world. ActionAid feels it has credibility for action on women and girls' issues, as well as a tradition for more edgy campaigning. These characteristics will help differentiate its brand in an increasingly crowded and complex 'marketplace' where everyone is competing for share of voice, supporters, and funds. Moreover, refocusing the brand on women and girls as beneficiaries, it is hypothesized, will help find new donors who have specific interests (Arutyunova 2017).

To support and articulate this renewal and redefinition of ActionAid's brand, the charity teamed up with its global PR consultancy via its London creative content team to focus on a single issue for which to find a bold, innovative, and creative solution. The issue was female genital mutilation (FGM). It was thoroughly in line with the organization's new core mission and was a big topic of social and political conversation. The challenge was that many other organizations were already campaigning on it. Additionally, ActionAid lacked the communications budget to drive a big and expensive campaign. Thus, the consultancy had the opportunity to execute an engaging creative strategy while focusing less on ActionAid's existing audience and more on younger millennials and Generation Z. The goal was to hijack these new, online audiences via their chosen and admired social media influencers. These influencers have their own YouTube channels and armies of followers across Instagram, Twitter, Facebook, and the blogosphere. The creative idea was hard-hitting: letting the young girls who face the threat of FGM tell their own story.

The campaign was called #BrutalCuts. To emphasize the life-threatening brutality of FGM, the campaign message was 'brutally cut' (with their support and consent) into the YouTube and other social channels of a host of lifestyle and fashion influencers. One minute a vlogger is commenting on her Tinder feed when she is suddenly interrupted by what audiences were least expecting: a young African girl asking for your help to be spared the horrors of FGM. #BrutalCuts reached into cinemas first, while other placements on channels such as radio, podcasts, and YouTube videos followed. This digital campaign stood out because it gained huge traction on multiple external channels – the campaign had a reach of over 152 million via social, digital, and outdoor media – while having almost no financial spend (Weber Shandwick 2016). In addition to supporting ActionAid's revitalized brand and gaining traction with widespread and new audiences via social media, the campaign helped ActionAid secure over £3 million direct funding. The funds will initially enable ActionAid to build safe centers for Kenyan girls escaping FGM, and will be extended to fund a programme of projects focussed on ending all forms of violence against women and girls across eight other countries over the next three years.

PR and brand management

Most non-profits have various constituent products (goods, services, and ideas), such as Talking Books within RNIB, Macmillan nurses within Macmillan Cancer Support, or Save an Elephant within WWF. All of these products are brands in their own right and PR has a lot to offer in using its expertise to strengthen these activities.

However, for most charities the organizational or corporate brand is the dominant brand in the same way that, for example, Virgin is the organizational brand encompassing all the Virgin products (trains, planes, banking, telecommunications, and more). The internal lead PR practitioner supported by the PR agency should have primary responsibility over this corporate or organizational brand, dominantly encapsulated in the non-profit name. Indeed the lead PR practitioner for the non-profit is effectively the **brand manager** of the organizational brand. This role should have the authority to apply the tools, methods, and frameworks described here. In addition, the brand manager must have the authority ultimately to 'police' the actions of other aspects of the non-profit central to the brand. Such aspects consist of the basics, such as style of typefaces and logo design and application, but it is also much more fundamental. Where any action of the non-profit is significantly outside the values and brand personality, the brand manager has a right and a responsibility to call attention to the issue and recommend adjustments to the behaviour, and in an emergency, be able to veto the behaviour.

For example, RNIB's brand has a vital component value of empowerment of blind and partially sighted people. This means never representing them through pathetic images. Whilst successful fundraising requires passion, unfortunately, in the distant past at RNIB, this passion was partly conveyed through presenting pitiful images of blind people in order to draw maximum sympathy (an approach then common among disability and overseas development charities at that time). It was the PR manager's role to lead on proposals to change the fundraising content to bring it in line with the desired brand personality, using allies at all levels of the organization including blind members of staff, blind trustees, frontline service deliverers, and crucially the chief executive. Perhaps most importantly the PR manager led a procedure to ensure problems of pathetic images did not reoccur. In this case, a panel of six blind people was set up to vet all claims and fundraising approaches before they went public.

Thus, PR's function is to be the organizational brand manager – the lead guardian and developer of the organizational brand – making sure no actions of the non-profit betray any audience's trust, especially that of beneficiaries.

Issues impacting non-profit PR relating to brand

There are a number of issues that impact practitioners managing brands in non-profits. These include issues of resources, declining trust in NGOs, and the need for creativity in the PR industry as a whole.

Harsh economic challenges create greater competition for potential funds. Economic challenges such as the recent 2008 financial crisis and international austerity policies impact fundraising and grant giving. These resource issues coupled with the increasingly tough challenges facing non-profit beneficiaries provide scope for maximizing the PR contribution. Beneficiary challenges range from the refugee crisis to social care; child abuse to rising homelessness; famine to climate change; unemployment to diversity and inclusion.

As aforementioned in the ActionAid case study, there is vulnerability to a decline in trust in non-profits. Traditionally, non-profits, especially charities, have bucked the trend of rising mistrust in business, governments, institutions, and – more recently – the media (Populus for NCVO 2016). The UK has shown how vulnerable trust can be: after several major scandals magnified by media interest, trust in charities fell sharply in 2016 (The Charity Commission 2016). Trust is vital to non-profits because they rely on trust as a source of credibility in a world of social media-driven fake news. Trust is needed for PR's role as effective, expert advocates and for mass public support and donations to non-profits. PR is the champion and guardian of trust in non-profits, and so it must be vigilant and fearless in vetoing any dodgy or unsubstantiated claims, while never taking any chances that might reduce trust.

There are other reasons why trust is so important to non-profits. Like most organizations, non-profits have multiple stakeholders with whom they need to maintain trust and confidence. If customers lose trust in an organization, they are more likely to go elsewhere. When a non-profit or the non-profit sector as a whole has its reputation damaged and people lose trust, donors in particular may have no primary service consumption experience against which to judge or evaluate the reputational accusations. This makes individual non-profits and the sector more vulnerable than most commercial companies because the payers are seldom the consumers of the charitable services.

Such reputational vulnerability is greater in non-profits than in many for-profits for another fundamental reason. Non-profits more often ask target audiences to 'buy' an idea, not a physical good or a service (Bruce 1994). They are not selling concrete products like baked beans or cars, but often vague things like human rights and life itself. When non-profits are campaigning or fundraising they are asking for a behaviour change, such as supporting a change in the law or giving more money. Thus, in marketing terms, the product is very intangible and the customer (a supporter or donor) has to trust the non-profit to implement the idea or product because they will experience no first-hand consumption.

For PR generally, a big issue impacting the industry is the need for creativity (Byrne 2014). These days creativity is the Holy Grail of the communications industry, with the Cannes Lions Festival of Creativity being the altar at which we seek enlightenment (and how to steal those great ideas from advertising that we could only dream of previously). Nothing drives creativity more than the passion, determined attitude and financial restraints of the non-profit sector. Creative brilliance is like water – it will always find a way to flow out. Creativity needs to strategically drive the branding process, making it important to find original ways to express brand values, personality, and mission.

For non-profit PR in particular, the revolution brought about by social media and digital communications brings changes that often work in a non-profit's favour since they both, in theory, are open-access, democratic platforms with no barriers to entry. Nevertheless, there is much noise in the marketplace to cut through, especially in an increasingly complex media and social media landscape. Most non-profits have to face these communications challenges without huge data and analytics resources, or without advertising agency creative support. Yet, if non-profits learn to work with social media and digital communications, then branding activities can expand across new venues and reach wider audiences, which means more fundraising outreach to meet the non-profit's goals.

What can non-profits learn from PR and advertising agencies?

Non-profits can learn from PR and advertising agencies in several different ways. First, have a non-profit's staff spend time in parts of an agency that they can learn from, like the planning, creative, video, or social media teams. Agencies are under pressure to innovate faster than their clients and each other. Otherwise, they add less value to clients or get eclipsed by faster moving, younger, digital native start-ups. Agencies have an imperative to adopt the newest trends and forecast the next ones while hiring the best creative talent around. Non-profits should make these goals a priority and learn to fish for themselves rather than be given the fish, to use a development sector saying.

Second, non-profits should look to where the agencies find inspiration. Find out what blogs the most creative agencies are reading and what media they are consuming to stay at the top of their creative game? One practical tip is to set aside a day in the summer and get your team together in a room with snacks and caffeinated drinks to watch the best creative communication that comes out of the summer's Cannes Festival. Watch the content that comes out of all sectors, not just the non-profit sector. Companies like Unilever, Proctor and Gamble, and Coca Cola spend billions on their marketing and communications ideas, and it is all there to access for free on the Cannes website for a limited time.

Third, non-profits should look at how PR and advertising agencies organize themselves. Agencies organize around their customers and clients. As suggested at the beginning of the chapter, non-profits can benefit from marketing's focus on putting the customer at the centre of their business. They succeed or fail by encouraging customer retention and loyalty, repeated customer spending, growing share of wallet (how much a customer spends on a particular company's goods or services), and not just meeting customer/client needs today but anticipating their needs tomorrow. Non-profits should always keep their ultimate mission at heart to keep focused on their beneficiaries and supporters.

One danger non-profits face is acting on gut instinct. Comparatively, the advertising industry has always acted on deep insights, behavioural science, anthropology, data, trends analysis, and future casting. Non-profits that are controlled by a few people who, despite caring passionately for the issue at hand, have little primary experience of the issue and essentially come from the same social background and education risk faltering. This is due to the lack of innovation and creative ideas that come from diversity of perspective. This is where it is essential to have your organization's staff gain experience in other departments and teams so that interdisciplinary work can happen.

Relationships between non-profits, for-profits, and PR agencies

Relationships between non-profits, for-profits, and PR agencies can be very productive ones. Each can learn from the other. The best relationships borrow and build on the knowledge shared between the two parties.

There are different ways of working with consultancies. Some consultancies work pro-bono with selected non-profits. Some PR consultants offer their advice by doing voluntary work in a personal capacity, sometimes through charities, like the Media Trust, that link PR professionals to non-profits. Other consultancies will work on a half and half paid and pro-bono basis, while some consultancy work is fully paid. Some consultancies specialise in the non-profit sector, but others may be large consultancies that employ some non-profit specialists. There is also the option of specialist freelance practitioners. Further, PR consultants can be invited to be trustees of non-profits.[2]

PR agencies are generally full of millennials and young people who care about societal issues like equality and diversity, and want to do more than just generate profits for their shareholders. Non-profits can benefit from this focus on social issues. Consider the great issues-based campaigns that have won at Cannes for the last few years. They cover several areas such as gender (such as the #LikeAGirl campaign), race (such as the 'no walls' and 'no hates' American brand advertising of the 2010s), climate change, social diversity, and LGBT rights (such as the 'The Proud Whopper' campaign with Burger King). If non-profits refocus on goals of social good, they will find longer-term success and better reputational credibility.

Key lessons for pairing a non-profit and a PR agency

1. Don't just find any partner; find a sympathetic partner who wants to work together for the long term. That way the non-profit knows they share values and principles and can share the agency's deep knowledge of an issue or sector.
2. Be bold. Don't get free access to a creative team and then try and rein them in or second guess them. Advise them on your brand values but let them do

their job. Make sure that the agency has an analytics team to test ideas first, and that the agency's planners add value to your earned media campaigns by creating a coherent strategy.

3.   Related to the above, be mutually respectful. Beware of agencies who want to 'do to' rather than 'do with' clients.

4.   Finally, insist on a free seat at the awards ceremony when your creative campaign wins big!

Conclusion

As marketing and public relations converge, each field learns from the other on how to best carry out the branding process. Branding is a fundamental part of the PR and marketing process, especially for non-profits. Non-profits cannot rely on the same things for-profit organisations can – it is harder for a non-profit to segment its audiences and to measure donor versus beneficiary satisfaction. Hence, the non-profit's brand is one of the best tools to use when fundraising and gathering support for a cause, and is a reliable way to easily communicate to the public. The PR function is the Brand Manager of the non-profit brand leading on proposing and monitoring brand development. The non-profit PR function needs to be vigilant in keeping the non-profit trustworthy; and it needs to manage the brand not only with creativity and interdisciplinary team-work, but also with marketing's help – thorough market research, positioning, segmentation, and targeting. Then, you can work out what people say about you when you are not in the room.

Discussion questions

1.   Why might the adoption of marketing methods be met with resistance in non-profits?

2.   Which are the most useful marketing tools to the PR professional?

3.   Are non-profits more vulnerable to loss of trust than commercial companies? Why or why not?

4.   What would you call all the people whose needs and wishes a non-profit has to meet? What is their priority in relation to other audiences? Why?

5.   How would you approach an advertising or PR agency asking for pro bono professional help? If successful, how would you work with them?

6.   Give an example of a successful relationship between a charity and a commercial company and explain why you believe it was successful.

Notes

1   Ian Bruce is Vice President of RNIB, and a former chief executive of RNIB.
2   Colin Byrne is a trustee of ActionAid.

References

Aaker, D. A. (2010). *Building Strong Brands*, London: Simon and Schuster.

ActionAid (2017). What We Do. [online] ActionAid UK. Available at: https://www.actiona id.org.uk/about-us/what-we-do

Arutyunova, A. (2017). Beyond Investing in Women and Girls: Why Sustainable Long-Term Support to Women's Rights Organizations and Movements is Key to Achieving Women's Rights and Gender Equality, in Z. Khan and N. Burn (eds), *Financing for Gender Equality: Realising Women's Rights through Gender Responsive Budgeting*. London: Palgrave Macmillan.

Berry, L. and Parasuraman, A. (1991). *Marketing Services: Competing Through Quality*. New York: The Free Press.

Booms, B. H. and Bitner, M. J. (1981) Marketing Strategies and Organisation Structures for Service Firms, in J. Donelly and W. R. George (eds), *Marketing of Services*, Chicago: American Marketing Association, 47–51.

Borden, N. H. (1964) The Concept of the Marketing Mix, *Journal of Advertising Research*, 4 (2): 2–7.

Bruce, I. (1994) *Meeting Need: Successful Charity Marketing (Charity Management)*. London: ICSA Publishing Ltd.

Bruce, I. (1995) Do Not-for-profits Value their Customers and Their Needs? *International Marketing Review*, 12(4): 77–84.

Bruce, I. (1997) Slide from MSc Teaching, Cass Business School, City, London University.

Bruce, I. (2011) *Successful Charity Marketing – Delivering Income, Services and Campaigns*. London, UK: ICSA.

Bruce, I., Laamanem, M., Ashcraft, R., Chen, M., Mersionova, I., Nel, H. and Smith, D. (2016) Resource Attraction and Marketing by Associations, in D. Smith, R. Stebbins and J. Grotz (eds), *Palgrave Handbook of Volunteering, Civic Participation, and Non-profit Associations*. Basingstoke, UK: Palgrave Macmillan, 992–1006.

Byrne, C. (2014) Increasing Creativity is PR's Biggest Challenge. [Blog] PR Moment. Available at: https://www.prmoment.com/category/blog/increasing-creativity-is-prs-big gest-challenge

Gainer, B. and Padanyi, P. (2005) The Relationship between Market-oriented Activities and Market-oriented Culture: Implications for the Development of Market Orientation in Non-profit Service Organisations. *Journal of Business Research*, 58(6): 854–862.

Cancer Research UK (2009) *Brand Guidelines August 2009*. London: Cancer Research UK.

Cancer Research UK (2016) *Beating Cancer Sooner Annual Report and Accounts 2015/16*. London: Cancer Research UK.

Cancer Research UK (2017) Our Strategy to Beat Cancer Sooner [online]. Cancer Research UK. Available at: http://www.cancerresearchuk.org/about-us/our-organisation/bea ting-cancer-sooner-our-strategy.

CIPR (2016) *The State of the Profession*. London: Chartered Institute of Public Relations.

Garsten, N. (2017) NGO Branding, Positioning, Values and Trust. 26th January. Lecture. University of Greenwich.

Grönroos, C. (2008) Service Logic Revisited: Who Creates Value? And Who Co-Creates? *European Business Review*, 20(4): 298–314.

Gummesson, E. (2002) *Total Relationship Marketing*. 2nd edn. Oxford, UK: Butterworth-Heinemann.

Harrison, T. (1987) *A Handbook of Advertising Techniques*. London: Kogan Page.

Hilton, S. (2004) The Social Value of Brands. *Economist Brands and Branding*. New York: Bloomberg, pp.47–64.

Investopedia (2017) Boil the Ocean [online]. Investopedia. Available at: http://www.inve stopedia.com/terms/b/boil-the-ocean.asp

KotlerP. and Levy, S. J. (1969) Broadening the Concept of Marketing. *Journal of Marketing*, 33: 10–15.

Kylander, N. and Stone, C. (2012) The Role of Brand in the Non-profit Sector. *Stanford Social Innovation Review*, 10(2) [online]. Available at: https://ssir.org/articles/entry/the_ role_of_brand_in_the_non-profit_sector

Lovelock, C. H. and Weinberg, C. B. (1984) *Marketing for Public and Non-profit Managers*. New York: John Wiley.

Mark, M. and Pearson, C. (2001) *The Hero and the Outlaw: Building Extraordinary Brands Through the Power of Archetypes*. New York City: McGraw-Hill.

McLaughlin, J. (2011) What is a Brand, Anyway? *Forbes* [online]. Available at: https://www. forbes.com/sites/jerrymclaughlin/2011/12/21/what-is-a-brand-anyway/#635adcb12a1b

Pallotta, D. (2011) A Logo Is Not a Brand. *Harvard Business Review* [online]. Available at: https://hbr.org/2011/06/a-logo-is-not-a-brand

Populus for NCVO (2016) *Trust Scores Compared to other Professions*. London: National Council For Voluntary Organisations.

Rados, D. L. (1981) *Marketing for Non-profit Organisations*. Dover, MA: Auburn House.

Rose, D. (2014) Formerly Known as the Spastics Society: The Importance of Charity Names. *BBC* [online]. Available at: http://www.bbc.co.uk/news/blogs-ouch-26788607

Sargeant, A. (1999) *Marketing Management of Non-profit Organisation*. Oxford: Oxford University Press.

Sargeant, A. and Lee, S. (2004) Donor Trust and Relationship Commitment in the UK Charity Sector: The Impact of Behaviour. *Non-profit and Voluntary Sector Quarterly*, 33(2): 185–202.

Weber Shandwick (2016) Brutal Cut. ActionAid UK/Weber Shandwick [video].

Weber Shandwick Branding Team (2017) *Weber Shandwick UK's Non-profit Branding Model*. London: Weber Shandwick UK Internal Documents.

The Charity Commission (2016) *Public Trust and Confidence in Charities 2016*. Research and Analysis [online]. The Charity Commission. Available at: https://www.gov.uk/governm ent/publications/public-trust-and-confidence-in-charities-2016

Third Sector Research (2013) *Charity Brand Index*. London: Third Sector Research.

Wymer, W., KnowlesP. A., and GomesR. (2006) *Non-profit Marketing: Marketing Management for Charitable and Nongovernmental Organizations*. Thousand Oaks, CA: SAGE.

7

STRATEGIC ILLUSTRATIONS OF NON-PROFIT SUCCESS?

An exploration into the evolution, purposes and ethics of case studies

Nicky Garsten, Kevin Read and Mazia Yassim

Case studies, are the 'golden ingredient of every charity story' observes non-profit media specialist, Gideon Burrows (2013). Case studies are used to exemplify third sector work, issues and causes. They have been used for centuries as part of non-profit communication strategies to secure social change and to attract support for causes. Their use is still widespread in the non-profit sector across shared, owned, paid for, and earned media.

The authors of this chapter explore how fit for purpose they are in the 21st century in relation to some ethical issues. Firstly, there is an increasing demand for authenticity by 21st century stakeholders (Quigley 2013: 193). Authenticity is an attribute of trustworthiness (Cornelissen 2014: 274). Secondly, the degree to which case studies are representative or not is an ethical concern. Thirdly, there can be tensions between communicators and fundraisers about how the needs of beneficiaries are framed. Vicky Browning and Joe Saxton (2012: 2) believe that these differences undermine 'many brand strategies'. Fundraisers so want to motivate donors that they justify 'any portrayal of clients'. Conversely, 'the comms and service teams often want to portray clients as barely in need of help'.

The forms of case studies range from succinct thumbnail sketches, to in-depth research reports (Smith 2009). **Short case studies about people** often encapsulate a perspective of a 'typical' stakeholder, like a beneficiary, employee, volunteer, donor, or beneficiary's employer. Practical guidance on presenting beneficiaries as case studies to the media is provided by, Gideon Burrows (2013) and with important emphasis on doing so ethically, by Joe Saxton (2012). Project-focused case studies tend to have more quantitative information. They can be lengthier, more in-depth research reports.

Case studies serve many purposes. Predominately they are used to secure interest (Barrell 2014; Burrows 2013), to persuasively build support (McLean 2016), prompt action and demonstrate impact (Barrell 2014; Burrows 2013). They are also used to assist reflective learning.

Despite the importance and variety of case studies in non-profit communications, no widely accepted, detailed definition of case studies exists in the non-profit literature about public relations. As Broom, Casey and Ritchey (2000: 6) state, 'clearly explicated concepts' are needed to research a topic.

In this chapter, the authors first consider existing definitions of case studies before offering a definition that is relevant to non-profit communications. They then explore the historical context of case studies before examining the purposes of case studies in non-profit communications. They go on to identify how individual stories can be impactful. Importantly, ethical considerations are then discussed.

Towards a definition of a case study in non-profit communications

Case study definitions are common in dictionaries and literature about academic research, rarities in textbooks about general PR planning, and are often brief in literature on non-profit communications.

The *Collins English Dictionary* (*CED*) defines a case study as 'a written account that gives detailed information about a person, group, or thing and their development over a period of time'. The *CED* states that the act of analysing case histories involves 'making generalizations'. Whilst these definitions do not embrace accounts conveyed through visual media or some case study content about issues, they helpfully identify that case histories provide examples and are often traced over time.

Case studies, that are in-depth case study histories, are defined in textbooks and articles about how to conduct academic research (Simons 2009; Yin 2014). Flyvbjerg (2006) in his study on case study research states that case studies are a 'detailed examination of a single example'. The phrase 'detailed examination' in this definition signals the importance of critical analysis in drawing up research-based case studies. The adjective 'single' conveys the concentrated focus of case studies.

Occasionally research-based case studies are considered in a general PR context (for instance, Smith 2009). PR planning expert Ronald Smith (2009) helpfully offers a definition of a case study. He specifies that a case study investigates how an organization has handled, 'a single event, product or situation'. This emphasis on the organization makes an institution's agency key. This focus is counter to alternative, critical perspectives on PR (L'Etang et al. 2016) that argue that PR should be focused on societies' needs as opposed to organizational preoccupations (Coombs and Holladay 2014). Smith also states that a case study enables others to 'learn from someone else's success'.

Whilst case studies are mentioned (for instance, Bonk et al. 1999: 24) or are discussed in detail in a range of books and guides about non-profit communications (Burrows 2013; Saxton 2012), they tend not to be defined in detail. Case studies are referred to by various terms in non-profit communications literature. For example, as 'real-life stories' by Bonk et al. (1999) or as 'testimonials' by McLean (2016). Browning and Saxton (2012) observe that a case study can, in part, be defined as 'a person's story' rather than as something that demonstrates an organizational action. This is a more ethical perspective, because the NGO is not positioned as central in either parts of the definition. Browning and Saxton also state that a case study can be a document.

The authors of this chapter suggest the definition of a case study in non-profit building on these definitions and on the findings of this chapter:

> A case study used for non-profit communications can range from a person's story to an in-depth, case history report. It often tells a story about the development of an issue, experience, condition, project, service, situation or event, over time. Case studies are often illustrative; person experiences may echo those of others and in-depth reports often provide more general learnings. Whilst a case study is often primarily researched using qualitative methods, quantitative data may also be woven into the narrative.

Case studies in historical context

In modern Britain, illustrative case studies have driven social change since at least the 18th century (Oldfield 1998). Over time, the channels through which case studies have been communicated have evolved. The expanding accessibility and multiplicity of channels have democratized the use of case studies.

The anti-slavery movement at the end of the 18th century was the UK's first nation-wide pressure group (Hague 2007). William Wilberforce (1823) and Thomas Clarkson (1839) recognized the need to raise awareness of the extent, and impact, of slavery. William Wilberforce drew on the testimonials of freed slaves (Equiano and Cock 1815) in his well-presented evidence that secured the support of the then Prime Minister, William Pitt. Clarkson used case studies innovatively on regional tours that focused on why the trade should stop. For example, he used the plan of the Brooks slave ship to show how slaves were transported to educate the emergent middle classes.

Similarly, closer to home there was the need to undertake rigorous studies to tackle prejudice and ignorance and for lawmakers to appreciate the extent of a specific social problem. Studies of the conditions experienced in England's emerging urban industrial centres, whether through the revolutionary lens of Engels (1892), the more reform-focused approaches of Mayhew (2010) [1851] and Rowntree and Sherwell (1901) sought to paint pictures of the everyday lives of the working classes. Beyond, the evidence-based approach that contextualized and gave scale to a problem was the need to link the observations to a specific call to action around a distinct issue. Many social reformers of Victorian and Edwardian ages, from Chadwick (1842) about public health, to Webbs (1910) on poor law reform recognized that whilst public sympathy was important, it was engagement with political circles that was vital.

Print and word-of-mouth were the dominant channels from the late 18th century until the early 20th century. Case studies were embedded in pamphlets and were added to major studies funded by philanthropists or governments. The ability for the wider public to access many of these studies may have been assisted by newspapers. However, issues of literacy and affordability would have been limiting factors.

New channels and approaches emerged. Film took the case study and its ability to explain and educate in a more democratic direction. A strong visual tradition was being established to both illustrate contemporary social causes that could reach the public and the political classes at the same time, with a powerful emotional appeal and rational, well-evidenced argument. Socially realistic documentaries were made in the 1930s by national bodies like the GPO (General Post Office) film unit and the British Gas Association (Bates 2011). For instance, in *Coal Face* the GPO film unit depicted the work of miners. Directed by Alberto Cavalcanti, it had words by W.H. Auden and music from Benjamin Britten (BFI Screenonline 2013–2014). Such new artistic approaches brought case studies alive.

The advancement of broadcasting and free public channels provided a unique platform to develop campaign films and documentaries that drew heavily on individual stories about the challenges that people faced, or some circumstances that they had overcome. The 1966 film documentary, *Cathy Come Home* was seminal (Paget 1999). Watched by 12 million people (Shelter n.d.), 'its impact ensured public empathy and support' for the then newly established charity, Shelter.

Modern multi-party campaigns sometimes use multiple case studies to highlight specific challenges that individuals, communities or societies face. For instance, Comic Relief's high profile Red Nose Day, brings together multiple organizations using multi-media to illustrate causes and explain the impact of fundraising. Celebrities front case studies, articulating clear calls to action that propel individuals to donate and raise funds. Comic Relief reported in July 2017 that it had raised £76 million.

Purposes of case studies in non-profit communications

There are many ways in which case studies can support the communications of NPOs. When communications are strategic, these help organizations to secure their objectives. Different purposes include the following.

Attracting stakeholders' attention. Compelling human stories may arouse the interest of potential donors or activists, volunteers or traditionally influential stakeholders, like journalists (Barrell 2014: 95; Burrows 2013) or politicians. Case studies have such 'weight' (Burrows 2013) and emotional appeal that they can be used to secure and augment media exposure digitally and off-line (Burrows 2013; Bonk et al.1999: 24).

Raising stakeholders' awareness of: causes and issues, an organization's or individual's need for funding, or the availability of support to potential beneficiaries. Case studies personify issues, says Burrows (2013). According to Merchant et al. (2010: 754), stories about beneficiaries help an organization 'to differentiate itself from others in the minds of existing donors, potential donors, and other publics'.

After a stakeholder's attention has been captured, and their awareness raised, they may listen to **calls to action** more responsively if moved by a case study.

Supportive, participatory activities (Burrows 2013), and other behavioural changes can be invited through highlighting individual stories. Supportive actions include: fundraising (like making a pledge or donation), campaigning (e.g., joining a protest or contributing content), recruiting volunteers, or enrolling potential beneficiaries.

Case studies educate stakeholders to prompt behavioural change. For instance, The Officers' Association (2016) has case studies of civilian employers who have successfully hired former military people to encourage other employers to do so. Case studies can also illustrate the dangers of certain behaviours. For instance, the RNIB ran an Eye Safety Campaign, and used case studies to illustrate the hazards of eye accidents in different environments, from factories to squash courts.

Demonstrating impact. Case studies can illustrate and evidence how an NPO's operations have made an impact (McLean 2016) on a person (Barrell 2014; Burrows 2013), group or situation, over a specific time-period. This impact can be related to the NPO organization's mission, objectives and brand. Charities in England and Wales are legally required to have specific purposes that result in public benefit (HM Government 2017. Case studies can demonstrate this benefit. Such case studies may be used to amplify the brand in owned, earned, bought and shared media. Saxton (2012: 7) highlights the power of the beneficiaries' perspectives: 'The ability to encapsulate what a charity is all about, and the difference it makes to a single person or persons, should never be under-rated.'

Increasingly, funding and grant providers are stipulating demonstrable impact as a condition of funding non-profit projects and activities. The impact of a project is monitored over a period of time and the project design, implementation and outcome is presented as a case study. For instance, The Change Foundation often uses research-based impact case studies to demonstrate to what degree its project objectives have been met as outlined in Case study 1.

The impact demonstrated by case studies may also motivate staff and volunteers. Research shows (Schwartz and McCarthy 2010) that the sense of making a difference is highly motivational.

CASE STUDY 7.1: THE CHANGE FOUNDATION'S IMPACT

The Change Foundation is a charity working with marginalized and at-risk young people. The Foundation uses sport and dance as a means to empower, educate, and train young people. The Street Team Programme (part of the Second Chance Project) aims to 'reduce reoffending rates of participants by supporting them in the transition from custody to community' (Meek and Sira 2013: 5). The project impact report published in 2013 is divided into three parts.

Part 1 outlines the programme and states the outputs. Participant numbers, volunteer hours, and number of qualifications gained by participants are quantified. Reoffending rates of the general prison population are statistically compared with those of the programme's participants. Then, lessons learnt throughout this three-year programme are identified.

In Part 2 advice is provided on 'setting up your own Street Team Programme'. The discussion here draws from the experience of various team members and lessons learnt throughout the programme.

Part 3 is entitled 'Real Lives'. Two detailed participant case studies and thumbnail synopses of another 12 participants are presented. These case studies are protectively anonymized. This confidentiality emphasizes the sensitivity of the work and client group (young offenders). The case studies highlight the programme's impact on all the participants' lives. Nevertheless, there is no shying away from mentioning that, in one or two cases, participants did reoffend and that they are now back on a similar programme.

Source: Meek and Sira (2013)

Sharing critical learning. Case studies can be used to draw out learnings from organizational initiatives (Smith 2009) that are related to an NPO's objectives. When these case studies are rigorously drawn up, organizational accountability is enhanced. The opportunity for improved organizational learning is created. Furthermore, when these case studies are made widely accessible, other NFPs and their partners can also learn.

CASE STUDY 7.2: CRITICAL LEARNING FROM SUNRISE AZERBAIJAN (AN OXFAM AND UNILEVER COLLABORATION)

In 2010, Unilever and Oxfam began a five-year project to 'learn how to do business with smallholder farmers in a way that improve livelihoods' (Oxfam GB 2014: 3). This involved establishing a new supply chain of dehydrated onions in Azerbaijan for some of Unilever's European Knorr products. However, this 'greenfield' development objective was never met.

The detailed case study, *Sunrise Azerbaijan* (Oxfam GB 2014), transparently identified learnings from the project. It was written independently by the specialist social enterprise, Reos partners. The writers sought to understand individual partner issues and how the project was run. They listened to the viewpoints of multiple stakeholders and laid bare a set of commercial and sustainability learnings for people running future smallholder initiatives.

The 28-page case study lays out reflections in a clear and constructive manner. The motivations, and processes involved in forming a partnership are explained. The impact of a variety of issues is discussed. These included macroeconomic forces, political conflict and the role of women. Honest reflections from both partners highlight a range of partnership challenges including managing priorities and decision-making, the level of central input and a difference in emphasis on overall objectives. Recommendations to help future initiatives are clearly identified. These range from being aware of optimism basis at the outset to allowing room for trial and error, through to ensuring exit strategies are in place from the start.

On the commercial side, the performance of initial trails in Azerbaijan is examined, as are the challenges associated with contracting versus surplus buying and new methods of farming. Following trials in 2011 and 2012, Unilever decided that the supply of dehydrated onions from Azerbaijan was not going to be economically viable. The report carefully explains this decision.

Hence, this case study openly reflects on mistakes and identifies learning points. It gives guidance on commercial and sustainable decision-making and is publicly accessible.

The power of case studies

There are many elements that have contributed to the staying power of case studies. These include their tangibility, narrative power and increased use of images.

Tangibility

Case studies focus on a single real-life subject, such as a person or a project and tell a story about it. This focus gives a granularity that aids comprehension. **Concrete** language can be used in case studies to illustrate what may be described in more **abstract** or general terms. For example, an assertion that an NGO is supporting a community is abstract. Contrastingly, identifying the precise outcomes of the support is concrete. Cognitive studies (Recchia and Jones 2012) show that understanding is deeper and more likely to be retained when specific features are referred to and context is provided.

Stories

Case studies need to be stories. This is because narratives about individuals engage emotions. They can convey ideas more powerfully than facts; and they are more likely to be memorable.

Compelling human stories trigger emotions (Hogan 2011). As Burrows (2013) notes 'people care about people'. Saxton (2012: 7) reflects: 'Case studies are one of the most powerful tools that any charity has....Not least because people's...hearts, wallets and use of time are moved by real people.'

There are ethical considerations about evoking stakeholders' emotions. Saxton (2012: 1) argues that the emotional intent should secure, 'empathy, not sympathy; admiration rather than pity'. He associates empathy with preserving dignity and sympathy with donation generation. More ethical considerations are considered at the end of this chapter.

Stories about individuals are used to raise funds (Merchant et al. 2010). Mother Teresa reputedly said: 'If I look at the mass I will never act. If I look at the one,

I will' (Slovic 2007). Whilst case studies often pivot on individual experience, organizations and projects can also be the subject of stories. For instance, Sunrise Azerbaijan featured in Case study 2, tells the story of a project whose main objective was not met. Furthermore, stories also aid memorability; they make ideas 'stick' (Heath and Heath 2007).

Pictures and film ahead of words

Photographs and film are powerful ways to portray the subjects of case studies. Scientific research confirms the advisability of using visuals. The brain processes visual information faster than words. The neuroscientist Medina (2008: 240) explains, 'Vision is by far our most dominant sense, taking up half of our brain's resources.' Consequently, 'we learn and remember best through pictures, not through written or spoken words.' This phenomenon is encapsulated by the term, **Pictorial Superiority Effect** (PSE). Medina (2008: 233) explains that this means 'the more visual the input becomes, the more likely it is to be recognized – and recalled'.

Notably, human case studies are often portrayed visually in digital fundraising communications. Fundraising materials, from e-mails (Weberling 2012) to videos, commonly use case studies. Visual communications can impact revenue. A Virtual Reality film that captured a Syrian refugee's daily experience in Jordan, called *Clouds Over Sidra*, helped the UN raise $3.8 billion (Watercutter 2016). Emotions are conveyed through faces. Images of beneficiaries' facial expressions are often used in charity appeals (Small and Verrochi 2009: 777).

Ethical considerations

Non-profits, perhaps above all other organizations, are expected to behave ethically. Values are essential to their work. Further, non-profits often act as 'social arbiters' in society (Hilton 2004). Ethical considerations in relation to case studies include: authenticity versus positive framing, representativeness and portrayals of individuals.

Authenticity versus positive framing: attempting to be 'really' authentic

Authentic communication is widely advocated, it is a generational expectation, and it is a feature of ethical persuasion. A common definition of authenticity is being **real** as opposed to being **fake** (Gilmore and Pine 2007; Boyle 2003). Stakeholders' expectations of authenticity are changing communications. Candour trumps corporate speak, particularly in the eyes of Millennials (Tyson 2016). Robert Phillips, former CEO EMEA of Edelman (2015: 241), asserts that message management now causes 'reputational decline' because honesty, engagement, transparency and accountability are paramount. Notably, the authenticity of a persuader is one of the five principles of ethical persuasion developed by Baker and Martinson (2001).

Transparency (Tyson 2016) and openness (Morgan 2013) are important features of authenticity. Kanter and Fine observed a few years ago that the non-profit sector had 'been slow to adopt almost any level of transparency' (2010: 76). One feature of transparent organizations they identify (ibid. 79) is that they 'communicate all results, good and bad'.

Notably, case studies are often referred to as 'real'. As seen above, their power comes, in part, from being 'real' stories by 'real' people. So how 'real' are they? It can be tempting to frame case studies only positively. Yet if a narrative is 100 per cent positive about a NPO's role, how accountable to, and authentic with its stakeholders, is the organization being? Further, how does such a bias impact on shared learning within the sector? Learning can be greater from failure than from success (Sandberg and Grant 2017).

An attribute of more in-depth, research-based case studies is that they provide an opportunity for learning. PR planning expert Ronald Smith (2009) points out that a case study enables others to 'learn from someone else's success'. Whilst this highlights the important aspect of learning from what has gone well, it does not extend to the more uncomfortable act of sharing learning from things that could have gone better.

Authentic communication is not easy (Quigley 2013: 192). It may feel as though there is a clash between furthering corporate objectives and being real. Situations are complex and human actions can be 'contradictory' (ibid.). Further, one person's perceptions of what is real may differ from another's. No-one is free from bias. However, this does not diminish the importance of trying to present nuanced case studies that balance competing demands. For instance, in Case study 1, on the Change Foundation, the fact that a project did have a 100 per cent initial success rate provides authenticity for the programme's continuation.

The illustrativeness of case studies

As already described, case studies are often described as being examples or as material from which generalizations can be made. When communicators select and enrol people as case studies, they are exhibiting a form of control. If they present the most satisfied client with a service or the most severe case of an issue is that truly illustrative? The authors here suggest that it would be good practice to indicate the level of representativeness that a case study has. For instance, to specifically acknowledge that a 'particularly satisfied' service user's view is being presented rather than implying that the happiest service user is typical.

Respectful portrayal of human case studies

The respectful portrayal of individuals is the subject of regulation, media attention, and guidance.

The selection and enrolment of case studies for fundraising communications is covered in the Fundraising Regulator's (2016) *Code of Fundraising Practice* in the

UK. The Regulator states that fundraising organizations must 'obtain permission for case studies, where practical' and comply with the Data Protection Act 1998. According to the *Code* when fundraising organizations use case studies, they must 'be able to prove that the case study is representative'. This means that when a specific person's story is being communicated, it is representative of that person's actual experience (personal communication).[1]

The balance between an NGO's brand and the beneficiary's perspective has attracted media attention. For instance, Johnson (2016) argues that charities need to make their beneficiaries rather than their own brands the stars of stories.

As outlined earlier in the chapter, there can be a tension between fundraisers and communicators about the portrayal of case studies. Research shows that guilt appeals using case studies can boost fundraising but these appeals can be perceived as patronising. The importance of respecting a service user's dignity and agency is stressed in useful guidance made by Charity Comms (Saxton 2012). A recommended process (Saxton 2012) for communicating the perspectives of clients and beneficiaries is provided. This includes: a designated person who is responsible for these portrayals; an advisory group of beneficiaries and a staff group 'to steer and review' guidelines. Images and words are both important. For instance, Saxton recommends (2012: 5) images of clients are kept reasonably up-to-date and that the representations are not passive. Descriptions of client groups need to be collaboratively decided (Saxton 2012). For instance, there may be debate about whether the terms like 'sufferer' or 'victim' are appropriate.

Given the sensitive nature of some NGOs' work, it is sometimes appropriate to keep case studies anonymous. For instance, the Samaritans offers a confidential service. As journalists tend to like using named sources, this can be a challenge when securing media coverage.

Conclusion

The use of case studies is a long-established part of the arsenal of NFP communications and warrants detailed definition to support examination. Case studies in their varied forms serve different purposes to highlight and advance non-profit organizations' work in a highly competitive environment. The authors have newly defined case studies specifically in relations to non-profit communications.

Lessons from nearly 250 years of the use of case studies can be discerned such that they may assist with the ethical and modern curation of multi-media engagement with diverse stakeholders. Case studies need to illuminate causes. They should provide fresh evidence and capture attention either through individual qualitative narratives or quantitative facts showing how individuals or a community are impacted. Equally, over dependence on the written word will no longer suffice. Looking for fresh or new ways to capture attention are important.

There are also ethical issues, particularly when human accounts are the subject. Whilst it can be tempting for non-profit organizations to draw up dramatic or glowing testimonial and thumbnail case studies, the authors have argued that a human case study used for non-profit communications should be an authentic and respectful representation of a person's story which exemplifies the wider group or context. More research-based case histories should be as transparent as possible, referring to learning from successes and things that have been more challenging.

Discussion questions

1. Identify a case study used for a social cause in the 19th century and one in 21st century. How are they similar and how are they different?
2. Find an example of a case study that principally uses a time-framed, explanation-building or pattern matching approach. What are the advantages and disadvantages of that approach?
3. What are some of the challenges of using case studies?
4. What can make a case study emotionally compelling?
5. What are some of the ethical considerations when using case studies?
6. Do you think that case studies still have a place in NFP organizations' communication in the 21st century?
7. What are some of the implications of using the term 'victim'?

Note

1 Telephone interview by Nicky Garsten with Edward Brown, from the Fundraising Regulator. 30th August 2017.

References

Baker, S. and Martinson, D.L. (2001) The TARES test: Five principles for ethical persuasion. *Journal of Mass Media Ethics*, 16(2–3): 148–175.

Barrell, J. (2014) *Make it Matter: Creating Communications Strategies in the Non-profit Sector.* London: Charity Comms.

Bates, S. (2011) GPO film-makes were pioneers, academic study claims. *Guardian* on-line. Available at: https://www.theguardian.com/film/2011/nov/10/gpo-films-pioneers-study (Accessed 5th July 2017).

BFI Screenonline (2013–2014) The GPO Film Unit: 1935. Available at: http://www.screenonline.org.uk/film/id/1356569/index.html (Accessed 18 July, 2017).

Bonk, K., Griggs, H. and Tynes, E. (1999) *The Jossey-Bass Guide to Strategic Communications for NonProfits.* San Francisco: Wiley.

Boyle, D. (2003) *Authenticity: Brands, Fakes, Spin and the Lust for Real Life.* London: Harper Perennial.

Broom, G., Casey, S. and Ritchey, J. (2000) Concept and theory of organization-public relationships, in J. Ledingham and S. Bruning (eds), *Public Relations as Relationship Management: A Relational Approach to the Study and Practice of Public Relations.* Mahwah, NJ: LEA.

Browning, V. and Saxton, J. (2012) Welcome, in J. Saxton, *Show and Tell: A Best Practice Guide to Portraying Beneficiaries and Service Users.* London: Charity Comms.

Burrows, G. (2013) *How to do Effective Public Relations and Media for your Charity or Not for Profit: A Complete Training Course and Tool Kit for Charities and the Third Sector*. E-book. ngo.media.

Burton, N. (2015) Empathy v. sympathy. *Psychology Today on-line.* 22 May. Available at: https://www.psychologytoday.com/blog/hide-and-seek/201505/empathy-vs-sympathy (Accessed 20 July 2017).

Chadwick, E. (1842) *Report on the Sanitary Condition of the Labouring Population of Great Britain: Supplementary Report on the Results of Special Inquiry into the Practice of Interment in Towns* (Vol. 1). HM Stationery Office.

Clarkson, T. (1839) *History of the Rise, Progress, and Accomplishment of the Abolition of the African Slave Trade by the British Parliament.* West Strand: JW Parker.

Comic Relief. Available at: https://www.comicrelief.com (Accessed 19 July 2017).

Coombs, T. and Holladay, S.J. (2014) *It's Not Just PR: Public Relations in Society.* 2nd edn. Malden, MA and Oxford: Wiley Blackwell.

Cornelissen, J. (2014) *Corporate Communication: A Guide to Theory & Practice.* 4th edn. London, Thousand Oaks, New Delhi and Singapore: Sage.

Engels, F. (1892) *The Condition of the Working-class in England in 1844. With Pref. Written in 1892.* Transl. by F.K. Wischnewetzky. Swan Sonnenschein.

Equiano, O. and Cock, W. (1815) *The Interesting Narrative of the Life of Olaudah Equiano; Or Gustavus Vassa, the African.* W. Cock.

Flyvbjerg, B. (2006) Five misunderstandings about case-study research. *Qualitative Inquiry,* 12(2): 219–245.

Fundraising Regulator (2016) *Code of Fundraising Practice.* Available at: https://www.fundraisingregulator.org.uk/code-of-fundraising-practice/code-of-fundraising-practice-v1-4-310717-docx/

Gilmore, J. and Pine II, B.J. (2007) *What Consumers Really Want: Authenticity.* Harvard Business School.

Hague, W. (2007) *William Wilberforce: The Life of the Great Anti-slave Trade Campaigner.* London: HarperCollins.

Hamlin, C. (1998) *Public Health and Social Justice in the Age of Chadwick: Britain, 1800–1854.* Cambridge: Cambridge University Press.

Heath, C. and Heath, D. (2007) *Made to Stick.* London: Arrow.

Hilton, S. (2004) The social value of brands, in *the Economist Brands and Branding.* New York: Bloomberg, pp. 47–64.

HM Government (2017) *Charities Act 2011.* Available at: http://www.legislation.gov.uk/ukpga/2011/25/section/4 (Accessed 10 July 2017).

Hogan, P.C. (2011) *Affective Narratology: The Emotional Structure of Stories.* Nebraska: University of Nebraska Press.

Johnson, M. (2016) Charities need to put beneficiaries before their brand when campaigning. Available at: https://www.theguardian.com/voluntary-sector-network/2016/jun/07/charities-control-let-beneficiaries-tell-own-story (Accessed 24 July 2017).

Kanter, B. and Fine, A. (2010) *The Networked Nonprofit: Connecting with Social Media to Drive Change.* San Francisco: Jossey-Bass.

Leat, D. (1996) 'Are Voluntary Organisations Accountable?' In D. Billis and M. Harris (eds), *Voluntary Agencies: Challenges of Organisation & Management* (pp. 61–79). Macmillan.

L'Etang, J., McKie, D., Snow, N. and Xifra, J. (2016) *The Routledge Handbook of Critical Public Relations.* New York and London: Routledge.

Mayhew, H. (2010) *London Labour and the London Poor.* Oxford: OUP.

McLean, B. (2016) *52 Habits of Highly Effective Non-Profits: Powerful Weekly Lesson to Attract and Engage Donors, Volunteers and the Media.* Corning, New York: Karmic.

Medina, J. (2008) *Brain Rules: 12 Principles for Surviving and Thriving at Work, Home and School*. Seattle: Pear.

Meek, R. and Sira, N. (2013) *Street Team Programme: 2nd Chance Project*. Cricket for Change.

Merchant, A., Ford, J.B. and Sargeant, A. (2010) Charitable organizations' storytelling influence on donors' emotions and intentions. *Journal of Business Research*, 63: 754–762.

Officers' Association (2016) *The Case of Lloyd's*. Slideshare. Available at: https://www.slide share.net/OfficersAssociation/transition-case-study-the-case-of-lloyds (Accessed 20 July 2017).

Oldfield, J. (1998) *Popular Politics and British Anti-slavery: The Mobilisation of Public Opinion against the Slave Trade, 1787–1807* (2nd edn, Studies in slave and post-slave societies and cultures, vol. 6). London: Frank Cass.

Owen, R. (1969) *A New View of Society: and, Report to the County of Lanark*. Penguin.

Oxfam GB (2014) *Sunrise Azerbaijan*. Available at: cs-project-sunrise-azerbaijan-case-stu dy-150814-en.pdf (Accessed 17 July 2017).

Paget, D. (1999) 'Cathy Come Home' and 'Accuracy' in British Television Drama. *New Theatre Quarterly*, 15(1): 75–90.

Phillips, R. (2015) *Trust Me, PR is Dead*. London: Unbound.

Quigley, S. (2013) The power of transparency, authenticity and empathy as drivers of cor- porate stakeholder engagement, in R. Gambetti and S. Quigley (eds), *Managing Corporate Communication: A Cross-Cultural Approach*. New York: Palgrave Macmillan

Recchia, G. and Jones, M.N. (2012) The semantic richness of abstract concepts. *Frontiers in Human Neuroscience*, 6.

Rowntree, J. and Sherwell, A. (1901) *The Temperance Problem and Social Reform*. Hodder and Stoughton.

Sandberg, C. and Grant, A. (2017) *Option B: Facing Adversity, Building Resilience, and Finding Joy*. London: WH Allen.

Saxton, J. (2012) *Show and Tell: A Best Practice Guide to Portraying Beneficiaries and Service Users*. London: Charity Comms.

Schwartz, T. and McCarthy, C. (2010) Manage your energy, not your time, in *HBR's 10 Must Reads On Managing Yourself*. Boston: Harvard Business Review, pp.61–78.

Slovic, P. (2007) 'If I look at the mass I will never act': Psychic numbing and genocide. *Judgment and Decision Making*, 2(2) April: 79–95.

Small, D.A. and Verrochi, N.M. (2009) The face of need: Facial emotion expression on charity advertisements. *Journal of Marketing Research*, 46(6): 777–787.

Shelter (n.d.) History. Available at: https://england.shelter.org.uk/our_work/history (Accessed 19 July 2017).

Simons, H. (2009) *Case Study Research in Practice*. London, Thousand Oaks, New Delhi and Singapore: Sage.

Smith, R. (2009) *Strategic Planning for Public Relations*. 3rd edn. New York and London: Routledge.

The Change Foundation. Impact. Available at: http://www.thechangefoundation.org.uk/ impact (Accessed 17 July 2017).

Tyson, M. (2016) Millennials want brands to be more authentic. Here's why that matters. The Blog *Huffington Post*. Available at: http://www.huffingtonpost.com/matthew-ty son/millennials-want-brands-t_b_9032718.html (Accessed 20 July 2017).

Watercutter, A. (2016) VR films work great for charity. What about changing minds? Wired.com. Available at: https://www.wired.com/2016/03/virtual-reality-social-cha nge-fundraising/ (Accessed 9 February 2017).

Webb, S. and Webb, B. (1910) *English Poor Law Policy* (Making of the modern world. Part 2 (1851–1914)). London, New York: Longmans, Green, and Co.

Weberling, B. (2012) Framing breast cancer: Building an agenda through online advocacy and fundraising. *Public Relations Review*, 38(1): 108–115.

Wilberforce, W. (1823) *An Appeal to the Religion, Justice, and Humanity of the Inhabitants of the British Empire: In Behalf of the Negro Slaves in the West Indies*. [Printed] for J. Hatchard and Son.

Yin, R.K. (2014) *Case Study Research: Design and Methods*. 5th edn. Thousand Oaks, London, New Delhi and Singapore: Sage.

8

INTERNAL COMMUNICATION IN NGOS

Planning an essential element of PR

Liam FitzPatrick

Introduction

Modern NGOs are very similar to organizations in other sectors. They have professional management teams, they worry about income, and costs and effectiveness. They are also as dependent on their staff being motivated and committed as other employers.

Voluntary organizations have additional internal communication (IC) challenges. Their workers often include unpaid volunteers. Dedicated staff may make personal sacrifices as every penny or cent not spent on beneficiaries has to be justified. Internal communication is rarely easy but, in a non-profit, it can be especially tough.

This chapter looks at the practice of IC and makes practical suggestions about planning and executing these communications. The demands on non-profit communications managers in relation to stakeholder segmentation and messaging are also identified and examined.

Defining terms

There are many similarities between the management of non-profit organizations and other sectors but one needs to be careful about lifting practice directly from one place into the world of non-profits. Values-based management, different revenue models and staff motivations can vary significantly (Ridder and McCandless 2010). Hence, general ideas about internal communication (IC) may need adaptation before they can be applied inside the sector.

What is meant by IC in general? Yeomans and Carthew (2014, cited by Yeomans and FitzPatrick 2017: 288) suggest that the strategic approach of employee engagement is 'building two-way trusting relationships with internal publics, with the goal of improving organisational effectiveness'. This involves having cognitive, affective and behavioural goals to help achieve organizational effectiveness (Bridger 2015: 6). These are points which are covered later.

Notably, the focus is on 'employees'. However, in the non-profit sector often volunteers undertake regular work and may have defined responsibilities despite not receiving a salary. Throughout this chapter we will assume that IC is targeted at paid and unpaid staff which is why the term **internal communication** will be used rather than **employee communication** (which is more commonly used in North America).

This chapter will focus on communication between non-profit organizations and their staff and volunteers This chapter will not examine the day-to-day interaction between individual colleagues and between teams. This is a complex subject worthy of the many specialist books on the subject (for instance, Clampitt 2012)

The importance of internal communication in organizational effectiveness

Good internal communication has long been seen as important. For instance, in the 1980s writers were highlighting the value of good IC to organizational effectiveness, employee commitment and involvement and service to customers and service users (Bland 1980; Yaxley and Ruck, 2015).

Today, leaders know that IC matters (Quirke 2012) and expect it to be done quickly and well (FitzPatrick and Valskov 2014: 5). This is also true of non-profits (Ridder and McCandless 2010).

Internal communication can help, but only if the outcome needed by the organization is identified and articulated in the plan. Practitioners widely suggest that the planning process for communications should always begin by defining the desired organizational results (Yeomans and FitzPatrick 2017: 293); importantly this involves prioritizing **outcomes** over **outputs** as results always matter more than the process of communicating (see Chapter 10 for more about the importance of outputs).

Communicators are urged (FitzPatrick 2016) to consider what they want stakeholders to:

- KNOW – (i.e. what is the cognitive outcome sought?)
- FEEL – (i.e. what is the affective result we are aiming for?)
- DO – (i.e. what behaviours do we wish to encourage?)

The roles of internal communication in non-profit organizations

Literature about relationships and stewardship in non-profits (Waters et al. 2013) and practitioner models (FitzPatrick 2016: 298) suggests that there are broadly seven main areas where an IC strategy can help a non-profit tap into the commitment and enthusiasm of its workers.

Six vital roles for IC in non-profits

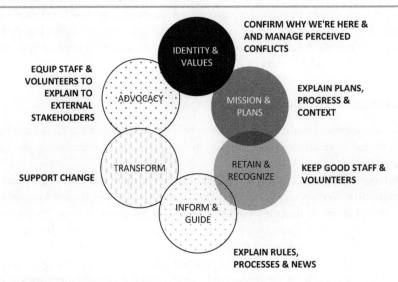

FIGURE 8.1 The Six Vital Roles for IC in Non-profits
Source: WorkingCommunication[1]

The six roles are:

1. Shaping identity and values (ensuring that paid staff and volunteers see how their own values align with those of the organization)
2. Explaining mission and plans (ensuring that staff and volunteers understand what the organization is attempting to do and how it translates into their individual or team roles)
3. Retaining and recognizing good people. Skilled and committed staff and volunteers can be hard to keep and the damage done by staff shortages can be significant in any organization. Monetary or extrinsic rewards seem to matter less in NGOs than they do elsewhere. Importantly, a sense of community is a major factor in retaining good volunteers and promotes collaboration (Garner and Garner 2011)
4. Informing and guiding people to do the right things in the right ways. People need clear direction about a range of things in any workplace; be that safety rules, operating procedures or general policies.
5. Supporting transformation or change. This is because change programmes often fail due to poor communication (Kotter 1996).
6. Creating external ambassadors and advocates. Workers and volunteers are disproportionally influential in shaping external attitudes towards an organization for better or worse (Dawkins and Lewis 2003: 16) and social media provides far reaching platforms from which opinions can be shared.

A non-profit internal programme may therefore set out to achieve results through using IC in a variety of ways. For example, in an international NGO (INGO) the principal challenge might be to ensure that staff are safe and following correct procedure (role 4). Another charity might have fundraisers who want to share ideas about unlocking new sources of income (role 5).

Understanding stakeholders

A communicator cannot hope to either deliver messages effectively or facilitate an internal conversation unless they have a strong understanding of their stakeholders.

A longstanding article of faith in public relations (Grunig and Hunt 1984) and IC is **mutuality**. Writers such as d'Aprix (1982) and Quirke (2012) have long stressed the idea that good internal communication is a two-way process. Practitioners tend to believe that messages are better understood and received when they are delivered in a conversation and recently, the concept of 'employee voice' has come to the fore (Ruck 2015), stressing that workers who have an opportunity to express their views are likely to be more loyal and committed to their organization and its mission (Waters et al. 2013). The opportunity to speak up in a positive way appears to be a crucial factor in retaining volunteers (Garner and Garner 2011). Often unpaid staff are neglected by formal channels and so may miss the opportunity to share their insights or have their commitment cemented by being listened to.

As a bare minimum FitzPatrick and Valskov (2014: 60) suggest a communicator should know:

- How many people work in the organization
- What they do (and in what proportions)
- What languages they speak
- What channels reach them
- What their recent experience has been as an employee or volunteer.

And it might be worth adding for the non-profit sector a further standard question:

- What is the nature of their employment relationship? For example, are they paid (full time/part-time) or volunteers; contractors or consultants, or local or corporate.

Understanding of contractual dynamics in employment relationships is important (Watson and Abzug 2016). In some NGOs, a large proportion of the workforce can be engaged as 'consultants' on short-term contracts. Without access to the benefits of permanent or stable employment enjoyed by their colleagues, they may be resentful and suspicious of corporate pronouncements or messages to the field from head office. Furthermore, their short tenure could limit their loyalty or their interest in the organization's long term plans or transformation. A practitioner who understands this will be able to give better advice about communications about new HR programmes or might be circumspect about how they ask staff to speak up for the organization.

Likewise, international organizations might have the challenge of employing people centrally and locally. Local staff may be paid well in local terms but their packages may not compare well with those of visiting colleagues from overseas. On the other hand, in lower income societies, a job with an NGO may be highly prized (although the number of these economies are reducing as is discussed in Chapter 14 on INGOs).

Understanding local staffing might be particularly important in organizations where local agents or staff come from a particular ethnic, faith, tribal or social group. For example, in a conflict zone, local staff drawn from a particular group might be ill-disposed to collaborate with beneficiaries from another community; a communications practitioner needs to understand this dynamic and be able to advise on communications processes to reach them.

IC professionals need to ensure that local staff are actually included in communications. Issues of literacy, multiple languages, management status, access to technology or work patterns are typical barriers. These can be overcome, for example with good quality briefing packs for managers and poster campaigns.

Consequently, having an insight into the channels that reach different groups of workers is very important. Not everyone will have access to tools such as an intranet or e-mail. Whilst mobile phones are almost ubiquitous these days, access to the internet may not be as available or might be censored. In locations with limited electricity or internet bandwidth, managers may not welcome being invited to download the director's latest video and might prefer written materials.

Communicators therefore need to think about how to segment their workforce in a number of different ways. For instance, fundraisers may have different concerns to operations staff, who might in turn see the world differently to campaigners. Managers and trustees may not worry about the same issues day-to-day as frontline colleagues.

Where volunteers are a key audience there is the additional challenge of work patterns. Some may help in a fundraising shop for just a few hours a month or be engaged on tasks such as driving which keep them out of touch of their colleagues for long periods of time. The communicator is unlikely to be popular if they insist that a chunk of this limited contact time is taken up with communications or briefing tasks. For volunteer staff, motivation particularly matters and needs to be understood by the communicator (Kang, 2016). Volunteers may get involved because they want to develop skills, increase their understanding, live out personal values or help others (Garner and Garner 2011). People with different motivations will react differently to challenges at work and place greater value on voicing opinions (Garner and Garner 2011) and feeling that they are part of a community.

Clear messaging

A core competence for a communicator is the crafting of clear messages. It is a popular truism in communications that powerful messages make a personal connection with the intended receiver of the message. A message does not need to include a benefit for staff (and trying to shoehorn an upside into every communication will quickly cause problems and undermine credibility). It is enough that the relevance of the message is immediately obvious.

In NGOs, communicators face an additional challenge in that often staff and volunteers may feel that nothing can override their own investment in the cause. Workers' loyalties may be associated with the achievement of their own responsibilities and aims. They might not extend to caring about corporate communications that can seem irrelevant to 'real' work conducted directly with beneficiaries. For example, a relief worker struggling to organize food supplies might resent receiving an HR communication about planning staff training, and a manager organizing a fluctuating pool of volunteers might see a message about IT security protocols as evidence that no one understands the real day-to-day problems facing the organization! Communicators know that co-workers are most interested in, or excited by, messages that resonate with intrinsic motivations (the reasons why people come to work in the first place).

Finding a way to make such communication relevant to colleagues with pressing operational concerns is a significant challenge in any organization but in a non-profit it is heightened by the immediacy of the challenges presented to front line colleagues. Communicators therefore need to address everyday realities in their messages. A communication about a new IT protocol might have to highlight how change can help beneficiaries; news of a change to accounting processes might be made more relevant if it can be tied to reducing waste for example.

Communicators commonly advise (FitzPatrick and Valskov 2014) that internal messages should have a number of features:

- A single uncomplicated memorable idea that probably includes a clear action and which touches on an emotional need
- A limited number of supporting messages which include a rationale, a sense of why should the audience care and an idea of the beneficial results being sought
- Clear proof points – evidence that backs up your claims and ensures your narrative is credible and trustworthy.

How you communicate is as important as what you communicate when it comes to maintaining credibility. Hours spent carefully wording a message about the importance of cost savings can be undone by an executive travelling on a business class ticket or an inappropriately glossy publication. An announcement about staff recognition can be reinforced by a personal visit from the chief executive or a statement about the importance of the staff survey can be reinforced by visible actions taken in response to feedback.

Channels and approaches

In the modern world, a communicator has at their disposal an enormous array of channels. Once organizations relied on a limited repertoire such as newsletters, memos and team briefings; now they can deploy intranets, social media, messaging apps, discussion boards, texting and much more. Sometimes it seems that the list is growing daily.

To keep things simple, it is often advisable to make sure that the communicators' repertoire of approaches provides options that allow them to:

- PUSH – send out information to colleagues whether they asked for it or not, such as news about changes to policies or celebrations of success. This might include email, intranet articles, printed magazines, posters or plasma screens for example
- PULL – where staff can find information or news when they are ready to receive it. Common approaches include intranets, specific social platforms like SharePoint, or Facebook For Work, online news and mobile apps
- FEEDBACK AND LISTENING – where staff can test their understanding, see how it is relevant to them, share their concerns, and where communicators can build up a picture of how people feel about an issue. The can do this, for instance in team meetings/briefings, by on-line forums (e.g. SharePoint or Yammer), during face to face events, or 'town hall' meetings with senior leaders. A two-way conversation is especially important in building employee commitment, loyalty and advocacy.
- COMMUNITY – where colleagues can enjoy being part of the organization and celebrate. Typical approaches include video, personal story telling, face-to-face events, social networks, on-line networks (e.g. Yammer or Jive), awards programmes, collaboration tools, print magazines/intranet features and creating beneficiary profiles.

The importance of supporting NGO line management

At the heart of good internal communication is the ability of colleagues to understand how a message is relevant to them and to be able to see what they need to do differently. This is best achieved when a worker can directly ask their manager to explain things and debate approaches. It has been a commonly agreed element of IC for a very long time (D'Aprix 1982, Quirke, 1996).

However, line or local managers are frequently blamed (D'Aprix 1982; FitzPatrick and Valskov 2014) for failing to explain properly the latest bright idea from head office. They are expected to fulfil their operational role of getting work done, of delivering for beneficiaries or bringing in funds, all at the same time as acting as animated noticeboards for management messages. The true value of a line manager lies not in being a push channel (a vehicle for making announcements and not listening). Rather, they have most impact when they can translate a corporate

The five questions

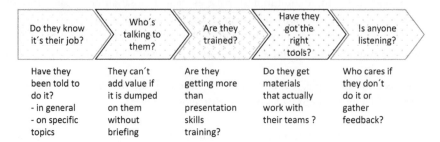

FIGURE 8.2 Supporting Line Managers
Source: Reproduced with permission from Kogan Page

message into something which their team understands, when they can provide clarification and they can listen and relay back the views of staff.

Figure 8.2 draws on the work of FitzPatrick and Valskov (2014: 119) to illustrate a number of factors that influence the effectiveness of line managers as corporate communicators.

Initially, line managers need to know that they are expected to communicate in general and on specific topics. This may not be obvious to many colleagues and may never be spelt out in their responsibilities and training. Often communications do not include clear instructions about what a line manager is being asked to do on a particular occasion (FitzPatrick and Valskov 2014).

Communicators tend to address this issue with briefing packages that lay out the request being made of local managers and instructions about what they are being asked to do. Even if the organization has included communication in its list of essential supervisory competencies, it is likely that local managers will need to underline the messages that first line managers are expected to discuss issues with their teams.

Secondly, many organizations seem to expect local managers to have an intuitive understanding of the issues being discussed in senior leadership meetings. Many communicators will recognize the tendency to email local managers a briefing pack and ask them to discuss the contents with their teams. Unsurprisingly, managers may often ignore such communications; the failure rate for such an approach is high unless there is an opportunity for managers to gather a more detailed background briefing (FitzPatrick and Valskov 2014). If a manager can add no value to a communique from head office they are quite likely to forward it on with or without comments to their teams, implying or explicitly suggesting that the contents is of little importance and can be ignored!

Organizations typically address these challenges in a number of ways. A leadership conference is an ideal opportunity for senior leaders to explain their thinking, provide clarification and to reinforce the importance of translating the message to the front line. A detailed briefing allows a local manager to own the information being shared and gives them confidence in answering questions that might come up from their own teams.

In international organizations the cost of bringing managers together frequently can be prohibitive and so other approaches such as regular management conference calls are often used. Crucially, good IC managers understand the need to make such calls engaging and so will work with senior leaders on the format to stop them producing uninteresting marathon broadcasts.

Communications managers often have to work hard to get time on agendas at conferences; bringing managers and supervisors together can be expensive and so operational leaders tend to be suspicious of demands to inject extra content or subjects into meetings. Effort is needed to show leaders how to prompt conference attendees to think about communicating; in particular, line managers often need help to realise that their job is to take a particular issue discussed at a leadership conference and translate it into terms that make sense and seem relevant locally.

Line managers are also sometimes surprisingly nervous about hosting discussions with their teams and will want some training. Such training works best when it focuses not on presentation skills but on the challenges of promoting a discussion, understanding the audience and handling questions (FitzPatrick and Valskov 2014: 123).

It is also important to give local managers tools which they can use when they are leading a team discussion. Traditionally, presentation slides have been a popular approach but they are only of use where a manager has the facility to show slides or to gather staff around a screen. They also often encourage management colleagues to provide far too much information and, where the whole team is on email, can be forwarded too easily without comment or endorsement.

Media, such as posters containing questions or discussion points (Simply Communicate 2012) enable local managers to host conversations in a more natural way and at times that suit shift patterns. IC leads often spend time discussing with local managers the tools that they find valuable and produce materials accordingly.

Significantly, IC managers also need to pull together the reaction and feedback that come out of local discussions. Where managers listen to the views of their teams they might reasonably expect that they in turn should be listened to by senior leaders; the role of the communicator is to ensure that a process exists for collating and presenting that feedback upwards.

Evaluation and tracking

As with other communications specialisms, IC is subject to a growing debate around evaluation and data (Ruck 2015: 107–116). The availability of traffic monitoring tools for digital media and the simplicity of survey programmes mean that increasing numbers of practitioners are gathering and interpreting complex data to understand what channels are working and which messages are landing.

Reviewing work by writers including Ruck (2015) and the UK Chartered Institute of Public Relations' Measurement (2012) suggests that there are four building blocks to evaluate internal communications activities. These include measurement of

- Sentiment about the communications experience (Did the audience like what they got?)
- Communications processes (Did we publish as often as we planned? How many people viewed it? Did people comment?)
- Out-takes (What actual impact did the communication have? Did attitudes change or did people act differently?)
- Outcomes (What impact did the communication have on the organization's objectives? Did it raise more money or help more beneficiaries?)

Importantly, the more valuable the data collected, the more difficult it is to obtain! It is relatively simple to find out if people enjoyed a presentation or see how many of them 'liked' a post on Yammer, but fundamentally this information does not shed much light on the value added by communication. Senior managers are more likely to be impressed when they are told that a particular IC strategy will increase donations, cut operational costs or improve effectiveness. Problematically, some non-profits do not have simple objectives in the way a commercial organization might (Ridder and McCandless 2010). Even when there are clear performance measures, evidence can be hard to gather.

Furthermore, it can be a challenge to argue that communications alone has changed behaviours. This is not to suggest that seeking to make the link between communications and organizational outcomes is futile, but rather that some intelligent lateral thinking is needed to see the true benefit of IC (Ruck 2015: 138).

CASE STUDY 8.1: COMMUNICATING INSIDE THE WORLD FOOD PROGRAMME – CHANNELS AND TOOLS

Funded by voluntary contributions, the World Food Programme (WFP) seeks to end hunger in a world of unprecedented stress (there have never been so many concurrent serious emergencies demanding its attention). Helping over 80 million people globally it has more than 14,000 staff, 90% of whom are embedded in the countries where assistance is provided.

IC plays a central role in connecting this dispersed workforce, highlighting common practices and standards and promoting access to information. IC is also vital in promoting change and fresh thinking internally.

The organization, as a UN entity, employs a large proportion of its staff on short-term contracts in order to be flexible and responsive as crises emerge. Although staff engagement is very high, IC has to work hard at promoting internal information sharing as the model of hunger relief evolves in such a fast-moving environment.

In recent years the organization has rebuilt its intranet. This was because, as with many other corporate entities, the intranet was more reflective of the needs of the organization than those of the stakeholders. For example, topics were not always hosted where one might naturally expect and some of the vocabulary used was not in keeping with the language skills of many staff.

Getting the language right is vitally important when much of the information exchanged internally is actually highly technical. The WFP works with logisticians, nutritionists and many highly specialized professions, so promoting clarity really matters as does supporting collaboration. Importantly, internal policies can be inevitably complex and technical and IC works hard to ensure that colleagues can easily identify which procedures they need to understand. Without an intelligent, audience-focused intranet, this is not possible.

The IC function is also actively concerned with providing colleagues with materials and information to help them explain the WFP's mission. Media statements and 'lines to take' are provided to staff and work is being done to improve the effectiveness of internal social media.

Staff news is provided on the intranet with content coming primarily from divisions (who can post their own material). The WFP also has launched its own social network on a bespoke platform and is working to understand how to promote participation. However, the IC team sees a major interest from colleagues in finding solutions to current and pressing problems; it is a need that the social platform should do well to meet.

Importantly, the WFP relies heavily on local managers to deliver corporate messages. The needs of field staff are at the heart of leadership thinking in the Rome HQ of the agency and communicators are expected to promote messages around training and development in an environment of accelerating change. Additionally, the size and diversity of the workforce mean that simplistic or common approaches do not work.

IC head Fionnuala Tennyson says 'ultimately it's about understanding users' needs; we're seeing increase in traffic because of a commitment to providing simple and useful information.'

CASE STUDY 8.2: THE CHILDREN'S SOCIETY – CLARITY OF PURPOSE

For over a hundred years The Children's Society has been working to give children a better chance in life in England. The charity's 850 staff run services, campaigns and research social work good practice as well as raising funds and operating over 100 shops on high streets staffed by volunteers.

IC has a mission to keep staff aligned to the evolving strategy of the charity. In recent years, the focus of the organization has changed slightly and staff and volunteers need to be reminded and excited about the core purpose.

The Children's Society specializes in innovating in the field of social work and so needs to attract and retain the best practitioners in their fields. Importantly, it is in the nature of the field that colleagues will transfer in and out of the charity as it takes on responsibility for projects from other bodies; so making these new colleagues feel part of The Children's Society quickly is often a priority.

Additionally, it needs to foster a culture of collaboration particularly around fundraising and in working with partner organizations.

IC invests a lot of time in operational communications and produces a thorough weekly update. The IC team is also heavily involved in supporting advocacy and, although recent change and transformation internally has taken up much focus, the communications team is increasing its emphasis on encouraging staff to report on their activities and on the impact they are having.

Much of the day-to-day internal communication is done through the intranet. The home page is used heavily for sharing news and updates. A weekly newsletter also highlights key topics. On the intranet, a weekly staff interview is a popular feature along with a simple polling facility. The charity also makes use of SharePoint (a collaboration platform). Experience shows that staff are particularly interested when the charity can report on the impact it is making on the lives of young people and share stories of success with staff.

IC is also concerned to reduce the flow of unwanted email traffic and has invested in a low cost platform that allows the team to target general messages to different audiences to understand whether they are being read and acted upon.

Progressively, more emphasis is being placed on equipping line managers to communicate; a line manager monthly update is distributed with key information for teams, a bespoke line management section on the intranet helps to guide managers, and leadership conferences are held to encourage managers see the importance of communicating effectively with their teams. Senior leaders are encouraged to spend more time in face-to-face discussions, and vehicles such as Senior Leadership Coffee Meetings are attracting interest among staff.

As with most organizations, meeting the needs and tastes of a diverse audience group is a challenge. Practitioners' first concern will always be for the young people with whom they work and so audits have highlighted demand for more focused messages, more face-to-face activity and more digital content; however, in a small team meeting these demands will always be problematic. Coupled with this is the need to be sensitive to the experience of practitioners who work with scarce resources – looking too polished can be misconstrued as being wasteful and is therefore avoided.

A recent refresh of the charity's strategy required careful treatment as it involved withdrawing from some areas of traditional involvement in the longer term. With such a committed workforce the communications relied heavily on face-to-face discussion and a heavy emphasis on listening and discussion.

Head of Internal Communications John Townsend says 'the big challenge here is to keep people engaged and connected at both the strategic and the most operational levels – and on a budget!'

Conclusion

Internal communication within modern non-profits is not markedly different from other sectors. Executive teams need to maximize income, manage costs and operate effectively on behalf of beneficiaries; good IC has a supporting role in helping achieve all of these objectives.

Yet non-profits bring their own particular challenges. Resources are permanently scarce and there are complex stakeholders. Workers will have a higher level of personal investment in the organization and its purpose and may indeed be making a conscious personal sacrifice; some may not be paid at all. This has implications for the shape and tone of messaging which the IC manager can deploy.

Nevertheless, as tools develop and management awareness of the value of IC evolves, the sector provides real opportunities to the IC practitioner who wants to work with committed colleagues in a challenging environment.

Discussion questions

1. Thinking about an organization with which you are familiar what might be the Chief Executive's biggest concerns and how can IC support him or her in addressing it?
2. Consider objectives for an IC programme in an organization you know. Can you differentiate between objectives that are about outputs and those that are about outcomes?
3. In the context of a non-profit operating in your country, what can IC do to promote a sense of membership and community among its workers (paid and unpaid)?
4. How might you brief staff in a non-profit about an external position taken by the organization? How might you explain it to volunteers as well as regular employees?
5. Plot out different internal stakeholder types for a non-profit you know. What do you need to understand about them before you can plan communications?
6. Imagine having to explain cuts to services and staff because of a change in strategy in an organization. How would you plan messages?
7. How should senior leaders prepare local managers to communicate a difficult message to staff?
8. How could an IC manager understand the effectiveness of their programmes?

Integra to change

I am grateful for the advice and comments I received from Victoria Cornwell, Sandy Gourlay, Fionnuala Tennyson, John Townsend, Alison Wallace and Chris Warham. The chapter is stronger for their contributions.

Note

1   The author is Managing Partner of WorkingCommunication.

References

Bland, M., 1980. *Employee Communications in the 1980s*. Kogan Page.

Bridger, E., 2015. *Employee Engagement*. Kogan Page.

Chartered Institute of Public Relations, 2012. *Measurement Matrix*. http://www.ciprinside.co.uk//wp-content/uploads/2012/07/Measurement-Matrix-FINALno-printmarks2.pdf (Accessed 14 August 2017).

Clampitt, P.G., 2012. *Communicating for Managerial Effectiveness*. Sage.

D'Aprix, R.M., 1982. *Communicating for productivity*. Harper Collins.

Dawkins, J. and Lewis, S., 2003. CSR in stakeholder expectations: and their implication for company strategy. *Journal of Business Ethics*, 44(2): 185–193.

Garner, J.T. and Garner, L.T., 2011. Volunteering an opinion: Organizational voice and volunteer retention in non-profit organizations. *Non-profit and Voluntary Sector Quarterly*, 40(5): 813–828.

FitzPatrick, L., 2016. Internal communications, in Theaker, A. ed., *The Public Relations Handbook*. Routledge.

FitzPatrick, L. and Valskov, K., 2014. *Internal Communications: A Manual for Practitioners*. Kogan Page.

Greener, T., 2000. *Internal Communication: A Practical Guide to Effective Employee Communications*. Blackhall Publishing.

Grunig, J. and Hunt, T., 1984. *Managing Public Relations*. Harcourt Brace Jovanovich College.

Kang, M., 2016. Moderating effects of identification on volunteer engagement: an exploratory study of a faith-based charity organization. *Journal of Communication Management*, 20(2):102–117.

Kotter, J.P., 1996. *Leading Change*. Harvard Business Press.

Quirke, B., 1996. Putting communication on management's agenda. *Journal of Communication Management*, 1(1): 67–79.

Quirke, B., 2012. *Making the Connections: Using Internal Communication to Turn Strategy into Action*. Gower Publishing.

Ridder, H.G. and McCandless, A., 2010. Influences on the architecture of human resource management in non-profit organizations an analytical framework. *Non-profit and Voluntary Sector Quarterly*, 39(1): 124–141.

Ruck, K. ed., 2015. *Exploring Internal Communication: Towards Informed Employee Voice*. Gower Publishing.

Simply Communicate, 2012. How Visual Thinking Maps can enhance internal communications. https://simply-communicate.com/visual-thinking-maps-can-enhance-internal-communication/ (accessed 17 April 2017).

Waters, R.D., Sevick Bortree, D. and Tindall, N.T.J., 2013. Can public relations improve the workplace? Measuring the impact of stewardship on the employer-employee relationship. *Employee Relations*, 35(6): 613–629.

Watson, M.R. and Abzug, R., 2016. Effective human resource management; non-profit staffing for the future, in Renz, D.O., *The Jossey-Bass Handbook of Non-profit Leadership and Management*. John Wiley & Sons.

Welch, M., 2011. The evolution of the employee engagement concept: communication implications. *Corporate Communications: An International Journal*, 16(4): 328–346.

Yaxley, H. and Ruck, K., 2015. Tracking the rise and rise of internal communication, in Ruck, K., *Exploring internal communication: towards informed employee voice*. Gower.

Yeomans, L. and FitzPatrick, L., 2017. Internal communication, in Tench, R. and Yeomans, L., *Exploring Public Relations: Global Strategic Communication*. Pearson Higher Education.

9

MAKING A DIFFERENCE IN THE WORLD – AND PROVING IT

PR measurement in the non-profit sector

Orla Graham

Introduction

Much of the work undertaken by PR teams in the non-profit sector is aimed at raising awareness, changing attitudes, challenging cultural norms and trying to make lasting differences in the world. Therefore, proving the impact and efficacy of PR is crucial.

In this chapter, the author explores the importance of evaluation for non-profit organizations; describes frameworks developed by professional bodies; examines how to design robust media evaluation programmes for non-profit organizations, and demonstrates the recommended approaches with case studies.

Evaluation matters in the non-profit sector

Measuring and evaluating PR activities is critical. It justifies budget, informs strategy, provides an objective view of the bigger picture, identifies potential issues and opportunities, and supports channel selection.

Resources are increasingly limited in non-profit organizations. Since communications teams are frequently being asked to do more with less, justifying the budget spent on both specific activities and on team salaries is critical. If a PR campaign costs about £25,000 to run but does not deliver the objectives of the organization, then it is essential for the team to learn why it did not work to ensure that mistakes are not repeated. Alternatively, if a PR campaign costs £5,000 and has delivered on the organization's objectives (such as creating awareness, petition signatures, donations or volunteer registrations), then it is equally important for the PR team to be able to demonstrate their success and prove their worth, thereby increasing the team's profile and likelihood of a seat at the table when decisions are made. Watson and Noble (2007) highlight that decision makers in organizations prefer to make such decisions based on evidence and not on anecdote.

Evaluation also allows for a continual and regular process of planning and learning. Frequent analysis provides the opportunity for course-correction, or refinement of communications strategies. Communications must be evolving rather than static. Regular examination of **PESTLE** (political, economic, social, techno-logical, legal and environmental) factors and **SWOT** (strengths, weaknesses, opportunities and threats) analyses assist on-going planning. For example, measuring the success of message delivery across key media titles on a regular basis makes it possible to understand if the right message is hitting home with the desired audience. If not, it is then possible to delve deeper to see why the messages are not resonating or if other messages might be more appropriate.

Without understanding the wider context of the media landscape and the non-profit sector, it is difficult to assess an organization's position. Analysing industry topics and issues can identify other arenas or debates in which to participate. Without an objective view of how PR activity relates to the wider world, it can be difficult to see the true picture. Tracking brand attributes, for instance, can allow an organization to see how it is viewed in relation to other organizations within the same space. This creates an opportunity to develop a unique identity and voice that cuts through noise.

An important, and often over-looked, aspect of evaluation is the ability to scan the horizon for potential problems or opportunities. Tracking issues relevant to the non-profit sector provides formative research that can contribute towards the development of communications strategies and the pre-empting of potential threats. For instance, charities might track discussion about street fundraising. This could be to identify which organizations are most associated with this type of fundraising, to analyse sentiment towards it, or to explore regional variations in the nature of discussion. Such observational research could inform decisions on whether and how to use street fundraisers.

In addition, evaluation can provide understanding about channel effectiveness. This helps focus time and effort (both scant resources in the non-profit sector). Ongoing planning is helped by tracking content in relation to the prominence of an organization across titles, key message delivered, and sentiment expressed (positive, neutral or negative).

Best practice

Evaluation is clearly important, but a robust and methodical approach is required to ensure maximum impact and efficacy of analysis. Employing best practice approaches, such as the Barcelona Principles and the Integrated Evaluation Framework are therefore critical.

Barcelona Principles

In 2005, at its annual international summit in Barcelona, AMEC (the international Association for the Measurement and Evaluation of Communications) announced what have become known as the Barcelona Principles; seven guiding tenets of best practice in evaluating PR and communications. AMEC re-launched the guidelines in 2015, reflecting evolving communications and media landscapes.

The principles (AMEC, 2015) are as follows:

'Principle 1: Goal setting and measurement are fundamental to communication and public relations'

PR practitioners must have focused aims, and be clear on how communications activities will lead to such goals. Using measurable objectives is encouraged to ensure a clear understanding of what success looks like.

'Principle 2: Measuring communication outcomes is recommended versus only measuring outputs'

Outputs have traditionally been the main focus of media evaluation, and refer to media activity metrics such as volume, sentiment, message delivery, spokespeople presence, the use of an image, or mention of a product. Whilst these are valuable to track, they alone do not tell the full story. **Outcomes** are metrics which go one step further, and involve measurement of an **action, behavioural or attitudinal shift** which has resulted from media activity.

'Principle 3: The effect on organizational performance can and should be measured where possible'

This principle links the two previous, recommending that 'outcome' metrics which demonstrate that an organization's objective has been achieved should be measured alongside media activity 'outputs' metrics. Choosing the right metrics, which link back to objectives, is key.

'Principle 4: Measurement and evaluation require both qualitative and quantitative methods'

It is necessary to measure both the content and quality of media coverage (what it is saying) as well as the volume and quantity (how much there is, how far it reaches).

'Principle 5: AVEs are not the value of communications'

This principle specifically eschews the use of Advertising Value Equivalents,[1] highlighting the flaws in the metric, and the danger in using the figure to attempt to prove the value of PR and communications activities. This has contributed a movement against the metric by the majority of the measurement and evaluation sector.

'Principle 6: Social media can and should be measured consistently with other channels'

Measuring social media can sometimes be seen as a complicated and confusing task. This principle highlights the importance of measuring social media consistently with traditional media channels, and applying all of the Barcelona Principles equally to all media types.

'Principle 7: Measurement and evaluation should be transparent, consistent and valid'

There must be clear understanding of how figures have been calculated, a consistent approach across all research and metrics, and replicable methodologies used. This principle is particularly important for ensuring that any results of media evaluation are taken seriously within an organization – the PR team cannot expect its results to be valued if they have been arrived at through spurious research tactics.

The Integrated Evaluation Framework

The Barcelona Principles provided guiding tenets for how to approach communications evaluation and were broadly welcomed by the PR community. To help practitioners understand how to use the principles in a 'real world' setting, AMEC developed frameworks, culminating with the 2016 launch of the Integrated Evaluation Framework (IEF), an online interactive tool and resource centre which allows communications professionals to map out objectives, activities, and how to measure these.

The Framework outlines each step of the process as follows.

Objectives

As in the first Barcelona Principle above, goal-setting is crucial to any successful PR endeavour. Outlining how the objectives of an organization filter down to the communications team is the first step in understanding how to evaluate. To identify success, a PR practitioner must know what success looks like.

Inputs

This refers to resources required before beginning any PR work (for example, defining target audiences, budget, timeframes). This is fundamental yet often overlooked. Understanding a project's baseline and parameters (like budget or resource limitations) can help shape and guide the direction of future strategy.

Activity

The individual activities that will be undertaken by the practitioner and/or formative research; for example, press releases, media events, baseline awareness surveys.

Outputs

This refers to media activity **outputs** such as volume (the number of articles), sentiment (the positive, negative or neutral tone of articles), message delivery, spokesperson presence, audience reach, or social media posts. Or simply, what is being said, by whom and to which stakeholders.

Out-takes

Out-takes are the initial response of an audience to the media activity delivered in **outputs.** Examples include social media engagement, web traffic, awareness, or public opinion surveys.

Outcomes

One step further from **out-takes, outcomes** look at evidence of the effects of media activity on an audience. This could be market research surveying trust, donations figures, online recommendations or advocacy (for example, petition signatures or letters to MPs).

Impact

Finally, this stage links **outcomes** to the organizational objective, to demonstrate how media activity has delivered an impact on the organization. Some examples include an improvement in reputation, meeting donation targets, or an increase in sales.

An approach used by NHS Blood and Transplant (NHSBT),[2] based on the Integrated Evaluation Framework, for measuring their Missing Type campaign, demonstrates how this works in practice.

The purpose of the Missing Type campaign was to raise awareness of the need for blood donors in the UK, particularly from young people and ethnic minorities. To get this message out and to encourage a corresponding rise in blood donations, NHSBT worked with high profile organizations to remove the letters A, B and O (the names of blood types) from branding such as Waterstone's shop signs, to street signs around London (including Downing Street). This was supplemented by case studies from donors and recipients; press releases with hard-hitting facts on how blood donations are used and why they are needed, and events aimed at ethnic minority groups.

To measure the success of the campaign, the framework below was used. A slightly simplified version of the Integrated Evaluation Framework (which

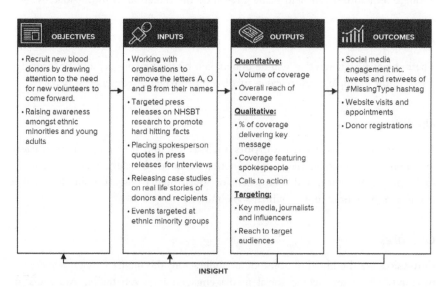

FIGURE 9.1 NHSBT Missing Type campaign – Media Evaluation Framework

combines out-takes and outcomes into one category), it provided a clear structure to ensure that any measurement of the campaign was linked directly to its objectives. This allowed the PR team at NHSBT to tell a compelling story about the impact of their work. Using a framework like this ensures clarity on how each step of a campaign can be measured to prove its success in delivering on the organization's objectives.

Evaluation within non-profit organizations

What does good look like?

To be able to measure success, it must be clear what the objectives are, and how metrics used within any evaluation link back to those objectives. Watson and Noble (2007) are among many commentators to emphasise the importance of setting out objectives before beginning evaluation.

Looking at the framework on the previous page that NHSBT used for its Missing Types campaign, there is a very clear link between its objectives and the metrics tracked in evaluating the campaign. The organization's aim was to increase awareness of the need for blood donations, communicate the difference it makes to people's lives, and encourage people (particularly young people and black and minority ethnic groups) to register as donors. If the PR team tracked only metrics such as positive coverage, the use of images, or mentions in high profile outlets, they may have come up with some 'good' results with large numbers, but these would not necessarily speak to whether the organization's objectives have been achieved. Kanter and Paine (2012: 19) also speak of the need for non-profits in particular to choose metrics which help make decisions, highlighting the need to resist the urge to 'data dump'.

Instead, metrics were chosen which directly linked back to those aims of increasing awareness and gaining new donors. This is an absolutely critical distinction to make when embarking upon an evaluation programme – or indeed, any communications activity. If a line cannot be drawn from the objective, to what achieving the objective looks like, it will never be possible to prove success, or learn from any failures. However, it is worth highlighting that an objective of evaluation can be to discover something new and unexpected, as discussed by Van Ruler (2014: 191). Goal-free evaluation 'prevents tunnel vision' and can help to re-focus strategies and priorities by refreshing baseline contexts.

Metrics which measure success should include qualitative, quantitative and targeting factors. Qualitative metrics look at what the content is saying – does it contain key messages? Does it contain a call to action (a link to a website where users can donate, for example)? Quantitative metrics look at the volume and extent of coverage – is there enough coverage to get the message across? Is it likely to reach enough people? Targeting metrics look at whether the right people are being reached – is coverage in the media titles that resonate with the target audience? Are influencers who will be able to help get the message across to the right people being reached and/or engaged with?

An effective analysis and evaluation programme will contain a range of these metrics (outputs data) but it must also include out-takes and outcomes data to show the impact of media coverage on an organization's objectives. For example, if the goal is to increase donations from 18–24 year olds, demonstrating that a campaign has achieved a range of message-rich coverage in titles relevant to that audience is only one part of the puzzle. It is also imperative for the communications team to establish that donations have simultaneously increased as a result of this coverage; otherwise, there has been no real purpose or impact to the communications work.

Outcomes metrics which are often used in conjunction with media results may include donations figures, web traffic, public opinion or awareness surveys, brand tracking, petition signatures, and volunteer registrations. It is vital to include metrics such as these which point to a change in audience behaviour or attitude. Positive media results are ultimately meaningless if they do not affect some sort of change within an audience.

Barriers to evaluation

Whilst the vast majority of PR professionals will agree that evaluation is useful and necessary, many also encounter challenges in carrying out any such programme. The most common is a lack of budget and resource. Evaluation requires sourcing media coverage, which can be expensive depending on volumes, and it also requires someone – in-house or externally – to analyse the content and provide the insight and learnings. At a time when charities are increasingly under tighter budgets, reduced funding and dealing with smaller teams, it can be difficult to find the necessary resource, financial or otherwise, to put towards evaluation. Data which demonstrates correlation between media activity and organizational results can be difficult to access in many organizations. The owner of the data may be unknown, the data itself may not exist in a format that makes it usable, or other departments may not be able or willing to share it. In addition, the necessary skills to analyse, interpret and draw insights from data (skills not necessarily associated with the creative PR industry) may not exist within the PR team.

These challenges are not insignificant, but they can be overcome. Media evaluation does not have to be expensive; if it is strategic and focused in its planning and execution, effective evaluation will always prove its own value. It should be seen no differently to hiring experts, software or necessary resources to analyse financial data in a company. If it cannot be measured, it cannot be improved.

CASE STUDY 9.1: UNICEF – PROVING GLOBAL IMPACT AND ADVOCACY

Overview

The world's leading organization for children, UNICEF[3] works in over 190 countries focusing on humanitarian and developmental assistance in developing regions. Ensuring a coordinated and effective approach in such a large organization is therefore vital. In 2014, UNICEF confirmed its new Global Communication and Policy Advocacy Strategy, marking the first time that all country offices were united under one strategy. This necessitated a consistent measurement approach to assess the success and efficacy of the strategy.

Evaluation for UNICEF focused on objectives and consistent global measurement, based upon four categories.

Voice: Be the world's most credible, trusted voice to drive change for children

Metrics included share of voice against comparators in mainstream and social media, proportion of coverage featuring key messages, spokespeople and celebrity Goodwill Ambassadors.

Reach: 1 billion people listening to UNICEF's voice

Metrics included opportunities to see (combined readership figures) of mainstream UNICEF articles, and potential impressions (combined follower count) of social media conversation.

Engagement: 50 million people acting in support of children

Metrics included web traffic (examining new and returning visitors to UNICEF's website), social media followers, and engagement metrics (the proportion of content interacted with).

Brand: Contribute to the positioning of UNICEF's brand

Metrics included the proportion of UNICEF content featuring particular brand attributes which speak to how UNICEF is perceived in media coverage.

Challenges and successes of engagement and attributes through analysis of a UNICEF video

Generally, analysis showed a difference in the types of brand attributes (the 'brand' objective) discussed in mainstream media compared to social media. Mainstream media tended to focus on factual, rational brand attributes, such as 'trustworthy' or 'expert', as much of the coverage reported facts and figures from UNICEF studies, and headlined these statistics. Social media, however, featured more emotional brand attributes (like 'caring' or 'passionate'), due to the use of provocative videos and images, led by emotional statements or questions.

For example, a video on UNICEF's Facebook page simply asked the question 'If you saw this little girl on the street, would you pass right by?' The video showed a child actress alone on the streets of Tblisi, Georgia, in two guises – as a well-dressed, 'rich' child, and as a poor, shabbily clothed child. When well-dressed, passersby asked if she needed help and offered to contact the police to find her parents. However, when dressed as a poor child, she was at best ignored and at worst abused by people – literally pushed away and shouted at. The experiment was halted when the child became upset by her treatment.

The video generated more negative actions (unfollows, unlikes, negative reaction emoticons) than any other post that quarter. However, it also generated substantially more debate than any other piece of content in the reporting period. Users commenting on the video discussed the issue of homelessness and children begging on the streets. They debated the 'right' approach, and how situations like this can differ regionally. Some disagreed with UNICEF's experiment, arguing that street children are often used by criminals to steal which can make passersby reticent to get involved, where others declared that they would help all children, regardless of their appearance. Some even vowed to change their attitudes and actions in the future.

This video was deemed successful precisely because of the size of debate provoked (speaking to the 'Engagement' objective). UNICEF's primary purpose is to create advocacy. Advocacy takes many forms – it can mean giving donations, increasing awareness and education on an issue, but significantly it must involve people taking **action**. UNICEF's aim is for people to be engaged with the issues facing children around the world, and to take a stand – donate money, write to representatives, post about issues on social media; be politically active and aware. Therefore, demonstrating that this video had achieved a substantially higher level of engagement and debate than other content was important to the PR and communications teams to provide evidence of what content achieves the desired results, and what does not.

Proving advocacy is not a simple task, however. In this instance, it was evident that this video had provoked the desired response, but this is just one example of content from a global team. Advocacy requires a step beyond social media engagement to enact real change in the world. Therefore, Gorkana recommended that outcomes data which exist in other parts of UNICEF – donation figures, brand tracking survey results – should be correlated with media activity results (outputs) to demonstrate the impact of the communications teams' work on the organization's overall goals.

Celebrity ambassador: assessment of voice

Many non-profit organizations use celebrities as ambassadors to help to spread their message, and amplify the impact of that message. UNICEF has A-list celebrity goodwill ambassadors who help the organization to achieve its 'voice' objective. However, market research conducted by UNICEF suggests that people struggle to correctly associate a celebrity ambassador with a UN agency. When asked to name a UNICEF ambassador, for instance, Angelina

Jolie is a popular choice among survey respondents, despite the fact that she is an ambassador for UNHCR, not UNICEF.

Part of the reason for this may stem from the fact that goodwill ambassadors are often given considerable freedom in how they amplify and promote UNICEF's messages. Analysis demonstrated no consistent link between the appearance of a goodwill ambassador in UNICEF coverage and the delivery of its key messages, whereas official UNICEF spokespeople did notably increase message delivery. Therefore, it was recommended that the organization should perhaps approach its work with these celebrities in a slightly different fashion.

The recommendation was to research the social media fans of goodwill ambassadors to better understand the topics of most interest to them and the channels which most resonate with them. This would allow the teams working with ambassadors to better target their messages and align ambassadors with issues which matter most to their fans. To make a crude example, there's no point in having Katy Perry promote an initiative to use sports to improve the lives of deprived children, if her social media fans are more interested in arts or education.

CASE STUDY 9.2: STROKE – A KILLER OVERLOOKED BY THE MEDIA

Stroke Association in the UK faced a different challenge to that of UNICEF. As it is a smaller, and UK-based charity, its issue is not how to make sense of and ensure the impact of the overwhelming volume of coverage it receives, but rather to get its name and mission into the public consciousness.

Stroke Association exists to prevent strokes and to provide information and support to those who have experienced strokes. Stroke remains one of the biggest health challenges of our time. It kills twice as many women as breast cancer and twice as many men as prostate and testicular cancer combined. Yet it does not get the recognition or funding of higher profile causes such as heart disease or cancer. Some 7% of deaths in the UK are due to stroke and it is the single biggest cause of disability in the UK. The economic cost is estimated as £9bn a year in the UK including direct NHS costs, other care costs, productivity losses and benefits payments. Yet just £48 a year is spent on medical research in the UK per every stroke patient compared to £241 per each cancer patient.

Communications framework

To combat this, Stroke Association[4] initiated 'Make May Purple for Stroke' (formerly Action on Stroke Month) to raise awareness of stroke, of the charity itself and to engage and build a 'stroke community' of those whose lives have been touched by stroke. Reductions in public sector funding made it even more important to ensure that a robust analysis could identify whether or not the campaign worked, to what extent and to learn from it for the future. For this to be possible, a framework was needed.

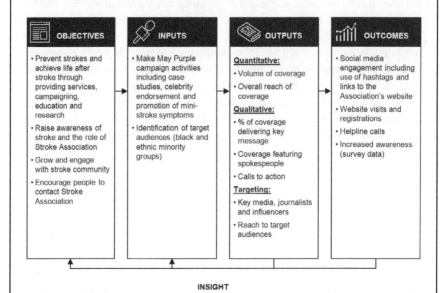

FIGURE 9.2 Evaluation Framework for the Stroke Association's 'Make May Purple' Campaign

This framework built on the learnings of previous campaigns by the charity, to inform the outputs and outcomes metrics which would have the most impact for the organization's objectives. This also included identifying a key target audience for the campaign – black and minority ethnic groups. Previous evaluation demonstrated that this audience was not as widely reached as other groups across the UK. This was a particular issue for the Stroke Association because those who fall into this group are at a much higher risk of stroke, so reaching them with their messages was vital to the campaign's success.

The results of the campaign, based on the metrics identified in the framework, were compelling. Reach to the target audience, black and minority ethnic groups, increased by 7 percentage points from the previous year's campaign. Pre- and post-campaign survey results also showed a positive uptick in awareness, which was aligned with increased reach to audiences, indicating a positive correlation between media activity and organizational impact. Awareness of Stroke Association increased by almost 18 percentage points after the campaign, to 80% of respondents being aware of the organization. Familiarity with mini-strokes increased by 11 percentage points, and awareness of the symptoms of mini-strokes increased by 6 percentage points.

These metrics pointed to a very clear relationship between the work of the communications team during the campaign and the positive results for the organization in reaching more people, increasing awareness of the danger of strokes, and spreading the word of the Stroke Association's role. Successful results were also seen in increased social media engagement from the previous year, as well as record web traffic results and a rise in the number of calls to the Association's helpline and the number of volunteers recruited.

From these examples, it is possible to see how strategically planned evaluation can provide real benefits to communications professionals and non-profit organizations. It can allow them to identify what works and what does not, identify where target audiences are and how best to communicate with them, and provides evidence to the rest of the organization of the value and impact of PR activity. Whether a large, global programme designed to provide a consistent and 'big picture' style overview of communications, or a focused campaign evaluation which looks at smaller scale activities and objectives, analysis is within the reach and ability of any non-profit organization if approached with the right mind set.

Thoughts for the future...

Although the principles of evaluation and analysis are, at their heart, quite straightforward – set measurable objectives, be clear in what good will look like and how it will be measured, and balance choosing impactful metrics with available resource and budget – there are many potential obstacles.

Getting access to data like web traffic, brand tracking or donations can be difficult, but even when it is available, proving the impact of PR over other communications disciplines like marketing and advertising is not easy. Ideally, there should be an integrated approach – PR should not sit in a silo; therefore, neither should analysis of it. Correlating various communications activities and results with outcomes data tells a richer story, and brings together teams who are ultimately working towards the same aim.

It is a challenge proving long-term advocacy (see UNICEF case study). Any quick wins in terms of, for instance, social media engagement or petition signatures must be considered alongside longer-term objectives like changing attitudes, and ultimately changing lives.

The use of controversy and provocation within non-profit communications is a fascinating one. Sometimes, as in the case of UNICEF's video, it can generate debate, make people question their attitudes and see a charity in a more dynamic light. However, there is always a risk of alienating long-standing supporters if the tactic is too sensational or too far out of left-field.

Taking learnings from other industries and sectors is something which is perhaps not considered enough within charity and non-profit communications. Analysis and research into areas like audiences and influencers is considered the norm for consumer and retail businesses, but perhaps less so in the non-profit sector; yet it is just as important. Similarly, benchmarking and making comparisons against other organizations working within the same sector is a standard approach in most commercial businesses, but does not happen as often within the non-profit world, despite the fact that it is equally, if not more, difficult to create a unique voice in such a crowded space.

Discussion questions

- Summarise each of the Barcelona Principles.
- Summarise each stage of the Integrated Evaluation Framework.
- Choose a non-profit organization and give examples of barriers to evaluation you think they might face.
- Name a recent charity campaign. What do you think might have been some of the metrics used to measure success? What may have been the outcomes the organization was hoping for? How would those be measured to define a successful campaign?
- Given the limitation that budget and resource often creates, what are some free sources of data/insights that can be used to conduct meaningful evaluation?
- What motivates you to donate or participate in charity campaigns? How might these be measured by a PR/communications team to learn what works, what doesn't and how successful they've been?

Notes

1   Advertising Value Equivalents, or AVEs, are a metric whereby a piece of editorial content is given a monetary value based on the cost of advertising in the given publication. This metric has been widely criticised across the media evaluation industry for a number of reasons, best summarised by Richard Bagnall in his article '16 reasons you should ditch AVEs' (2016).
2   The author is senior client insights manager at Gorkana. NHSBT was a client of Gorkana for the evaluation of this campaign.
3   UNICEF was a client of Gorkana – this summary of its evaluation programme is based upon joint Gorkana/UNICEF entries for AMEC awards during 2015–2016.
4   Stroke Association is a client of Gorkana.

References

AMEC (2015) Barcelona Principles, available at: https://amecorg.com/barcelona-princip les-2-0-infographic/ (Accessed 7 July 2017).
AMEC (2016) Integrated Evaluation Framework, available at: https://amecorg.com/am ecframework/ (Accessed 7 July 2017).
Bagnall, R. (2016) 16 reasons you should ditch AVEs, available at: https://www.ragan.com/ Main/Articles/16_reasons_you_should_ditch_AVEs_49335.aspx (Accessed 7 July 2017).
Kanter, B. and Paine, K. (2012) *Measuring the Networked Non-Profit*, San Francisco: John Wiley & Sons.
Van Ruler, B., (2014) 'Agile public relations planning: The Reflective Communication Scrum', *Public Relations Review*, 41, 187–194.
Watson, T., and Noble, P. (2007) *Evaluating Public Relations*, 2nd edn, London: CIPR/Kogan Page.

PART III

PR in the broader non-profit sector

10

PR FOR HOUSING ASSOCIATIONS

The communications challenges of profit for purpose

Patrick Law

Introduction

Given their rich heritage, scale and social importance, non-profit UK housing associations deserve to be better known and understood amongst opinion formers and the general public. This reputational deficit and how it is being addressed, at a time when more demands are being placed on the sector, is the subject of this chapter.

The history of housing associations in the UK stretches back 150 years and encompasses some of the greatest names in philanthropy such as Joseph Rowntree, George Peabody and Edward Guinness. Today, the sector is a hybrid (Mullins 2010) providing access to low cost housing for millions of people, services to vulnerable people, charitable activities and profit generating housing developments. Housing associations may be more commercial than traditional Third Sector organizations but they remain driven by a strong social purpose.

This hybrid model, neither entirely state, charity nor commercial, creates significant public policy and communication challenges. At times the model is a fashionable example of the 'third way' (Lund 2016), however more recently the policy environment has become more challenging. Austerity measures cut state funding and housing benefits; and an ideological change promoting home ownership above social rent questioned the very purpose of housing associations. One chief executive has referred to providing low cost housing against a backdrop of continuous policy change 'as trying to dance on a magic carpet' (Murtha 2013). A more brutal appraisal is that housing associations have faced something of an existential crisis.

The industry's communications response, led by the housing association trade body, the National Housing Federation (NHF), has been to articulate the case for the sector. Individual associations have also wrestled with their own communications agenda. In such a challenging environment, they have sought to increase efficiency but also to communicate their sense of social purpose more effectively to win support internally and externally. Mergers between associations are also creating significant communications issues. On top of these developments, associations continue to face a challenging 'business as usual' communications agenda that ranges from improving transparency and issue management through to campaigning activities and embedding social media.

This chapter discusses these communications challenges and how the industry and the individual associations are responding; it first maps out the background and the public policy context.

Overview of UK housing associations

Housing associations are 'independent, not-for-profit companies set up to provide affordable homes for people in housing need' (NHF, FAQ). Across Britain there are over 1,700 housing associations varying in size from managing fewer than 10 homes, to around 130,000 homes. Taken together they manage about two million homes for five million residents and most of these homes are rented at a significant discount to market rents.

The biggest housing associations are major businesses and significant developers in their own right: buying land, obtaining planning and building homes. Increasingly, open market housing is developed with the explicit objective of making a profit. This helps associations cross subsidise affordable housing but also to continue to offer community initiatives such as employment training and social regeneration. The diversity of the sector is best illustrated by the fact that there are still many small, highly localised associations embedded in their communities often supporting those with specific needs including older people or those with disabilities.

Many associations have their origins in the 1960s and 1970s and were set up in response to the housing needs of people being poorly served by both the private rental sector and public housing. This community ethos remains a powerful force within many associations today. The most rapid period of growth for associations came after the election of new Conservative Government in 1979 that wished to see local councils have a smaller role in the provision of subsidised housing and introduced policies to achieve this. As a result, a large volume of housing stock was transferred from local authorities to housing associations. Associations were also permitted to raise private finance. Today, as the NHF has argued (2015), associations are 'amongst the most successful public private partnerships in England's history, securing £75 billion in private investment'.

Internationally, social housing provision varies considerably with the state, commercial companies and local municipalities all playing a role in different countries. The closest parallels to the UK model (the subject of this chapter) are in the Netherlands and the Republic of Ireland.

Criticism of associations and their communications response

Housing associations under attack

The 2015 UK General Election saw housing emerge as one of the major issues of the campaign. A major plank of the Conservative's platform was the extension of low cost home ownership schemes and a proposal to extend the right to buy to housing association tenants that had previously only existed for council tenants (Conservative Party 2015). Home ownership was promoted above all other tenures. The prevailing view seemed to be that expressed by Alex Morton (2010: 52), the Prime Minister's housing adviser, who had previously written that 'social housing increases child poverty, mental health issues and inequality of opportunity and wealth'.

There was also wider media criticism of the sector. A *Daily Mail* front page (Martin 2015) talked of 'Housing Fat Cats' Hypocrisy' and a 'Furious backlash at PM's right to buy revolution from housing chiefs with lavish homes and six figure salaries'. *The Spectator* magazine attacked housing associations on multiple fronts. Their chief executives were overpaid, they were inefficient and above all they just did not build enough homes, given the level of public subsidy. It even described housing associations as the 'true villains of the property crisis' (Clark 2015).

After the election, emboldened by an unexpected victory, the Government embarked on a radical reform agenda including the right to buy that put the sector and the Government on a collision course. Provoking further criticism from the sector, George Osborne's post-election budget unexpectedly cut rental income for housing associations and reduced housing benefits (Kelly 2015).

Rather than face the uncertainties of legislation over the right to buy, in October 2015 the sector reached a voluntary agreement with the Government. The deal was brokered by the NHF and backed by its larger members like L&Q and Peabody. However, it proved controversial and a number of smaller NHF members were highly critical of the agreement (Zeffman 2015). In reality it can be argued that the deal bought the sector time and enabled a reengagement with the public policy agenda.

CASE STUDY 10.1: L&Q'S SHORT-TERM ISSUE MANAGEMENT

At the 2015 National Housing Federation conference, members voted to voluntarily support the Right to Buy. One week later, L&Q hosted its annual dinner at the Labour Party Conference. Key stakeholders attended and many voiced concerns about the sector's support for Voluntary Right to Buy. Some went as far as saying that they would never work with housing providers locally after feeling let down by the social housing sector. Despite having anticipated and planned for this response, having heard concerns first hand, L&Q redoubled its stakeholder engagement work. After the dinner, L&Q sent members of its communications team immediately back to London to progress the engagement plan. Every area they worked in across London was mapped and key political stakeholders were identified and geographically grouped; particularly local council leaders and key MPs. The principles of the campaign were speed (some meetings took place within the week), listening to the genuine sense of grievance and offering tangible commitments. The latter consisted of a pledge that L&Q would ensure no loss of social housing as a result of the right to buy agreement, that they were committed to providing more work for more Londoners and that they would work with local authorities to build more homes.

(Source: Jennifer Riddell 2017)

The sector's communications response

During this period, the sector lost control of its own narrative. The positive case for housing associations was not successfully made and without a compelling story of their own, an alternative version emerged. This portrayed associations as organizations failing to build homes, weighed down by their own failings and inefficiencies; part of the housing crisis rather than a potential partner in solving it. Inevitably this led to soul searching within the NHF and individual associations. It also led to a change of approach and a major communications initiative – 'Owning Our Future'. First of all, the NHF set out to understand perceptions, then defined more carefully the purpose and value of the sector before reengaging with traditional supporters and starting to win new allies.

Asking the audience

The first step for the NHF was to establish how associations were perceived amongst opinion formers like politicians, journalists and think tanks. So, a qualitative opinion audit was commissioned which revealed a perceptual gap between how associations saw themselves and how they were perceived by others. The detailed findings were:

1. **"Housing associations are being defined by others rather than themselves**
    Most interviewees felt the sector was bad at defining itself and in the absence of a strong story, other narratives can thrive – particularly around efficiency, innovation and contribution to new supply."
2. **"The sector has no instinctive political allies – but both right and left are there to be won over**
    Many Conservative politicians do not feel a close affinity with the sector but all felt it had an important role to play in meeting housing need. Labour politicians were more likely to have a positive view of housing associations but they are not currently acting as strong advocates for the sector."
3. **"For housing associations, familiarity breeds appreciation, not contempt**

On all sides of the political spectrum, the stakeholders who interact most with housing associations tend to like them more, even though they are also more likely to have had negative experiences as well as positive. Engaging and telling our story works."

4. "Everyone wants to see the sector build more homes

All interviewees felt housing should be a top government priority and saw housing associations as central to delivering more homes. Conservatives were more likely to underestimate how much housing associations build than Labour, but all groups felt that increasing housing supply was the prime function of the sector."

5. "Politicians, opinion formers and the media share our ambition to be more innovative and dynamic

Calls for housing associations to set out our shared vision and take a greater leadership role on housing issues came from across the board, echoing our own drive for more innovation, dynamism and creativity.

If you share our sense of purpose, we want to work with you. If you want to end the housing crisis, you need to work with us."

Source: NHF (2017), How we're perceived now

Research was also undertaken amongst the general public. There was a high level of awareness of associations, but also a view that they did not provide housing for 'people like me', their services were aimed at poorer groups, and support was significantly lower amongst young people.

Defining purpose

Armed with an insight into their reputational strengths and weakness, the NHF worked with its members to define a sharper sense of purpose for the sector. It was co-created in workshops throughout the country involving Chief Executives and communication professionals.

This was the position that was agreed:

Housing associations are united by a single purpose – to ensure everyone in the country can live in a quality home that they can afford.

For over a hundred years we have delivered on this, whether that's building low cost homes for Victorian workers or helping young families get on the housing ladder today. We meet shifting housing needs by building more homes, by providing extra support when it's needed and by innovating to tackle the challenges people face.

In changing times, we deliver where the private sector won't and the public sector can't. We generate income which doesn't go to shareholders so we can reinvest all our profits in homes and communities. That's what we have always done; it's what we will always do.

Source: NHF, Tell the HA story

Messaging and communications

Importantly the core positioning was reinforced by specific pledges and demon-strations that associations were delivering on the public policy agenda (NHF, Deliver on the substance)

- Work towards building 120,000 homes per annum – half for rent and half for sale
- Improve quality in terms of repairs, maintenance and service (often a key source of opinion former criticism)
- Improve efficiency and innovation to ensure value for money (a key priority for the Government)
- Create strong thriving communities supporting economic growth, promoting employment and skills and providing extra support for residents where this is needed.

In each area, a stronger evidential base was created. Importantly the sector is now communicating quarterly to Downing Street and the Treasury how many new homes the sector is delivering. Previously this data was not collected or communicated.

As part of the campaign, the NHF played an important role supporting associa-tions make their case more effectively. A tool kit was produced to support medium to small organizations. The kit's elements included:

- A short film outlining the sector's vision, featuring a range of CEOs who participated in building the core messaging
- Materials outlining the impact and benefits of the sector including publications and infographics
- Access to an influencing academy that provides high level communications advice and practical training in story telling
- A new online tool for associations to conduct a power analysis that pinpoints stakeholders and provides the steps to develop influencing plans.

Outcomes

The sector has come a long way since the post 2015 election dark days. The NHF campaign started to define and tell the housing association story more successfully. The Housing White Paper (DCLG 2017) struck a new tone, recognising the value of housing associations and that social rent as a tenure has a future. The Con-servative Manifesto (Conservative Party 2017) went further, pledging not just a bigger role for housing associations but also explicitly acknowledging the need for more affordable/social housing. However, the position is fragile and as a former CEO of the Housing Corporation recently argued, the sector has to deliver to ensure that recent progress for the sector is not undermined (Douglas 2017). The challenge is now to embed their social purpose, improve the quality of services while becoming more commercial. Walking this tightrope is at the heart of the communications challenges of the individual associations and is discussed in the remainder of the chapter.

Communication challenges of today's housing associations

It is not difficult to find public criticism of today's housing associations. The very nature of their positioning as socially responsible businesses invites severe criticism when housing safety is questioned, quality standards are not met or services are reduced as funding is cut. They are under pressure to build more homes but some of the homes have been of a poor quality. Some criticise associations for being too commercial (Hilton 2016) and others, including the then Prime Minister David Cameron, as too inefficient (Gardiner 2015). They need to become housing developers selling homes on the open market to cross subsidise other more philanthropic activities, yet the very act of being more commercially driven in parts of the business can have an impact on the more traditional third sector culture.

Communicating purpose

Given the changing and conflicting demands, a number of housing associations have invested in redefining their objectives and values. They are finding it increasingly important to reassert and communicate their social purpose, particularly in the light of their increasingly commercial activities and the criticisms that brings. For example, Rushanara Ali, MP for Bethnal Green and Bow, warned of a 'trend towards bigger, more remote and less accountable housing associations with multi-million pound turnovers and substantial assets and reserves behaving like companies that are not serving their communities' (Ali 2016).

CASE STUDY 10.2: REDEFINING HYDE HOUSING BRAND

At Hyde Housing, this need to re-examine what the organization stands for was particularly acute. First, it was originally proposing to merge with L&Q and East Thames but decided to withdraw from discussions and continue as an independent organization. Secondly, its 50th anniversary gave an opportunity to lay out its future direction. So, Hyde Housing embarked on a process of defining its brand in terms of vision, mission and social purpose. As the Chair of Hyde Group, Mark Sebba said (2017): 'House builders, local authorities, investors and peers need to know what we stand for in order to form successful partnerships. But most of all we must encourage and foster an engaged, motived and enthused team.'

Hyde's new strategic plan (2017a) covers its vision, mission, values and objectives. It tackles the issue of profit/surplus head on, arguing that 'The money that we make is used to build more homes for those excluded from the market. For every million pounds surplus we make, we can build 150 new homes.'

The new values of the organization are a sharp contrast to some more generic corporate wording

- "We're Do-ers – We back up our intention with action. We're proactive, take responsibility and make it easy for others to do so too.
- We're Professional – We aspire to be a brilliantly run social business, so we are not afraid to take tough decisions, we always do what needs to be done, and we think carefully about every penny we spend.
- We're Ambitious – For what our organization and individuals can achieve, and for what others can do for themselves.
- We're Open – To dealing with the real issue, to new ways of solving problems, to other points of view, and to best practice from others.
- The Hyde Group values diversity and we make sure our services are accessible to all." *(Source: Hyde 2017c)*

Employees were the initial focus of the communications programme's role out. For three months, the new vision was trailed emphasising the fact that Hyde was changing. A teaser campaign included an animated dismantling of the old brand's identity on computer 'wall paper' screens. Previous brand collateral was removed from offices. Prior to the launch, senior managers received packs equipping them to brief their staff on the new direction and brand. Then on launch day all staff received a CEO e-mail at 8am and all the new communications collateral was put in place including the intranet, the external websites. Externally, the role out was carefully managed. Stakeholders were briefed on the new direction for Hyde without majoring on the new visual identity (Law 2017a).

Communicating mergers

With so many high-profile mergers between associations now in place or in planning, there are a number of important communication lessons to be drawn. The first is having the communications function involved from the earliest possible moment. Communicators help to shape the messaging. They develop an executable plan for all audiences from the date of announcement. Importantly, these plans also cover leak scenarios. Communicators work with corporate advisers to identify what types of leak could trigger an announcement and rehearse the handling of these scenarios. If an earlier announcement is required by a leak, then it is vital that all the necessary communications material is already produced and plans can simply be brought forward. For instance, there were rumours prior to the merger of L&Q and East Thames. However, the companies concerned believed these were insufficiently detailed and well sourced to necessitate bringing forward their announcement (Nixon 2017). Major, sensitive announcements cannot be handled as business as usual within a communications department; a small specialist team needs to be established who have signed relevant undertakings in terms of commercial confidentiality.

The second lesson is clearly communicating the logical argument for a merger. Merging two or more housing associations is not an end in itself! Commercial and social benefits have to be carefully set out. For instance, the Peabody press release (2016a) announcing the proposed merger of Peabody and Family Mosaic, stated that the merger would help the organizations add services, 'providing better value for money to residents and other stakeholders. The larger group would also have better resources to build more homes and provide local community services, including helping more people into work through training, apprenticeships and volunteering.' There is an emphasis on providing better value for money in this statement, notably on providing local community services and helping people into work. This is a broader vision that chimes more with traditional housing association values. It links with the emphasis that Peabody places on creating and reinforcing communities in their major redevelopments such as Thamesmead.

The third communications lesson is patience and staying in control. Mergers typically take around 18 months. It is important that the communications process is phased with regular updates. In particular, managing employees' expectations to ensure a sense of progress is important. Bringing together teams of people and integrating them is a communications task in its own right which has to be properly planned and resourced. A strong working relationship between the communications teams of the separate organizations has to be created.

Issues management

Given the amount of change in the housing association sector, there is a very significant issue management agenda. This can arise from poor quality new build through to the perceived unfairness of the treatment of individual residents or changes in services as associations improve efficiency. The way in which these issues are managed is likely to have a very significant impact on the associations' reputation.

During 2017, a number of high profile issues around quality and service arose on new developments built by housing associations. *The Guardian* newspaper highlighted the plight of residents and cases of damp, mould and even infestation, linking problems back to the perceived change of management ethos (Harris 2017: 6). In a number of extreme cases housing associations have now agreed after lengthy campaigns to demolish recently built homes and rehouse the residents. Housing associations that have a well-defined social purpose, a strong cultural emphasis on customer service, coupled with strong issue resolution processes will be better able to manage difficulties and avoid crisis communication.

Transparency and trust

Given the level of scrutiny the sector is under, associations are experimenting with new ways to build trust. This will become more important as associations are given greater freedom, operating under the lighter touch regulatory regime necessary to ensure associations and their debts are not classified as public sector. One approach is increasing transparency and levels of engagement with residents and stakeholders particularly around governance, performance and operational and service changes.

Bromford, based in the Midlands, has adopted an approach of publishing considerably more information than required by statutory obligations and annual reports. Every three months the organization publishes performance information on its website in an easy to read style using infographics. Active involvement is promoted with the 'you said, we did' area of its site being regularly updated so that customers can see that there is a purpose in providing feedback. As a result of this engagement, Bromford has seen a 45 per cent increase in customer feedback. The organization has also introduced the Bromford Lab where it shares online the challenges it is looking to address and search, via crowdsourcing and employee engagement, for creative solutions. As Philippa Jones, the CEO of Bromford, recently wrote (2016) 'we get a lot of value from sharing and collaborating with stakeholders rather than working in isolation'.

Peabody takes a more procedural approach. A Residents Council represents residents' views in terms of services, business priorities and strategic objectives to Peabody's Executive Team and Board (Peabody 2016b).

The online revolution

Given the pressure to improve efficiency, it is perhaps surprising that housing associations have not been faster adopters of online services and social media. However, after a slow start associations are starting to use these techniques to revolutionise their organizations, from changing service provision to listening to residents online through to recruitment and employee engagement.

The Orbit Group has pointed out that it costs 16 times as much to write a letter compared with providing a service online. Halton aims to have 90 per cent of residents accessing service through social media and its website by 2018 (Clifton 2015). In a specific example of using new approaches to improve efficiency, Hyde launched an Anti-Social Behaviour (ASB) online tool kit in April 2016. It has been used to educate residents and staff as to what is and is not ASB with the result that reported cases fell significantly in the first six months of the programme. Where cases continue to be reported, the process is simpler for residents and the likelihood of prompt remedial action much higher (Hyde 2017b).

Curo, a smaller association based in Bath, has been one of the earlier adopters. Some 80 per cent of staff are now recruited through LinkedIn and related social media, mainly via the strong social media presence of their senior staff. They have also adopted clear policies and processes around social media and strong issue management protocols so that service issues or online criticism can be captured and rapidly dealt with (Law 2017b).

Muir Group, a Scottish association, provides all staff with social media training and gives them considerable freedom to express themselves. Their approach is based on the confidence that Muir's employees have a strong adherence to their core values (Smith 2015).

A number of associations are now starting to use social media to support employee communications. Bromford, regarded as one of the leaders in the sector, has used Yammer as an internal social networking and knowledge sharing platform. It has helped its employees across multiple sites share best practice more effectively (CIPD 2014).

The housing associations that are succeeding in the new media world are tending to adopt a clear set of protocols without being over prescriptive. These are likely to include the following elements.

- Principles and policies that clearly set standards and best practice but that do not impose rigid central control.
- A social media strategy that establishes what the organization wishes to achieve and how it will go about that in practice.
- Investment in online listening and reporting to ensure that the organization fully understands its social media footprint.
- The training of employees, including senior staff, to ensure an understanding of dos and don'ts of the online world.
- Protocols to manage online criticism and issues management. This is to ensure that an internal escalation process is followed where necessary.

Whilst some housing associations have adopted this type of approach, the sector is not yet at the vanguard of the social media revolution. Few have the confidence to start debates online and to adopt a more engaging conversational approach. One exception is the Swan Housing Association 'Time for Change' campaign that succeeded in obtaining planning permission for the Laindon shopping centre. A dedicated website was commissioned, including a 3D fly through, so residents had a hub of information and could give feedback as plans developed. Facebook advertising was used to drive attendance at engagement meetings which in turn led to 83 per cent of people who submitted feedback during the consultation saying they supported the plans. The overall result was that after years of mistrust over the redevelopment, Swan obtained a unanimous planning consent (Swan 2017).

CASE STUDY 10.3: COMMUNICATIONS IN SPECIALIST HOUSING ASSOCIATIONS

A number of associations focus on the housing needs of disadvantaged groups and campaign on their behalf. For instance, Habinteg is an association that specialises in disability and although the majority of residents are not people with disabilities, all their homes are accessible and over one third are designed for wheelchair users.

This provided Habinteg with a platform for a focused campaign, led by Connect, to promote the need to increase the number of 'disability friendly' homes being built. It was a multi audience approach aimed at government, parliament, local government, tenants and the media. At a high level a meeting was secured with the Minister for Disabled People who agreed to raise the issue of accessible housing with the Minister for Housing and Planning. To build pressure for change a range of parliamentarians were briefed particularly select committee chairs.

The passage of the Neighbourhood and Planning Bill in 2016–17 provided a good opportunity to secure legislative change. To support the campaign, using Freedom of Information requests, it was revealed that only three per cent of councils outside London had plans to deliver and monitor the number of accessible homes built in their area. An interactive map was created of the best and worst performing councils together with a tool kit to help councils improve their policies. A national day of action for Habinteg residents was organized – backed by use of social media. Using a Twitter thunderclap, the hashtag #for-accessiblehomes started trending and, including Instagram, the message was delivered 31,874 times. More traditional media channels were also used with national, sector and local media coverage particularly around a joint letter signed by 15 influential organizations.

The Government was persuaded to amend the bill to include an obligation on the Secretary of State to issue guidance to local planning authorities on how to address housing need arising from old age or disability. The overall outcome was a change in the law, new guidance from government and greater awareness of the issue of specialist housing.

Source: CIPR 2017

Conclusions

Housing associations face significant challenges ahead: building more homes, providing services to tenants more efficiently whilst maintaining their not for profit ethos. As they grapple with these issues, to succeed in the eyes of their stakeholders, associations have to explain their unique position more successfully both collectively and individually. That will mean defining their social purpose more clearly, particularly as profitable activities are required to cross subsidise other activities. It will mean being more proactive in telling their story of building homes and communities backed by compelling evidence of their contribution to society. It will also mean being more transparent in terms of accountability and innovating more in how that story is told. As Stuart Ropke (2017), chief executive, Community Housing Cymru observes: 'If we genuinely want to tell our story better perhaps the prerequisite is a sector that is recognised as open, transparent and accountable beyond the housing world.'

Questions for discussion

1.   How successfully is the sector grappling with the communication challenges of social purpose and profitability?
2.   What types of communication challenges will associations face in future, bearing in mind the pressures they face?
3.   How might associations embrace social media more fully?
4.   What role could there be for campaigning in housing associations?

References

Primary sources

Law, P. (2017a) Conversation with Carol Jones, Director of Communications, Marketing and Public Affairs, Hyde

Law, P. (2017b) Conversation with Gerraint Oakley, Managing Director, Curo

Secondary sources

Ali, R. (2016) *Hansard*, 31 October

CIPD (2014) Putting social media to work. Available at: https://www.cipd.co.uk/knowl edge/work/technology/social-media-report [Accessed: 11 July 2017]

CIPR (2017) *Public affairs excellence award winner.* Available at: https://www.cipr.co.uk/con tent/awards-events/excellence-awards/past-winners/full-results-2017 [Accessed: 11 July 2017]

Clark, R. (2015) Why housing associations are the true villains of the property crisis, *Spectator Magazine*, 25 July. Available at: https://www.spectator.co.uk/2015/07/housing-a ssociations-have-failed-to-build-houses/# [Accessed: 3 May 2017]

Clifton, H. (2015) Getting social, *Inside Housing* [online]. Available at: https://www.inside housing.co.uk/home/home/getting-social-44198 [Accessed 6 June 2017]

Conservative Party (2015) *Manifesto*. Available at: https://www.bond.org.uk/data/files/ Blog/ConservativeManifesto2015.pdf [Accessed 11 July 2017]

Conservative Party (2017) *Manifesto*. 7 February. Available at: www.conservatives.com/ma nifesto [Accessed 11 July 2017]

DCLG (2017) *Fixing our Broken Housing Market*, Cm 9352

Douglas, S. (2017) Criticism of White Paper misses point, *Inside Housing*. Available at: https://www.insidehousing.co.uk/home/home/criticism-of-white-paper-misses-the-point-49871 [Accessed 6 June 2017]

Gardiner, J. (2015) Cameron launches attack on housing associations, *Building*. Available at: http://www.building.co.uk/cameron-launches-attack-on-housing-associations/5077604. article [Accessed 6 July 2017]

Harris, J. (2017) 'I'm scared this building is going to collapse', *Guardian G2*, 6 February, p.6

Hilton, A. (2016) Housing Associations must beware the risks of going commercial, *Evening Standard* [online]. Available at: http://www.standard.co.uk/business/anthony-hilton-hou

sing-associations-must-beware-the-risk-of-going-commercial-a3379256.html [Accessed 6 July 2017]

Hyde (2017a) About us. Available at: https://www.hyde-housing.co.uk/corporate/a bout-us/strategic-plan-2017-20/about-hyde/ [Accessed 6 June 2017]

Hyde (2017b) Online anti-social behaviour tool kit, UK Housing Award Entry

Hyde (2017c) Vision, mission and values. Available at: https://www.hyde-housing.co.uk/ corporate/about-us/strategic-plan-2017-20/vision-mission-and-values/ [Accessed 6 June 2017]

Jones, P. (2016) Real transparency means building tenants' trust and sharing and collaborating with stakeholders, *NHF Blog*. Available at: http://www.housing.org.uk/blog/real-transpa rency-means-building-tenants-trust-and-sharing-and-collaboratin/ [Accessed 4 July 2017]

Kelly, L. (2015) Social housing rents to fall by 1% a year, chancellor announces, *Guardian*. Available at: https://www.theguardian.com/housing-network/2015/jul/08/social-housin g-rent-fall-chancellor-budget [Accessed 4 July 2017]

Lund, B. (2016) *Housing Politics in the United Kingdom: Power, Planning and Protest*, Policy Press

Martin, D. (2015) Housing Fat Cats' Hypocrisy, *Daily Mail*, 15 April, p.1

Morton, A. (2010) *Making Housing Affordable: A New Vision for Housing Policy*, Policy Exchange

Mullins, D. (2010) *Working Paper 16: Housing Associations*, Third Sector Research Centre

Murtha, T. (2013) Steps to success, *Inside Housing*. Available at: https://www.insidehousing. co.uk/home/home/steps-to-success-34718 [Accessed: 2 May 2017]

NHF (2015) Evidence on Welfare Reform and Work Bill. Available at: https://www.pub lications.parliament.uk/pa/cm201516/cmpublic/welfarereform/memo/wrw23.htm [Accessed: 2 May 2017]

NHF (n.d.) FAQ. Available at: http://www.housing.org.uk/about-us/faqs/ [Accessed: 2 May 2017]

NHF (n.d.) How we're perceived now. Available at: http://www.housing.org.uk/get-invol ved/promoting-our-sector/owning-our-future/current-perceptions/ [Accessed 6 June 2017]

NHF (n.d.) Deliver on the substance. Available at: http://www.housing.org.uk/get-invol ved/promoting-our-sector/owning-our-future/deliver-on-the-substance/ [Accessed 4 July 2017]

NHF (n.d.) Tell the HA story. Available at: http://www.housing.org.uk/get-involved/prom oting-our-sector/owning-our-future/tell-housing-associations-story/ [Accessed 6 June 2017]

Nixon, N. (2017) Presentation to NHF Communications and Marketing Conference, London, 7 March.

Peabody (2016a) Peabody and Family Mosaic to merge. Available at https://www.peabody. org.uk/news-views/2016/dec/merger [Accessed 6 June 2017]

Peabody (2016b) Help improve Peabody's services. https://www.peabody.org.uk/news-views/2016/jan/help-improve-peabodys-services

Riddell (2017) Presentation to NHF Communications and Marketing Conference 2017, London, 7 March.

Ropke, S. (2017) How can we tell our story better? *Inside Housing*. Available at: https:// www.insidehousing.co.uk/home/home/how-can-we-tell-our-story-better-50066 [Accessed: 6 June 2017]

Sebba, M. (2017) Housing associations need better branding, *Inside Housing*. Available at: https://www.insidehousing.co.uk/home/home/housing-associations-need-better-bra nding-50210 [Accessed: 6 June 2017]

Smith, K. (2015) Musing on mice, men and social media at Muir, *Allthingsic*. Available at: https://www.allthingsic.com/muir/ [Accessed: 11 July 2017]

Swan (2017) Laidon Shopping centre redevelopment, *Time for Change*, award entry, https://www.laindonfutures.co.uk/latest-news [Accessed: 5 July 2017]

Zeffman, H. (2015) Right-to-buy deal backed by only 55% of housing associations, *Guardian*. Available at: https://www.theguardian.com/society/2015/oct/17/right-to-buy-deal-backed-by-only-55-of-housing-associations [Accessed: 5 July 2017]

11

TRADE UNION PR

The working voice

Nigel Stanley

Trade unions are longstanding non-profits in the UK. Trade union historian, Henry Pelling (1992: 9), reflects that in the eighteenth century "the need for combination grew" when guilds became less powerful and when wages became less regulated. Today, freedom of association, which includes the right for workers to come together, is standard for human rights declarations.

This chapter explains the role of trade unions. It describes their historical development as this has a big impact on how the media regard them. It looks at their public relations needs by examining what they do, the audiences they need to reach, and suggests what makes union communications effective.

The rationale for trade unionism is that the relationship between employer and employee – or master and servant to use the legal language of the nineteenth century – is inherently unequal. Joining with colleagues to present a united front to the boss goes some way to equalise that relationship.

The weapon that gives workers power in the workplace is strike action. One worker protesting can easily be sacked, but if the whole workforce – or large sections of it – withdraw their labour, it is harder to dismiss them all. But strikes are generally a last resort. While they hurt the employer – and have wider effect on society and the economy – union members suffer loss of pay.

Employers negotiate with unions – in a process known as **collective bargaining** – to reach agreement. Unions normally have a shrewd idea of what employers can reasonably deliver, just as employers can judge a union's bottom line. Strikes are normally avoided therefore, but it is the right of union members to withdraw their labour that gives unions bargaining power.

It is a lazy stereotype to see unions as all about strikes. A union member can go from starting work to retirement without ever striking, yet still benefit from not just fair pay but representation in a grievance, access to training, a decent pension and legal rights won by union campaigning such as parental leave.

Trade unionism – some history

Modern trade unionism traces its history to the nineteenth century. Starting with skilled artisans, union expanded to less skilled workers, mainly men but women too with the match girls' dispute (Pelling 1971: 97). Unions grouped together in 1868 to found an umbrella organization the Trades Union Congress (TUC). In 1900, they joined with various socialist groups to form the Labour Party as a voice for workers.

After the First World War, a weak economy and large numbers of returning soldiers drove down conditions. In 1926 the TUC called all its members out in the General Strike in support of Britain's miners who were fighting cuts in their pay and conditions. But after nine days the strike was called off in defeat.

The Second World War brought a new role and strength for unions. Pelling (1971: ch11) describes this as "power with responsibility" as unions worked to maximise production.

The post-war years were a union golden age with a determination that the policy and economic mistakes made after the First World War would not be repeated (Hennessy 2006). The UK's post-war welfare state was based on the blueprint of the 1942 Beveridge Report. There was very little difference between his proposals and the proposals of the TUC Beveridge told the TUC in 1942.

The UK's post-war consensus broke down in the 1970s with the oil shock – a big increase in the cost of oil caused both inflation and a recession. Workers wanted to maintain the value of their wages against unprecedented inflation which peaked at more than 25 per cent. This led to sharply increased levels of industrial action with significantly higher numbers of days lost to strikes until the mid 1980s (ONS 2016)

Economic crisis and inflation dominated the decade of the 1970s. A deal between unions and a Labour government to limit inflation broke down leading to a series of disputes in early 1979 – the "winter of discontent". Images of uncollected rubbish and stories about strikers refusing to bury the dead had a strong impact. Conservative leader Mrs Thatcher won the 1979 election running not just against Labour, but the post-war consensus.

The 1984–85 miners' strike against pit closures was the biggest since the war. This bitter and prolonged dispute polarised the nation. The refusal of the leader of the National Union of Mineworkers, Arthur Scargill, to back a ballot of all members was controversial, but so was the policing of the dispute and the tactics of the government (Hencke and Beckett 2009).

Its defeat coupled with wide scale deindustrialisation and mass unemployment accelerated union decline through the 1980s and 1990s. Conservative governments introduced a series of laws regulating unions and making strikes more difficult.

UK union membership peaked in 1980 (ONS 2015) but then fell sharply, before stabilising somewhat after 1997 as the public sector grew (Willman and Bryson 2007). The 2008 crash and subsequent austerity hit membership again.

Unions today

A good measure of union effectiveness is density, the share of the workforce that is in a union. Charlwood (2013: 16) estimates density in 1980 as more than half. It is now less than a quarter. Highest workforce densities are among professional occupations (approaching a half) and public sector employees (over a half). Lowest densities are private sector employees (one seventh) and senior management (one seventh) (ONS 2015).

Union organization is much stronger in the public than the private sector not only in the UK but also across many economies. Women workers are more likely to be unionised than men. The typical union member today is a woman educated to degree level in her 40s working in the public sector.

Collective bargaining with employers is still the prime purpose of trade unionism. This produces better – and fairer – pay, the "sword of justice" effect: "unions narrow the wage differentials between women and men, blacks and whites, those with health problems and those without, and between manual and non-manual workers" (Metcalf et al. 2000).

There are various benefits to union membership. Union members were a third more likely to have received training with benefits to the employer according to Stuart et al. (2015) thanks to government and employer support for union learning.

People want to be able to call on expert representation if something goes wrong, such as workplace injury, unfair discrimination, a disciplinary issue or grievance – workplace insurance.

Unions deliver through both paid staff and volunteers – the elected shop stewards and representatives (reps). Union full-time officers assist reps and lead negotiations with big employers. Specialist staff cover areas such as communications, health and safety, the law and pensions. Unions elect their leadership. The chief executive – usually the General Secretary – will be elected by postal ballot – a UK legal requirement.

Unions group together in umbrella bodies to strengthen their voice and share services such as research, training and legal advice. In the UK, the TUC is the single umbrella for UK unionism (Taylor 2000), but other countries may have more than one federal body.

The UK is unusual in having some unions that directly affiliate to a political party, Labour. But most do not. Some are explicitly non-political, while others take political stances but stop short of affiliating. UK law requires unions to set up a separate political fund if they wish to give money to political parties or campaign in ways designed to influence an election. Such a fund has to be set up by a ballot, and individual members can opt-out of the proportion of their membership fees that go to the fund.

Despite the explicit party allegiances of some unions, the TUC seeks to influence governments of all parties. Individual unions will press governments on issues which affect their members, ranging from non-ideological issues such as problems that musicians have taking instruments onto aeroplanes to big political issues.

Union public relations

Unions have multiple audiences, a range of interests and face preconceptions about unions. A list of union **publics** include the following.

The general public

There are few sections of the public that unions can ignore. People need to be engaged as voters, citizens and consumers. When there is a strike, employers will go on the attack – particularly important when many use a service such as public transport or are parents of children at school.

Many public policy issues have an important impact on the workplace. Unions seek to influence political decisions by shifting public opinion. This might mean trying to raise a union issue up the news agenda, or more strategically promoting a consensus around an issue. In the UK, a national minimum wage was introduced against the historic opposition of the Conservatives and many business voices in 1999. By 2015, the policy had won such national consensus that a Conservative Chancellor announced its biggest ever increase.

Members

Unions are voluntary organizations. For many being a union member is a small part of their identity except when there is an important issue at work. Unions need to project a positive and engaging image to their own members, reinforcing the benefits of membership. They directly communicate with their members with magazines, meetings, one to one contact, email and social media. Securing positive media coverage helps validate unions with their members.

Unions need to communicate fast with their own members when in dispute or campaign mode, particularly if employers, sections of the media, or politicians are attacking. As well as direct contact, unions use workplace reps to cascade their message. Getting them on side is part of the communications challenge.

Potential members

Unions always need new members. Some unions have a defined target audience but many need to cast their net more broadly as technology and economics are both destroying jobs – often unionised – and creating new ones.

Unions recruit members in many ways. Union reps recruit in the workplace – a union pitch can be part of the induction process for new staff where there are good relationships. To break into new or weakly unionised workplaces, unions employ organizers. They use familiar marketing and advertising techniques including television and cinema advertising.

Policy makers and opinion formers

Unions – particularly umbrella bodies like the TUC in Britain – lobby government and other decision-making bodies, such as regulators and enforcement agencies. They are likely to use in-house public affairs experts to build relationships, but modern governments tend to take a great deal of notice of what the wider media says about an issue.

The case study shows how unions can achieve far more by working in alliance with other groups, getting the media on side, and getting other players, such as investors and politicians, to take up their cause. The more surprising they are as union allies, the more effective they can be. The UK's Communications Workers' Union was able to work with the Womens' Institute and the Country Landowners' Association in a campaign against privatisation of the Royal Mail in 2010 as they shared union concern about rural post office closures (Parker 2008).

Employers

The prime purpose of a union is to regulate the relationship between employee and employer. Unions must therefore engage with employers, both individually and collectively. Employers have a range of attitudes towards unions. Some are extremely hostile – and some positive, seeing the benefits of partnership. Most will treat unions in a pragmatic way as one more issue that they have to deal with as managers.

Today's employers are complex organizations. Unions may sit on Europe wide Works Councils and negotiate pay at the national level, but most interaction is likely to be with local managers and human resources staff resolving workplace issues or dealing with individual problems such as disciplinary and grievance hearings.

Positive stories about unions making a contribution towards productivity through the promotion of skills and settling issues before they become bigger problems are harder to measure than strike days, but just as important in the union story. Managers who have to take notice of the views of their staff and cannot simply operate in a command and control top down mode may well become better managers.

The relationship between unions and employers is therefore complex and nuanced. Employers and their staff have both common and opposing interests. In the defence or nuclear power industries both will want their company to win government orders, but can still argue about the future of a pension scheme. Unions need employers to see them as useful partners with whom they can do business but with the potential to wield a big stick.

The communications context

In the UK, unions often face a difficult media environment with some outlets extremely hostile to trade unionism. There are a number of reasons for this.

The UK's national newspapers tend to be partisan. Media expert, Charlie Beckett (2016), comments

> To people not used to British newspapers they can sometimes feel a bit like that drunken, loud-mouthed guy in the bar who is anxious to tell you what he thinks and what you should think, too. But readers seem to like it.

Hostility to trade unionism is a historic part of what makes a UK newspaper right-wing. Until the 1980s highly unionised hot metal printers were very powerful and unpopular with proprietors. But new computer technology made their skills redundant.

In 1986, News International moved some major newspapers' production overnight into a new plant in Wapping in East London. Six thousand employees were already on strike over the plans (Oatridge 2002). Some unions were derecognised and thousands of printers were made redundant. This provoked a bitter year-long strike with echoes of the then recent miners' dispute as pickets and police clashed outside the plant. This ended in defeat for the unions, described by McSmith (2010: 198) as "the most significant victory by a private employer in any industrial dispute in post-war Britain".

Unions during this period were slow to realise that they needed to get their side of the story across. Many thought their economic power was sufficient. This allowed a series of trade union clichés to develop which still feed coverage today. Unions have "bosses" rather than leaders, who "order" workers on strike rather than implement a ballot result (a legal requirement before any strike in the UK).

The 1970s and 1980s still form many media stereotypes, and the Glasgow Media Group has argued there is a systematic bias against unions (Philo et al. 1995). Since the middle 1980s there has been a big decline in strikes, yet it is never hard to find reference to a "winter of discontent" in sections of the media. This author once calculated that if 1979 was a full winter of discontent then "the most we have managed since 1990 is a long weekend" (Stanley 2010).

Coverage of union affairs has declined. Specialist journalists, normally called industrial correspondents, used to cover unions daily, but their number and status has fallen this century. They understood unions – their personalities, how they worked and the dynamics of disputes (Jones 2011).

While expert coverage has declined, there are many more outlets today and particularly broadcast and social media bring new opportunities. Social media campaigning can mean communicating with those who already agree with you, but union members who need persuading and informing, will likely listen to their union. Social media can rapidly generate new networks and spread content that can be vital during industrial disputes, when members may face a hostile media and employer misinformation.

Union traditions, structures and hierarchies do not always fit with the disintermediating informality of social media. But the #SportsDirectShame element of the case study shows that unions can embrace it.

CASE STUDY 11.1: SPORTS DIRECT AND INSECURE WORKING PRACTICES

Union organizers helped drive media exposure of poor working conditions, including a failure to pay the minimum wage, at the Sports Direct warehouse – a UK retail chain – on TV (for instance, Channel 4, 2015) and in a number of reports in the *Guardian* (Goodley and Ashby 2015; Parker and Moore 2015). Unite, the union concerned, had already been campaigning against abuse of zero-hours contracts and low pay with shareholder activists groups such as Share Action (Butler 2015).

This was then taken up in parliament, with condemnation from MPs from all political parties. Unite ran a social media campaign #SportsDirectShame, and kept up the pressure with action outside shops and though a petition. Founder and chief executive Mike Ashley provoked even more press coverage by initially refusing to give evidence to a House of Commons Committee (Goodley 2016).

Investors already had concerns about corporate governance standards at the company. Successive reports on poor practice led to the share price falling, putting further pressure on the company, and leading investors to work with unions. Sports Direct workers won a significant settlement of unpaid back pay, though concern continues (Kollewe and Butler 2017).

The story ran for months. It helped reveal wider poor treatment and insecurity at work, exposing other companies which were guilty of similar practices. The **gig economy** where services such as meal delivery or taxi rides are provided through digital platforms between customers and nominally self-employed contractors also caused concern, given the very strong control the platforms can have over their workers.

Growing political concern about the "modern labour market" led to the Conservative Prime Minister, Theresa May, commissioning a major review in 2016 (Department for Business, Energy & Industrial Strategy 2016).

Public attitudes to trade unionism

The hostility shown in parts of the media to trade unionism does not represent the general views of the public. Polling company IPSOS-MORI (2017) has asked the same set of questions about trade unions over four decades (albeit with gaps). A question about whether unions "are essential to protect workers' interests", produces overwhelming support with more than 70% consistently agreeing. The proportion of people who agree that they "have too much power in Britain today" has declined from 70% plus agreeing in 1975–85; to only 30–40% agreeing between 2010 and 2017. This is partly because unions have lost power and membership numbers (IPSOS-MORI 2017).

Effective trade union public relations

Trade unions face complex communications challenges in addition to those faced by not-for-profits in general. Media bias (Davis 2002) and stereotyping are a common obstacle faced by trade unions. Other challenges vary by union. What works for a small specialist union – say professional footballers – may not work for a big general union. Nevertheless, there are some general principles that can help and which are identified below.

Understand your brand and stick to it

Unions need to have a strong sense of who they are, and what they want people to think about them. Unions sometimes dislike marketing terms, but then this can be part of the union brand! Unions naturally have many of the values that commercial brands seek. Unions may not want to hire expensive branding consultants (although this can be useful with the right agency). Nevertheless, they should be clear about how they want to be regarded and should consistently act in ways to reinforce this.

Unions share common beliefs. Yet each has its own characteristics. For many the brand will be based on perceptions about their members. A nursing organization will want to capture the positive reputation of nurses, while a union organizing vulnerable workers against tough employers will have a different personality. National federations or big general unions cannot so easily base their identity around their members' jobs and need to think more carefully.

One useful exercise for unions is not just to think what they are, but what they are not. For instance, an umbrella body for unions might make a list like the one below.

TABLE 11.1 Trade Union Attributes

What we are	*What we are not*
We speak for people at work	We are not just a collection of vested interests, a union of unions
We are experts in the world of work. Our views are based on thorough research, and knowing the people we represent.	We are not "rent-a-quotes", ready to say anything over the top that will get us publicity.
We are effective campaigners who can help set agendas, have real influence and can make a difference, even if we do not get everything we want.	We are not "outsiders" with no influence.
We may make a reasoned and evidence-based case but we are passionate in our commitment to social justice and our opposition to exploitation, unfair discrimination and bad treatment in the UK and abroad.	We are not neutral commentators, experts or a think-tank; we have a mission.

A danger for unions is that it is easier to gain coverage when conforming to media stereotypes. Even broadcasters genuinely looking for balanced perspectives can have a view of what makes a good union interviewee. Unfortunately, that may not be a softly spoken, reasonable woman who speaks about facts and personal experience.

Be authentic

The strength of unions is that they represent "ordinary" people. This is at a time when trust in authority figures and experts has declined.

The opponents of unions always frame their arguments about the union as an organization, hence the concentration on union bosses. Many union leaders are able communicators, but can still be seen as professional expert voices or worse as quasi-politicians. A typical member talking about a particular workplace or job will be more believable. A lack of media "polish" can help authenticity. As many organizations now forbid employees speaking to the media, this may have to be anonymous, but that can make it powerful.

This is particularly pertinent during an industrial dispute, when sections of the media will want to talk about "union bully boys" rather than why members are striking. A 2007 BBC Trust review of business coverage led by Sir Alan Budd found that much business and industrial reporting tried to balance views between business and consumers, at the expense of a union or worker voice.

> As an example, we point to the coverage of the threatened strike action by British Airways cabin crew (January 2007). Too much emphasis was placed on how much flights were likely to be disrupted and insufficient attention was given to examining the claims of staff in a full and fair way....
>
> Around 29 million people work for a living in the UK and spend a large proportion of their waking hours in the workplace. However, little of this important part of UK life is reflected in the BBC's business coverage ... the audiences are served in their identity as consumers. But they are not that well served in their role as workers.
>
> *(BBC 2007)*

More general stories fronted by union officials should be backed up by case studies. The TUC's long campaign for equal pension rights for same sex couples is brought alive with a case study.

> ...married couple Peter Armstrong-Luckhurst and his husband Kristofer, entered a civil partnership in 2009 and converted this to a marriage in 2014. Armstrong-Luckhurst has paid into an NHS pension scheme for 16 years, and has also bought another four years' worth of pensions' credits. As a heterosexual couple,

if his spouse died, he would be entitled to £5,585.91 per year from this pension. As it stands, Kristofer would only receive £793.18 a year.

(Personnel Today *2015*)

Have clear objectives and think strategically

Coverage is rarely an end in itself, unions are usually campaigning for a purpose. Some media coverage can help secure change, but some may hinder. Difficult negotiations to end an industrial dispute are rarely aided by commentary on their progress. Both sides will probably need some room for compromise, and want to present an eventual deal as a win rather than a retreat (even if this is closer to reality). Even accurate reporting may get in the way of this, and a media blackout is a sign of progress.

The same can apply to political campaigns. Any government may not be keen to "give in" to union campaigning if that is how an issue has been framed. Instead they may well be prepared to "respond to widespread concern" about an injustice, even if the same issue is at stake. This is when you look for allies to carry a joint message. In the Sports Direct case study, the investment funds who criticised employment practices (using information from union and media exposes) were crucial.

Thinking strategically means knowing when to stop, rather than continuing when no more progress can be made. This also leads to unions failing to celebrate advance. It is unusual to win absolutely everything you want, but any progress is usually worthwhile and should be claimed as such. Do not commemorate glorious defeats at the expense of celebrating partial advances. People join unions for instrumental reasons not to be part of a great cause.

Do your research but tell a story

Unions need to know what they are talking about, and be able to back up their claims. Negotiations with employers need you to be on top of the detail. Influencing government requires them to agree there is a problem and that change is required. Potential allies will want reassurance that you understand their objectives and concerns.

Good research can drive campaigns. Every country produces a wealth of official statistics that can provide fascinating detail about the world of work. Understanding public opinion – measured through quantitative and qualitative polling – can refine a message so that it resonates. Understanding those you seek to influence – their attitudes, motivations and resources – is a prerequisite for successful campaigning.

However, dry facts and statistics will not cut through unless they tell a story which engages your audience emotionally. It may make them angry, or as in this case study, it may be something with which they identify.

Nigel Stanley

CASE STUDY 11.2: WORK YOUR PROPER HOURS DAY CAMPAIGN

Britain's TUC ran its first annual Work Your Proper Hours Day in 2003 to draw attention to how much unpaid overtime there is in the economy. This is measured by the Labour Force Survey – the major official source of statistics about work.

A relatively simple calculation shows that on average a worker who does unpaid overtime would work for free well into February each year if they did all the unpaid work at the start of the year. This gives a date for Work Your Proper Hours Day. The same statistics show how much that overtime would be worth of it were paid. As they are broken down by occupation, separate figures can be worked out for groups such as teachers or accountants – of great appeal to trade press.

The TUC developed this campaign to try and shift perceptions of trade unionism. Unpublished research commissioned showed that workers support trade unions, but many non-members think they are irrelevant to them. They had an image of trade unions as confrontational and interested in a narrow range of issues, particularly pay. But long hours, work-life balance and excess workloads were problems for many who do not strongly identify with unions.

The campaign recognised white-collar and professional workers are not paid overtime, and few want to be seen as clock-watchers. Doing a good job can sometimes mean extra hours, but many say this can be exploited. So the campaign did not demand overtime pay or that staff should refuse extra work. Instead the campaign called for people to "work their proper hours" for one day a year to highlight that their work was too often being taken for granted. Managers should use the day to properly recognise staff loyalty by taking them out for a drink or coffee after work or during a proper lunch-hour.

Conclusion

The size and power of trades unions has declined markedly since the middle 1980s but public attitudes towards them have become much more positive. Media coverage of union affairs has also declined but the stance of most newspapers in particular has remained negative. There are many positive trades union attributes which need to be promoted in ways that will be recognised not only by members but also other audience segments who are likely to be sympathetic. In particular unions need to do their audience research and tell true stories to exemplify their case and to defy stereotypes. In short "be authentic".

Discussion questions

1. What are the recent media stories you can remember that feature a union?
2. Can you remember or identify through research a recent story that was generated by a union? What were they trying to show, and why did they raise this issue?

3.   Repeat this exercise for a union federation such as the TUC.
4.   What could unions do to improve their image?
5.   How should unions explain their involvement in politics?
6.   What could unions do to make themselves more attractive to young people?
7.   If working for a union, how would you prepare a communications strategy for a strike against the closure of a pensions scheme.

References

BBC (2007) *Report of the Independent Panel for the BBC Trust on Impartiality of BBC Business Coverage.*   http://downloads.bbc.co.uk/bbctrust/assets/files/pdf/review_report_research/impartiality_business/business_impartiality_report.pdf

Beckett, C. (2016) Why press bias is a Great British tradition. https://medium.com/@CharlieBeckett/to-people-not-used-to-british-newspapers-they-can-sometimes-feel-a-bit-like-that-drunken-loud-88569e03a63d#.2kq27jkxx

Butler, S. (2015) Union files pay claim to Sports Direct over zero hours contracts. *Guardian* on-line. https://www.theguardian.com/business/2015/aug/07/union-files-pay-claim-to-sports-direct-over-zero-hours-contracts

Channel 4 (2015) *Sports Direct – Investigation Reveals Harsh Working Conditions.* http://www.channel4.com/info/press/news/sports-direct-investigation-reveals-harsh-working-conditions

Charlwood, A. (2013) *The Anatomy of Union Membership Decline in Great Britain 1980–1998.* London School of Economics and Political Science http://etheses.lse.ac.uk/852/1/Charlwood_anatomy_union_membership_decline.pdf

Davis, A. (2002) *Public Relations Democracy: Public Relations, Politics and the Mass Media in Britain.* Manchester: Manchester University Press.

Department for Business, Energy & Industrial Strategy (2016) Taylor review on modern employment practices launches. 30th November. Press release. https://www.gov.uk/government/news/taylor-review-on-modern-employment-practices-launches

Goodley, S. (2016) Sports Direct founder Mike Ashley snubs call to face MPs. *Guardian* online. 21st March. https://www.theguardian.com/business/2016/mar/21/sports-direct-founder-mike-ashley-snubs-call-mps-parliamentary-select-committee

Goodley, S. and Ashby, J. (2015) A day at 'the gulag': What it's like to work at Sports Direct's warehouse. *Guardian* online. https://www.theguardian.com/business/2015/dec/09/sports-direct-warehouse-work-conditions

Hencke, D. and Beckett, F. (2009) *Marching to the Fault Line: The Miners' Strike and the Battle for Industrial Britain.* London: Hachette.

Hennessy, P. (2006) *Never Again: Britain 1945–1951.* London: Penguin Books.

IPSOS-MORI (2017) *Attitudes to Trade Unions 1975–2014.* https://www.ipsos.com/ipsos-mori/en-uk/attitudes-trade-unions-1975-2014

Jones, N. (2011) *The Lost Tribe of Fleet Street: Whatever Happened to the Labour and Industrial Correspondents?*London: Nicholas Jones

Kollewe, J. and Butler, S. (2017) Mike Ashley brushes off 60% dive in profits as shares in Sports Direct rise. *Guardian* online. 20th July. https://www.theguardian.com/business/2017/jul/20/sports-direct-weak-pound-profits-mike-ashley

Metcalf, D., Hansen, K. and Charlwood, A. (2000) *Unions and the Sword of Justice: Unions and Pay Systems, Pay Inequality, Pay Discrimination and Low Pay.* London: Centre for Economic

Performance. http://eprints.lse.ac.uk/20195/1/Unions_and_the_Sword_of_Justice_Unions_ and_Pay_Systems,_Pay_Inequality,_Pay_Discrimination_and_Low_Pay.pdf

McSmith, A. (2010) *No Such Thing as Society*. London: Constable.

Oatridge, N. (2002) *Wapping '86: The Strike that Broke Britain's Newspaper Unions*. Coldtype. http://www.coldtype.net/Assets/pdfs/Wapping1.pdf

ONS (2015) Trade union statistics. https://www.gov.uk/government/statistics/trade-u nion-statistics-2015

ONS (2016) Labour disputes in the UK. https://www.ons.gov.uk/employmentandlabourma rket/peopleinwork/workplacedisputesandworkingconditions/articles/labourdisputes/latest

Parker, G. and Moore, M. (2015) Sports Direct working conditions come under fire from MPs. *FT* online. https://www.ft.com/content/e21150dc-a28c-11e5-bc70-7ff6d4fd203a

Parker, J. (2008) The Trades Union Congress and civil alliance building: towards social movement unionism? *Employee Relations* 30(5): 562–583.

Pelling, H. (1971) *A History of British Trade Unionism*. 2nd edn. London: Penguin Books.

Pelling, H. (1992) *A History of British Trade Unionism*. 5th edn. London: Palgrave Macmillan.

Personnel Today (2015) Equalise pension survivor benefits for same-sex couples, urges TUC. http://www.personneltoday.com/hr/equalise-pension-survivor-benefits-sex-coup les-urges-tuc/

Philo, P., Hewitt, J. and Beharrell, P. (1995) *"And now they're out again": Industrial news, Glasgow Media Group Reader, Volume 2: Industry, Economy, War and Politics*. London: Routledge.

Stanley, N. (2010) Rats burying the dead in mounds of rubbish. *The Journalist*. October/ November 2010, p.13.

Stuart, M., Valizade, D. and Bessa, I. (2015) *Skills and Training: The Union Advantage: Training, Union Recognition and Collective Bargaining*. London: TUC. https://www.tuc.org. uk/sites/default/files/Skils_and_training.pdf

Taylor, R. (2000) *The TUC: From the General Strike to New Unionism*. London: Springer.

TUC (1942) Notes of statement by Sir William Beveridge to General Council at their meeting on 16 December, 1942. http://contentdm.warwick.ac.uk/cdm/ref/collection/ health/id/1913

Willman, P. and Bryson, A. (2007) *Union Organization in Great Britain*. London: Centre for Economic Performance. http://eprints.lse.ac.uk/19762/1/Union_Organization_in_Grea t_Britain.pdf

12

SOCIAL ENTERPRISE PR

Doing business whilst doing good

Tove Nordström

The non-profit sector is broad, both in terms of areas of work as well as how various organizations are set up and how they are functioning. Due to funding shortages, financial sustainability is increasingly becoming a key focus and concern, with many organizations consequently exploring other revenue streams. At the same time, due to a shift in the general public's view of corporate responsibility, the private sector is looking to become more socially responsible. With these two trends we are seeing growth within the social enterprise movement.

Social enterprises fall between the non-profit and the business sectors. Understanding what they are, how they have developed, what they do and what their challenges and opportunities are is essential to conducting relevant PR. This chapter considers the development of socially responsible business; definitions of social enterprise and its policy setting; PR challenges and solutions for the social enterprise sector; sector opportunities; and two case studies.

The development of socially responsible business

The topic of social business is one of growing interest with those in favour debating those who are not and with evident internal struggles. Efficiency and business sense is debated as are various definitions. For as long as there have been businesses there have been business men and women who have pursued a social purpose, people who would be recognized as social entrepreneurs. Some of the best known early ones were the Quakers, whose movement started in the 1640s with a strong focus on social activism and a way of running businesses that made life better for those who worked for them. Another example of early adopters can be seen in the Scottish weavers at Fenwick in Ayrshire who, in 1761, started buying oatmeal collectively. The oatmeal was bought in large sacks and they went on to sell the contents on to their members at a lower price than could be found in local shops. The Fenwick Weavers Society because of its approach is considered one of the first co-operatives, and it was later followed by the Rochdale Society of Equitable Pioneers. The Rochdale Society was set up in 1844 and its founders wrote the Rochdale Principles, a set of principles that have led the way for the modern co-operative movement (Ashton 2010). The principles were: open membership; democratic control; dividend on purchase; limited interest on capital; political and religious neutrality; cash trading; and promotion of education. They were set up to guide how the Society would be run, in a time when local workers were making a stand against the capitalist ideologies of the Industrial Revolution. The mill workers who founded the Society aimed to serve their community with goods their fellow community members normally could not afford. They set up a co-operative store, initially with only a few goods on offer, and were able to quickly grow it into a success. By 1854, over 1,000 similar stores had opened and the co-operative move- ment in the UK was seeing local successes across the country. They were all based on the Rochdale Principles that had brought a social conscience to business, and these can be widely seen in co-operatives and social businesses today (BBC 2010).

In modern days, we have had the likes of Milton Friedman argue that the sole responsibility of business is to increase profits (Friedman 1970). But since the 1970s, despite Friedman's words, we have seen an increase in businesses putting more emphasis on their wider responsibility in society. Many will argue that this is the response of business at a time when the general public tends to not trust big companies (Scoble and Israel 2006). The most recent Edelman Trust Barometer (Edelman 2017) shows a decrease in trust across the board with the general public showing a lack of trust in business and media, as well as government and non-profit organizations.

To see this trust in its context, the issue of transparency is important. The general public will not necessarily demand detailed disclosure but most will want assurance of honest behaviour (Gower 2010). Genuine openness, rather than just staged transparency, is crucial (Christensen 2002). Coombs and Holladay (2010) have seen an increased importance of transparency from the general public concerning not just financial information but additional information such as decision-making and the consequences of actions made by an organization.

Acting ethically as a public organization is evidently important in order to achieve support from society (Gallagher 2005) and to avoid bad reputation. Many will see ethical behaviour as simply the right thing to do (Treviño and Nelson 2004) or, as the likes of Kant, as a moral obligation (Guyer 2007), and we can see an increasing ethical focus across most types of business. But some go further, incorporating it into the core of the business, and this is where we are seeing developments of the social business.

Nobel Peace Prize laureate and social entrepreneur Muhammad Yunus argues that "to make the most of the structure of capitalism complete, we need to introduce another kind of business" (Yunus 2007: 21). Contrary to Friedman, he suggests that social business is the answer, where a company is cause-driven rather than profit-driven. Paul Allen agrees and sees it as the future of business, stating that "enterprises solely concerned with profit are like dinosaurs, and caring about people and planet is no longer a niche pursuit" (2007: 24).

The global financial crisis of 2007/8 saw a stronger shift in thinking towards the idea that the economy needs to serve society and this thought underpins social enterprise PR strategy towards the general public. Globally, we have come to realize that current capitalism has brought wealth to some, but not to many others, which is causing increasing inequalities. A business response to this is the social enterprise that "can be seen to represent a viable, and potentially, radical alternative to mainstream enterprise" (Kay et al 2016:220). And at the same time, the social enterprise is seen by some, such as politicians, as an alternative to non-profits, allowing organizations to develop a more sustainable model where they generate their own income rather than depending on grants and donations (McBrearty 2007).

The ethical business is also seeing a growing interest from potential employees, and especially amongst the younger generation. A majority of millennials – born 1981 to 1996 – want to work for companies making a positive impact and they would prefer purposeful work to a high salary (Jenkin 2015). Millennials are looking to make the world more compassionate, innovative, and sustainable and they are looking for work that matches their values (Poswolsky 2015). This provides the basis of social enterprise PR strategy towards employees.

An increasing number of corporate businesses are recognizing this trend and are in response looking at developing a more responsible approach to business. Many are putting a stronger focus on the triple bottom line, a phrase initially introduced in 1994 by John Elkington, founder of UK consultancy SustainAbility. Elkington argued that companies should be looking at three different bottom lines: the traditional profit and loss account; the 'people account' looking at the level of social responsibility; and the 'planet account' measuring how environmentally responsible the company has been (*The Economist* 2009). Robert Ashton argues that the triple bottom line is 'increasingly becoming a concern for organizations of all kind, not just those with a strong social or environmental purpose' (2010: 12–13).

The triple bottom line is an approach especially taken by business movements such as the B Corporation movement that started in the USA in 2006 and has grown globally. It was introduced to define a new generation of businesses with B Corporations being granted certification based on high standards of social and environmental accountability, performance and transparency (Chesters 2017). The B Corporation website states that there are over 2,000 B Corporations across 50 countries covering 130 industries with companies like Etsy, Kickstarter, Ben & Jerry's, and Patagonia already certified.

Such certification systems are a powerful PR tool for businesses to show customers, employees and partners that they are operating with a positive purpose for the wider society, showing their values through the status of their business.

Defining social enterprise and its policy setting

As the previous section sets out there have been businesses with a social purpose for as long as there have been businesses, but what has changed is what we call them. The language and definition of social enterprise has been debated for a long time and this debate continues with practitioners and academics in the field trying to distinguish the activities of a social enterprise from other social services (Keohane 2013).

A social enterprise can take many shapes or forms, which means that the matter of identifying the sector is somewhat difficult. This is partly due to the nature of the organizations, partly because of the varied areas of work they engage in, and partly because of the different ways they are funded (Jones and Keogh 2006).

In the UK, one of the early social entrepreneurs was Elizabeth Gilbert who, after losing her sight due to scarlet fever as a child, wanted to support blind people through employment. She believed in empowering people to help themselves and founded The Association for Promoting the General Welfare of the Blind in 1854. The business still exists under the name Clarity, producing cleaning and beauty products and employing blind, visually impaired and other disabled people (Clarity 2017).

An initiative in the UK which makes a significant PR contribution is Social Enterprise UK, an umbrella organization that promotes social enterprises and gives good practice guidance. It defines social enterprises on its website as follows:

> Social enterprises trade to tackle social problems, improve communities, people's life chances, or the environment. They make their money from selling goods and services in the open market, but they reinvest their profits back into the business or the local community. And so when they profit, society profits.
>
> *(2017)*

Alongside the actual work of a social enterprise, it is often also expected that ethical values run through the core of the enterprise (Martin and Thompson 2010). A social enterprise is therefore not necessarily just a business with some social objectives but a business model where people of shared values work together to achieve equality and fairness (Kay et al. 2016).

Despite efforts by umbrella organizations like Social Enterprise UK to define the sector, there is a lack of a shared definition across society and the confusion around the work of social enterprises does not just cause debate but it can also be a distraction to the crucial work of the sector. External stakeholders may struggle to define or identify what the social enterprise does and there is sometimes also an internal tension between the social mission and the drive to generate profit (Mitchell et al. 2016).

Across Europe there is a lack of understanding of the concept of a social enterprise, often impacting negatively on the growth of the enterprise as well as its relations with its customers (European Commission 2015). But despite this, the sector is growing with governments and investors across Europe seeing the sector as an effective alternative to both public and private sector business (Seager 2014). Many European countries have over the last few years legally or formally recognized the concept of social enterprise and the European Commission uses the term to cover businesses where a social mission is the reason for its existence and where profits are reinvested to achieve this social mission (European Commission 2015). There has been prominent development in countries like Greece where recent economic turmoil has resulted in growing unemployment and poverty. State support has decreased and instead, a larger number of social enterprises have come in its place to support those affected. But in terms of a definition there is still some uncertainty as even though a law in 2011 recognized social enterprise as a legal concept in Greece for the first time, the definition was drawn too tightly for many organizations working in the ethical entrepreneurship sector to be included (Hurley 2017). Despite a strong social business movement, the Netherlands is one country that has no separate legal structure for social enterprises. In countries such as Sweden, where social problems traditionally have been the responsibility of a strong state, developments within social entrepreneurship have mainly happened over the last few years. It is increasingly being seen as an approach that can change systems and improve support structures (Mantel and Lamptey 2013) with organizations like Social Entrepreneurship Forum (SE Forum) promoting the approach as the future of good business.

The social enterprise movement worldwide has grown substantially over the last few years, with entrepreneurs setting up businesses where the key focus is the social purpose, with people wanting their business to do more than just make money, and with non-profits developing a trading arm to fill financial gaps (Ashton 2010). Because of the fact that social enterprises can take many shapes and forms, the term should be seen primarily as a concept and an approach to business rather than a legal term. In terms of the legal aspect, the most common legal forms in the UK are:

- Company limited by shares (CLS)
- Company limited by guarantee (CLG)
- Community Interest Company (CIC)

CIC is a legal structure that was created specifically for social enterprises with the structure providing a clear signal to partners and investors that the business operates for the benefit of the community (Department for Business, Innovation and Skills 2011). It has grown in popularity since its establishment in 2004 and according to the CIC Association website there are over 12,000 CICs in the UK.

Today there are in total about 70,000 social enterprises in the UK, contributing £24 billion to the economy and employing nearly a million people. It is a movement that is growing quickly with close to half of all social enterprises being five years old or less. They have a strong social mission with many working in some of the most deprived communities in the country and a majority employ at least one person who is disadvantaged in the job market. For 16 per cent of social enterprises in the UK, half of the employees will fit into this category, which shows a strong focus on diversity. Another sign of the sector's diversity is the fact that 40 per cent are female-led (Social Enterprise UK 2015), compared to only seven female CEOs on the FTSE 100 (Cohen 2016).

Social enterprises cover all aspects of society in terms of the areas they work in, but a majority work in the leisure and culture, health and social care, and education sectors (NatWest SE100 2015). In Europe on the other hand there is a strong focus on work integration of disadvantaged groups amongst social enterprises, with a large number also working within social welfare services (European Commission 2015).

PR challenges and solutions within the social enterprise sector

The previously mentioned confusion around a clear definition of social enterprise is not just an issue when it comes to business growth, as the confusion also leads to less defined communications. The tension between the social and the commercial side of the business is a barrier to clear communications, with many social enterprises complicating their story of social value and delivery because of their dual focus of social and business (Mitchell et al. 2015). Not engaging in communications activities to make this clear could undermine the organization's ability to become sustainable (Powell and Osborne 2015) and the social enterprise should ask itself key questions such as how it is positioning itself, who its customers are and what they value (Mitchell et al. 2015) to ensure this is clear from the start. With the two sides of a social enterprise – social and business – it needs to clarify who it is and what it is for, as lack of clarity would confuse the messaging further and would make the focus on its primary purpose more difficult (Black and Nicholls 2004).

Social enterprises that have not internally defined who they are are subsequently more uneasy about pursuing communications activities if this results in them presenting themselves as 'too commercial' (Powell and Osborne 2015: 33). But the argument of emphasizing strong business credentials is highlighted by the fact that customers and clients may question the viability of a social enterprise compared to a corporate business, and the social enterprise therefore needs to come across as professional (Ashton 2010).

Similar to non-profit organizations, social enterprises often lack resources and budgets to engage in extensive communications activities (Mitchell et al. 2016) and many social entrepreneurs, especially those that come from a more social background, may lack in communications expertise, resulting in limited efforts to promote the business and ensure sustainability in a competitive market. Over half of UK social enterprises admit they are poor or average at marketing and branding (Social Enterprise UK 2015) so there is a need for many to up their game. Communications efforts have a potential contribution to make to social enterprises but this is 'largely unrecognised or misunderstood' (Powell and Osborne 2015: 35). Due to a lack of resources devoted to communications, communications activities of social enterprises are rarely planned or conducted in a strategic manner, and even though some are used to build relationships, the efforts would not achieve competitive advantage (Powell and Osborne 2015).

Most social enterprises are primarily looking to attract new customers or clients (Social Enterprise UK 2015) so the brand needs to stay relevant and may need to reach a broader audience than its current core group. The brand therefore needs to be defined based on what existing and potential audiences should think and feel about the social enterprise (Social Enterprise UK 2012).

There are several reasons why customers may choose a social enterprise over a regular corporate business. It may meet an existing need in a new and interesting way, it may be considered trendy in the customer's group of friends to buy from social enterprises, or the product may simply be of similar cost and quality (Ashton 2010). But the decision will often originate from the customer starting out asking questions around the ethical aspects of a purchase: How will it impact the planet? Is the product responsibly produced and have the people who made it earned a fair wage?

Corporate businesses as well as the more ethical ones are increasingly communicating their successful triple bottom line through strategic transparency PR, which means the competitive market for social enterprises is growing. To remain competitive and increase its following the social enterprise cannot afford to neglect developing a strong brand based on the equal mix of social and business. Just relying on the social good aspect will not be enough and it is crucial to have a brand and a product or service that can compete with the corporate equivalent.

Taking advantage of the sector's opportunities

The growth of the sector should, despite the growing number of competitors, be seen as an opportunity as it will eventually mean a clearer definition and subsequently a clearer understanding amongst customers and stakeholders. Taking advantage of sector wide initiatives can therefore be beneficial in order to raise awareness, increase relevance and grow a customer base. One clear example in countries like the UK and the Netherlands has been the Buy Social campaign; the campaign shows the benefits of buying products from social enterprises and promotes various social enterprises via online channels and the hashtag #buysocial that is used across social media.

A clear advantage for a social enterprise is that its social purpose, and therefore story, is at its core and this is essentially what makes a social enterprise different and can build a deeper emotional connection with its stakeholders. But it is equally important to relate to the needs of customers, as focusing too much on its social story can make the actual product or service irrelevant. The product or service needs to be as good, if not better, as its corporate counterpart and cannot depend on just trying to make social good. The social enterprise cannot just rely on its legal status or depend on just saying that it is a social enterprise. It needs to ensure its stakeholders understand how the social problem it seeks to solve is solved by the success of its business. A great and innovative product or service that makes business sense and has a strong brand with a clear story will do this.

Working out what the value proposition is from the start will help the social enterprise in finding its place in the market. It is important not just to know what it does but also what benefits potential customers or users will get from its products or services. Due to many social enterprises struggling with resources, focusing on a few key channels will be beneficial in order to focus efforts and get most value out of them. The use of digital channels is for this reason valuable as they can be of low cost, and something like a well-designed website that is easy to navigate with clear messages about a social enterprise's purpose can reach a large audience without spending money on other channels like advertising (Ingenhoff and Koelling 2009). Using social media also has its financial advantages and these channels are especially useful to engage in conversations, which is important for non-profits and social businesses as these conversations activate passion and encourage people to act on causes they care about (Kanter and Fine 2010). But using all social networks will often not be possible due to the lack of resources so a targeted approach will be necessary, especially in order to stay authentic as well as professional.

Finding the right social channels to use will essentially depend on where an enterprise's key stakeholders are as this is where it can engage with them. The social enterprise needs to know who the key stakeholders are, what their wants and needs are, where on social media they spend their time, what they are interested in, and what conversations they engage in.

An important advantage for a social enterprise to make the most of is the fact that the reason for its existence is a strong story in itself. It may be the founder's personal story of why it was set up, the cause it is supporting, the impact it is having on its community, or how doing good is good business. Telling this story in words as well as through engaging photography is an important aspect of the social enterprise's communications activities as well as business growth, with nearly half of social enterprises surveyed in the 2015 NatWest SE100 report stating they had won business by being able to demonstrate their social impact.

The communication activity itself is also an opportunity due to the growing issue of trust and transparency. Being visible and having open conversations will build trust and activities such as blogging on its website will give the social enterprise personality and a more human face (Scoble and Israel 2006).

Showing personality and the social need for its existence will engage stakeholders in its aim to do social good. But to stay competitive, its business story is equally important, if not more so. Its product or service needs to be leading in its sector to gain market share and the communications activity needs to align with this. It needs to show that, essentially, the social enterprise is the best in its field and the fact that it also benefits society is an added bonus in a time where stakeholders are increasingly demanding this from any business or non-profit organization. With the social enterprise being a mix of the two it needs to show it is the sustainable answer to the profit versus social good dilemma to grow market share and continue using business to be the force of good it can be.

CASE STUDY 12.1: DIVINE CHOCOLATE

One of the most well-known social enterprises in the UK is Divine Chocolate, with a social mission outlined on its website as 'to grow a successful global farmer-owned chocolate company using the amazing power of chocolate to delight and engage, and bring people together to create dignified trading relations, thereby empowering producers and consumers' (2017).

Divine was set up in 1998 and is the only Fairtrade chocolate company that is to 44 per cent owned by cocoa farmers who are part of the Kuapa Kokoo cooperative in Ghana. The Fairtrade certification means farmers get a better deal for their cocoa, but with company ownership, farmers also get a share of Divine's profits as well as a stronger voice in the wider cocoa industry.

Divine has also actively worked to empower women amongst its 85,000 farmers and has introduced gender quotas in village committees (Slavin and Ley 2017). Its gender equality focus can also been seen through its communications with an 'empower women cocoa farmers' logo on its 70 per cent dark chocolate bar. In Spring 2017, marking International Women's Day, Divine also launched a limited-edition bar featuring an illustration of a female cocoa farmer on the front of the pack, as well as stories of women empowered by Kuapa Kokoo on the inside of the wrapper (Perkins 2016).

As a consumer product, Divine is able to use its packaging to promote its ethical credentials, however, to compete with corporate brands it has seen a shift from initially prioritizing the ethical credentials to instead pushing the quality of the product. This shift has also been necessary as corporate competitors have introduced Fairtrade cocoa and are now competing on more similar terms (Mannion 2015).

CASE STUDY 12.2: THE SOAP CO.

The Soap Co. is an ethical luxury soap brand with two main aims of creating beautifully designed products of the highest quality and employment for people who are visually impaired, have disabilities, or are otherwise disadvantaged. The products are made in the UK with natural extracts, recycled and recyclable materials are used where possible, and The Soap Co.'s profits go back into the business.

From the start, the brand has been of high importance, with the packaging embracing a simple design style to appeal to the millennial, trend conscious customer, and with the use of braille linking back to the social mission of the business. The packaging has contributed to the success of the brand and won a D&AD Pencil for Design and Inclusive Packaging Design in May 2016, but the main focus has been on ensuring the products are as high quality as they can be, to be able to compete with other luxury brands. The Soap Co.'s communications emphasize this over its social mission but the ethics of the enterprise are integral and transparency is a priority. This can be seen on the informative website as well as through personal touches such as the name of the maker being stamped on the side of soap bars and a note with the story of the person who packaged your product included in your delivery box.

As a small business with small budgets, The Soap Co.'s communication focus has been on social media. The brand was initially launched with the #Soap-CoInspired campaign that brought together a network of female entrepreneurs, founders and CEOs to share what inspires them. This gave The Soap Co. a chance to reach a wider network of potential customers within the target audience of female millennials with a conscious and entrepreneurial mindset. A similar approach was also used for the Christmas 2016 campaign #Give-GoodGifts where The Soap Co. brought together bloggers, retailers, vloggers and customers to celebrate gifts that were both beautiful and had a wider social impact. Varied content could therefore be created, and again, the company could reach already existing networks of the people and businesses taking part.

Source: The Soap Co.

Discussion questions

1. Are the Rochdale Principles still valid today; how might they be modified/added to?
2. How would you define a social enterprise?
3. Give a couple of examples of social enterprises you know of, and their key characteristics.
4. How can you prevent big businesses colonizing the social enterprise sector for narrow brand advantage?
5. What are some challenges facing social enterprises and their communications?
6. How would you suggest a social enterprise should communicate its story?

References

Allen, P. (2007) *Your ethical business: How to plan, start and succeed in a company with a conscience.* UK: NGO Media.

Ashton, R. (2010) *How to be a social entrepreneur, make money and change the world.* UK: Capstone Publishing Ltd.

BBC. (20 July2010) *How Rochdale Pioneers changed commerce forever.* [Online] Available from: http://news.bbc.co.uk/local/manchester/hi/people_and_places/history/newsid_8838000/8838778.stm

Black, L. & Nicholls, J. (2004) *There's no business like Social Business: How to be socially enterprising.* UK: The Cat's Pyjamas.

Chesters, L. (2017) Keeping it real. *Ethos.* 1 February 2017.

Christensen, L.T. (2002) Corporate communication: the challenge of transparency. *Corporate Communication: An International Journal*, 7(3): 162–168.

Clarity. (2017) History. [Online] Available from: http://clarity.org.uk/about-us/history/

Cohen, C. (2016) Just who are the 7 women bosses of the FTSE 100? [Online] Available from: http://www.telegraph.co.uk/women/work/just-who-are-the-7-women-bosses-of-the-ftse-100/

Coombs, W.T. & Holladay, S.J. (2010) *PR strategy and application: Managing influence*. UK: Wiley-Blackwell.

Department for Business Innovation and Skills. (2011) *A guide to legal forms for social enterprise*. London: Department for Business, Innovation and Skills.

Divine Chocolate. (2017) Inside Divine. [Online] Available from: http://www.divinechocolate.com/uk/about-us/inside-divine

Edelman. (2017) *Edelman Trust Barometer*. [Online] Available from: http://www.edelman.com/trust2017/

European Commission. (2015) *A map of social enterprises and their eco-systems in Europe*. Luxembourg: Publications Office of the European Union.

Friedman, M. (1970) The social responsibility of business is to increase its profits. [Online] Available from: http://www.colorado.edu/studentgroups/libertarians/issues/friedman-soc-resp-business.html

Gallagher, S. (2005) A strategic response to Friedman's critique of business ethics. *Journal of Business Strategy*, 26(6): 55–60.

Gower, K.K. (2010) Truth and transparency. In: Fitzpatrick, K. & Bronstein, C. eds., *Ethics in Public Relations: Responsible Advocacy* (pp. 89–106). California, USA: SAGE Publications, Inc.

Guyer, P. (2007) *Kant's groundwork for the Metaphysics of Morals*. London: Continuum International Publishing Group.

Hurley, P. (2017) A Double Helping. *Ethos*. 1 February 2017.

Ingenhoff, D. & Koelling, A.M. (2009) The potential of web sites as a relationship building tool for charitable fundraising NPOs. *Public Relations Review*, 35(1): 66–73.

Jenkin, M. (5 May2015) Millennials want to work for employers committed to values and ethics. [Online] Available from: https://www.theguardian.com/sustainable-business/2015/may/05/millennials-employment-employers-values-ethics-jobs

Jones, D. & Keogh, W. (2006) Social enterprise: a case of terminological ambiguity and complexity. *Social Enterprise Journal*, 2(1): 11–26.

Kanter, B. & Fine, A.H. (2010) *The networked nonprofit*. San Francisco, CA: John Wiley & Sons, Inc.

Kay, A., Roy, M.J. & Donaldson, C. (2016) Re-imagining social enterprise. *Social Enterprise Journal*, 3(2): 237–253.

Keohane, G.L. (2013) *Social entrepreneurship for the 21st Century: Innovation across the non-profit, private and public sectors*. US: McGraw-Hill.

Mannion, L. (2015) Marketing unwrapped: top tips from Divine Chocolate. [Online] Available from: https://www.pioneerspost.com/business-school/20150724/marketing-unwrapped-top-tips-divine-chocolate

Mantel, N. & Lamptey, R.A. (2013) Social entrepreneurship: on the rise in Sweden? [Online] Available from: https://www.theguardian.com/social-enterprise-network/2013/jun/04/social-entrepreneurship-rise-sweden

Martin, F. & Thompson, M. (2010) *Social enterprise: Developing sustainable businesses*. New York, NY: Palgrave Macmillan.

McBrearty, S. (2007) Social enterprise: a solution for the voluntary sector? *Social Enterprise Journal*, 3(1): 67–77.

Mitchell, A., Madill, J. & Chreim, S. (2015) Marketing and social enterprises: implications for social marketing. *Journal of Social Marketing*, 5(4): 285–306.

Mitchell, A., Madill, J. & Chreim, S. (2016) Social enterprise dualities: implications for social marketing. *Journal of Social Marketing*, 6(2): 169–192.

NatWest SE100. (2015) *NatWest SE100 Annual Report 2015*. [Online] Available from: https://se100.net/analysis/annual-2015

Perkins, C. (2016) Divine Chocolate bar celebrates 'women's empowerment'. [Online] Available from: https://www.thegrocer.co.uk/stores/ranging-and-merchandising/divine-chocolate-bar-celebrates-womens-empowerment/546529.article

Poswolsky, A.S. (4 June2015) What millennial employees really want. [Online] Available from: https://www.fastcompany.com/3046989/what-millennial-employees-really-want

Powell, M. & Osborne, S.P. (2015) Can marketing contribute to sustainable social enterprise? *Social Enterprise Journal*, 11(1): 24–46.

Scoble, R. & Israel, S. (2006) *Naked conversations: How blogs are changing the way businesses talk with customers*. Hoboken, N.J.: John Wiley & Sons, Inc.

Seager, C. (7 January2014) Best bits: What will social enterprise look like across Europe in 2020? [Online] Available from: https://www.theguardian.com/social-enterprise-network/2014/jan/07/live-discussion-social-enterprise-europe-2020

Slavin, T. & Ley, R. (2017) Female cocoa farmers 'key ingredient in Divine Chocolate's success'. [Online] Available from: http://www.ethicalcorp.com/female-cocoa-farmers-key-ingredient-divine-chocolates-success

Social Enterprise UK. (2012) *Start your social enterprise*. London: Social Enterprise UK.

Social Enterprise UK. (2015) *State of Social Enterprise Survey 2015: Leading the world in social enterprise*. London: Social Enterprise UK.

Social Enterprise UK. (2017) FAQs. [Online] Available from: https://www.socialenterprise.org.uk/Pages/FAQs/Category/FAQs

The Economist. (17 November2009) Triple bottom line. [Online] Available from: http://www.economist.com/node/14301663

The Soap Co. (2017) https://thesoapco.org

Treviño, L. K. & Nelson, K. A. (2004) *Managing business ethics: Straight talk about how to do it right*. 3rd edn. Hoboken, NJ: John Wiley & Sons, Inc.

Yunus, M. (2007) *Creating a world without poverty: Social business and the future of capitalism*. US: PublicAffairs.

PART IV

Around the world

Global and national non-profit communications

13

INGO COMMUNICATIONS

Global strategic planning

Joe Barrell

Introduction: there's no such place as international

All good communicators know that the best strategies are built around audience insight – an understanding of who you wish to target; what you want them to **think, feel or do**, and what will motivate them to engage. This poses a challenge for international communications teams, owing to the sheer size and diversity of their target audiences. How could one department, or one strategy, meet the needs and expectations of local NGOs in Burkino Faso, policy makers in Brussels, and five-pound-a-month donors in the United Kingdom?

This is the **defining challenge** of international communications teams in international non-governmental organizations (INGOs). The fact that there is **no such place as international** differentiates international communications teams from national teams. Each national, country-based team is securely anchored to its own market, usually with a measurable, concrete plan, and a nuanced understanding of the local social and political contexts shaping their work. They may too share similar characteristics with the audiences they are trying to reach.

International communications teams have to work hard to assert their purpose in all INGOs. They must carve out their own international role, distinct from that of national colleagues yet also show how they enhance national-level communication efforts. This can be a challenge: there are blurred lines and definitional challenges (Is the United Nations HQ in the USA or is it 'international'?), which can lead to confusion and duplication if not carefully managed. Further, there are seldom hierarchical reporting lines between international and national teams, as most INGOs operate a federated structure with different offices being separate legal entities; neither gets to tell the other what to do. This means collaboration requires a willingness on all sides, where all get the benefits of cooperation, and enjoy good working relationships. These relationships are not always equal: the communications teams of larger national offices will likely be far better resourced than the international team, as most INGOs prefer to keep their staff as close to the 'front line' as possible.

Defining a clear purpose for international communication teams can therefore be difficult, and this inevitably begs the question: 'Why do we need one at all?' There are a lot of very good answers to that question, explored in this chapter, which covers:

- The **current context** that international communications teams are operating in;
- What international communications teams do. This includes their **three modes of communications**, their **purposes**, their **functions** and some of their **strategies**.

No two INGOs work in the same way, and few will consider all the issues described in this chapter relevant, or include all the functions described. INGOs are structured differently too. Some international communications teams work out of international headquarters, while others are lean, virtual teams, distributed around the world in regional, national or local offices. Still, common themes and approaches do exist, and this chapter emphasises those likely to be present in most large INGOs.

The material in this chapter is based on extensive interviews with international communications directors over several years, some desk research, and the writer's own experience of leading global communications for international NGOs.

Context of INGO communications

This section looks at five global trends shaping the work of international communications teams: a new tone set by the Sustainable Development Goals; the growing issue of intra-national inequality; a proliferation of humanitarian crises testing the sector's capacity to respond; compassion fatigue and the decline in trust in institutions; increasingly blurred lines between 'programme' and 'fundraising' countries.

The Sustainable Development Goals

The United Nation's Sustainable Development Goals (SDGs) is a global intergovernmental agreement that will shape the development agenda until 2030. The 17 global goals (United Nations n.d.), which include 169 targets, provide a framework for how the world will tackle development issues in the coming years. Like the Millennium Development Goals (MDGs) before them, the SDGs include targets for addressing some of the perennial development issues like poverty, hunger, health and education. However, the SDGs place a stronger emphasis on big systemic challenges, such as environmental protection, economic development, strengthening institutions, access to justice, and tackling inequality.

The SDGs provide important context for communicators working in INGOs because they will define much of the policy making, funding, partnerships, and development approaches pursued by the sector in the coming years. While the issues the SDGs focus on are not new, they do set a new tone. They move away from a more traditional development paradigm of the North–South transfer of resources to a more sophisticated story of sustainable economic growth and social justice. For communicators, they mean that the narratives around global development, the environment, and human rights will need to change to keep in step with the shifting agenda. The SDGs also place new importance on working in partnerships: between international and local NGOs, between NGOs and government and, increasingly, between NGOs, social enterprise, and the private sector.

Intra-national inequality

While global poverty remains unacceptably high, global development efforts have had a positive impact and progress has been made. For example, the first Millennial Development Goal to halve the proportion of people living in extreme poverty by 2015 (from the 1990 rate), was achieved five years early in 2010 (United Nations 2015: 15). Owing to rising average incomes, the number of countries defined by the World Bank as 'low income countries' (LICs) continues to decrease as well. In the 2018 fiscal year there were 31 LICs (World Bank n.d.), compared to 64 in 1994. All but four of them were in sub-Saharan Africa.

However, as economic growth has continued, poverty eradication has not kept pace. This has translated to an ongoing shift in distribution of global poverty toward middle-income countries (MICs). Development economist, Andy Sumner argues (2012:19) that this implies 'substantially more domestic resources available for poverty reduction'. In short, there are still a great many extremely poor people living in middle-income countries that could be doing more to help them.

The role of international NGOs is evolving with the changing shape of poverty, and the new SDG framework. INGOs are delivering fewer direct interventions, like the provision of health services or nutrition programmes, outside of emergency contexts. Instead, most are further emphasising systemic, sustainable development programmes. For example, **system strengthening** (e.g. helping countries improve their education or health systems); **community empowerment** (helping marginalised communities claim their rights), or promoting the rights of those facing discrimination (such as women and girls, minority ethnic groups, refugees and disabled people). Meanwhile, among the major funders of development, there has also been a shift in preference from a traditional 'aid' model towards development interventions that promote economic development, such as grant-giving schemes and training programmes that support community-level entrepreneurship and reduce aid dependency.

Of course, there is good news in all of this. Extreme poverty is declining, and many development indicators, such as infant mortality rates, are improving, albeit too slowly (United Nations 2015). But the changing shape of poverty has also brought inequalities **within** nations – as well as **between** nations – into sharper focus.

This context has numerous implications for international communications teams in NGOs. Reflecting current development challenges can be more complex and demand more nuance than traditional approaches. Many supporters of international charities prefer a simpler paradigm – and are still more likely to respond to an emotional message and a simple ask ('your £10 will save this child's life') than amorphous concepts like inequality or economic development. In some markets, framing overseas development issues in systemic, societal terms can seem opaque – and for more ideologically conservative audiences can feel too political, even statist, interrupting the idea of the passive victim for whom the donor, alone, is the solution. The proposition that the best way to tackle poverty is better governance, a skilled-up public sector, inward investment, and respect for inalienable human rights does not pluck the heartstrings as resonantly as a photograph of someone in hospital. While dire depictions of suffering do tell an important part of the human story of poverty, there is growing unease that on their own these depictions tell a distorted story, and sustain an image of the developing world as hapless, unsophisticated, and dependent on the generosity of richer countries. Many INGO communicators see their task as bridging this gap between the evolving reality, and an older, more familiar, post-colonial image of poverty.

Proliferation of humanitarian crises

A proliferation of humanitarian crises is shaping the sector more than ever. This is largely due to conflict, but also to hunger crises, struggles for the control of natural resources, outbreaks of disease, and environmental degradation. At the end of 2016, more than 128 million people around the world were affected by 'conflict, displacement, natural disasters and profound vulnerability', according to the United Nations (2016), while the first half of 2017 alone saw four extreme food crises (Associated Press 2017). As a result, both the INGO community and the agencies of the United Nations have become overwhelmed, and lack the capacity to mount an effective response in every situation.

This has, in part, led to a recent drive toward localisation of humanitarian response. At the World Humanitarian Summit (2016: 22), the expression 'As local as possible, as international as necessary' was coined. The commitment was a part of a Core Responsibility from the Summit to reinforce, and not replace, national and local systems. This imperative for the INGO community and UN system seems to mark a convergence between principles of long-term development and short-term humanitarian response. These are two arms of the sector that are still organized separately and that have different working cultures. In practice, 'As local as possible, as international as necessary', means humanitarian departments place greater emphasis on resourcing local community-based capacity over flying in foreign workers, a well-established principle among their development colleagues.

For INGO communicators, this organizational change means equipping local communities with skills and equipment to gather and distribute communication material, such as photography and eyewitness accounts, to fuel international emergency appeals. But despite this shift toward national-level resourcing, navigating simultaneous crises and feeding the 24-hour global news cycle is now a feature of daily life for international communications teams. The proliferation of humanitarian crises also means wrestling with compassion fatigue.

Compassion fatigue and decline in trust

In rich countries, where INGOs do most of their fundraising, there is growing concern that the public's capacity to engage is also overstretched, having been constantly exposed to one disaster or another. Achieving 'cut through' is a growing challenge for INGOs, when constant crisis seems to have become the norm, and any good news barely gets a mention.

This is exacerbated by changing expectations among the public. New generations of digital-native supporters are demanding more transparent engagement with INGOs, with some coming to see them as unnecessary intermediaries. INGOs are responding with a new trend, **'disintermediation'** – reducing the presence of intermediaries between donors and beneficiaries – and going to ever-greater lengths to position themselves as **connectors**, instead of as **gatekeepers**, trusted to do the right thing, whatever that may be. Some INGOs are trying to offer supporters a more 'real' experience of their programme. This includes offering virtual reality tours of emergencies (UN OCHA 2017; BBC Media Action 2017), direct contact with communities through social media, or fundraising models that appear to invite supporters to choose who gets their cash and what it should be spent on (Oxfam 2017). While crowdfunding is still in its infancy, almost half of UK charities, community groups and social entrepreneurs see it as an important future income source (Bone and Baeck 2016).

More broadly, INGOs have not escaped the general global decline in trust of institutions, and international aid has in some countries become strongly associated in the public mind with corruption. In the UK, for example, just one quarter of the UK public (27%) now believe INGOs are 'open and honest', while almost one third (29%) believe charities exaggerate problems in developing countries to raise more money (Eden Stanley 2017).[1] Even among the most loyal supporters of NGOs, there are doubts that their support is making much difference; 75% of the UK's INGO supporters believe, according to Eden Stanley research (ibid.) that corruption prevents aid reaching the people that need it most. Rebuilding trust has become imperative for international communicators (as well as national communication teams). This is addressed internationally in numerous ways, from agreeing key messages to be used globally, often emphasising impact and accountability; to managing reputational risks as they arise, knowing that a flare-up in one market can rapidly impact others owing to the borderless state of digital media.

Blurred lines between 'programme' and 'fundraising' countries

The distinction between **programme countries**, where NGOs do their good work, and **fundraising countries**, where they raise the money to pay for it, has become blurred. Increasingly INGOs are raising funds in the same country that the money will be spent. Typically, this is happening in large, middle-income countries like India or Brazil that have both widespread poverty and an affluent middle class populous enough to sustain a public fundraising programme.

It used to be simpler. Most communications resource in developing countries was deployed extracting **case studies** for use in fundraising appeals in high-income countries. There was less capacity assigned to directly supporting development programmes, for example through disseminating public health information, or facilitating peer-to-peer communications in behaviour change programmes. Meanwhile, in high-income countries, activity centred on engaging institutional funders and individual supporters or building public pressure through the media to support political lobbying that was usually about aid policy.

However, the picture is no longer as straightforward. The three main modes of INGO communications – fundraising communications, advocacy communications, and development communications (described below) – are now much more likely to be applied in developing countries. This trend marks a continued shift in emphasis for international communicators, from telling rich people about poor people, to more universal and multifaceted strategies that demand sophisticated planning and management, as well as new specialisms that are discussed below.

What do international communications teams do?

This part of the chapter looks at the workings of international communications teams. It describes the **three modes of communications** (advocacy, fundraising and development); **four areas for objective setting**; and the **key functions and strategies** used to achieve them.

Three modes of INGO communications

Broadly, INGO communications fall under three modes, although there is little cross-sectoral standardization and INGOs frame them differently.

- *Advocacy communications*

Advocacy in both high-income and developing countries can mean influencing politicians and civil servants directly through lobbying activity, or indirectly through the media or public petitioning. In developing countries, INGOs may equip and train communities to advocate for change at a local level, sometimes mobilizing them to build political pressure on national governments or international institutions. International communications teams tasked with coordinating activity around global events, such as major multinational summits of the G7 or the UN, may invite people from local communities to participate in their global campaigns.

- *Fundraising communications*

This is an established discipline for national teams in high-income countries. It includes engaging sections of the public, high net-worth individuals, or grant-giving organizations, and making the case for support to donate to their programmes and support functions. In the developing world the principles are the same. All fundraising relies on establishing need, coupled with compelling, credible storytelling. However, the tactics used in the developing world can be very different owing to differences in media, regulation, and the structure of markets. In India, for example, some telephone fundraisers have a fleet of motorcyclists at the ready, who will be at your door within half an hour to accept your generous gift, should you show interest.

- *Development communications*

This is a very broad term describing communications strategies in developing countries where the aim is to improve development outcomes. This is by no means a new field, but among INGOs there is a growing awareness that communications can have a more direct role in achieving change in the developing world, and more resources are being assigned to it. This can take many forms. For example, addressing HIV/AIDS through campaigns to destigmatise the use of condoms; tackling gender-based violence by assisting peer-to-peer empowerment projects, or setting up radio services to inform disaster-struck communities about how to make drinking water safe or how to access health services and aid distributions (CDAC 2017).

The purpose of international communications teams

All international communications teams express their purpose differently. Nevertheless, most are engaged principally in building trust in their organization and increasing profile and influence. This in turn supports national and regional teams in achieving more specific, local goals linked to fundraising, policy influencing or development outcomes. There are myriad strategies for achieving this that are touched upon in this chapter.

Some INGOs assign specific responsibility for protection of their name, logo and corporate identity to the international office. As such, international communications teams may have an enhanced role in developing and managing their brand; promoting and policing compliance internally, while tracking its performance in their markets around the world.

When describing their purpose, international teams typically talk about some or all of the following four areas:

- Increasing brand awareness with selected global-level audiences, or positioning their organization as leaders in a specific field

- Building influence with global institutions, often in the UN system, to promote changes in policy or practice
- Strengthening communications capacity and championing communication practice amongst colleagues in national teams
- Managing content flows within the organization to make best use of resources and ensure coherence of message.

The key functions and strategies of international communication teams

Brand building and reputation management

In the context of a global trend of declining trust in institutions, and a resurgence of protectionism (particularly in the USA and Europe), international aid, and the INGOs that administer it, have become an easy whipping boy. In response, many INGOs have placed global brand and reputation management higher up their priority list, mindful of the potential damage that loss of public trust could cause.

Global brand strategy is an evolving function, and a strategic approach where nuanced questions like brand values or differentiation are deliberately considered, still tends to give way to more operational concerns at a global level. International communication teams are likely to be preoccupied with day-to-day compliance to visual identity and messaging standards, while their counterparts in national teams – particularly in the major fundraising markets – do most of the heavy lifting (such as audience research, creative development and media investment) associated with a hardworking brand-building strategy.

This is an inevitable result of two factors: first, national teams usually control their organization's brand budgets, with international teams seldom having requisite resources to invest in high quality creative work or advertising media. Second, global brand strategies are necessarily loose frameworks – consistent enough to create a coherent impression across national boundaries, but flexible enough to allow local difference. Getting this balance right remains a work in progress for most international communications teams.

Coordinating global efforts around major events

International teams are uniquely placed to coordinate campaign activities connected with major global summits, like meetings of the G8, UN assemblies, or the World Economic Forum in Davos. This might include anything from developing key messages, to managing media relations, to coordinating digital campaigns across multiple markets. All of this happens in collaboration with national teams.

Supporting 'in-country' communications

Along with growth in digital connectivity, many developing countries are also seeing their 'old media' industries booming. Television is widely used across sub-Saharan Africa, with 84% penetration (Nielsen 2016: 20). Growing middle-class populations have pushed up newspaper sales in India (WAN-IFRA 2016), while cheap technology has seen an explosion in radio – particularly community radio – across much of Africa and elsewhere.

Many INGOs have seized on these opportunities, and raised their investment in mass communication in programme countries. In some INGOs, the international communication team supports this activity by providing skills, staff and resources. While some middle-income countries are now able to sustain fundraising pro-grammes (notably India and Brazil), most 'in-country' communication follows one of these modalities:

- Regional- or national-level advocacy may include building political pressure through media work, directly lobbying decision makers and their advisers, or mobilizing communities to advocate for their own rights.
- Behaviour change communications, which are used to challenge and change social norms. This can include anything from reducing gender-based violence by asserting the rights of women and girls, to tackling public health risks by promoting safe burial practices during disease outbreaks (see Case study 2).
- Information as aid, an emerging field, which deploys communications as an integral part of humanitarian response. Advising disaster-struck communities about how to stay safe and where to get help is every bit as important as the physical distribution of food and hygiene supplies, which on their own are seldom enough to meet the needs of the entire affected population.
- Information and communications technology for development, or ICT4DEV, is the use technology to improve development outcomes. A growth of inno-vation in this area has led to new technology applications in agriculture, environment, education, health and political participation. Mobile technolo-gies that enable peer-to-peer micropayments, apps that allow farmers access to market prices and shorten their supply chains, or crowd-sourced emergency warning systems, are three commonly cited examples among many.

Providing or coordinating surge capacity in emergencies

When humanitarian crises occur, a borderless media market demands ever greater co-ordination to ensure consistent messaging, which in turn supports fundraising and delivery of aid. An INGO's readiness to rapidly gather and distribute content from disasters to meet the demands of a 24-hour news cycle in multiple time zones is a defining factor in the success or otherwise of their emergency appeals. With each new disaster, the larger INGOs will race to get their story into the news, in the knowledge that the first to market usually raises the most money. In some INGOs, responsibility for coordinating emergency communications falls on inter-national teams, who manage their dissemination networks and are seen to be 'neutral' and least likely to favour any national office over another in the jostle for visibility.

Many international communications teams were created out of the need for global coordination of media work around humanitarian responses, and this is often where they are most effective. This is particularly true in the case of rapid-onset emergencies – whether caused by sudden natural disasters or conflict – where the sheer urgency and scale of need focuses teams on a singular objective and inspires them to do their best work.

International teams often take the lead in co-ordinating the communications response in an emergency, which can require deft handling of multiple competing interests in difficult conditions. They may be responsible for deploying communications staff – from the global team or national offices – into the emergency area to gather and distribute stories for dissemination, provide information to the affected communities, or support journalists covering the events. Meanwhile, their colleagues back at the office distribute content and media lines to national teams, while drumming up interest among their media contacts.

Developing and distributing content for national markets

As communication channels proliferate, both in digital and broadcast, a steady flow of high quality content is essential for INGOs to meet the voracious appetites of both the global media, and national teams producing marketing and communication material for their local audiences. Communication resource management is a maturing discipline for international teams, with digital systems for content storage and distribution enabling INGOs to compile video, photographic and editorial material for use in multiple markets.

Content is typically stored as case studies – providing human stories gathered from communities in the developing world, which are woven into communications for any number of purposes. Use of these case studies requires rigorous management of intellectual property rights (for example in the case of photography), and ethical and safeguarding issues must be considered – particularly when individuals are identifiable (Saxton 2012).

Content development – or *story gathering* – requires significant staffing, and most larger international teams coordinate a network of communications experts based at strategic locations around the world. These staff both gather content themselves, and provide communication skills training to their own networks of field-based staff, and to the communities they serve. With internet connectivity getting better, and video technology becoming cheaper, these networks are reaching ever deeper into communities, shortening the time lag between content creation and dissemination – and creating the impression of a narrowing gap between donor and beneficiary.

Internal communications and capacity building

As international teams are less 'market facing' than national counterparts, many spend most of their time looking inwards: communicating with and building capacity of communications staff around the world. As well as supporting specialist communications staff, this will involve developing the skills of non-communication colleagues too, for example providing media training for programme staff.

Most international teams play a convening role, building and servicing their network of communication staff. Many organize annual conferences where they meet face-to-face, share skills and develop strategies together. This convening role is important to international teams as it is how they exert influence, given they usually have no direct authority over their national colleagues. Putting people in a room and inviting them to solve problems together is a tried and tested way of improving alignment, and strengthening relationships.

Most international teams also have well-developed internal communications plans, which they use to similar ends. Likely they will run the global intranet and email bulletins, which can help build a sense of common identity among widely distributed teams.

Managing global partnerships

All INGOs do some of their work within international partnerships, whether with each other, with media organizations, or with major funders, to drive both advocacy and programme delivery. Global partnerships around specific thematic areas (such as disease eradication) increasingly include private sector organizations, a trend that looks likely to continue in the coming years, owing to the emphasis of the Sustainable Development Goals on developing a cross-sectoral response.

Some international communications teams lead the development of joint strategies around these partnerships, managing partnership relationships, negotiating relative brand visibility, or coordinating communications resource.

Media relations

As a general principle, managing relationships with national media brands will usually fall under the remit of the national team in any given market. The office in India looks after the *Hindustan Times*, the Swedish office manages *Aftonbladet*, and so on. Some international communications teams manage relationships with global media outlets, such as Associated Press, CNN, or Al Jazeera, and sometimes national outlets with significant international reach, such as BBC News or Time.com.

Nevertheless, there is a very mixed picture, and INGOs distribute responsibilities differently. Where international teams are small, they will usually share responsibility for managing global media outlets with better-resourced national teams. Conversely, where a national team has very limited capacity, the international team may take responsibility for some of their domestic media relations, or coordinate media relations in major news 'hubs' with broader regional influence, such as Nairobi, Dakar, Brussels or Delhi.

Digital and social

With a few exceptions, most international teams are still grappling with how to respond to a rapidly evolving digital landscape, especially the use of social media. Few INGOs have managed to achieve a coherent global digital presence, and instead different national teams tend to work independently with minimal international coordination. As a result, most INGOs have numerous national websites, campaign microsites, and social media presences that – for their audiences – can be a source of confusion, and – for the organization – one of reputational risk. A few INGOs address this by developing a single platform approach, deploying content management systems that allow national teams to share and repurpose content, while providing a consistent brand experience to their audiences.

International communications teams typically understand these challenges, and their efforts to improve standards usually favour persuasion over coercion. Promoting good practice, offering skills training, or providing content, have been more effective strategies than more 'top-down' rigid approaches. The benefits of this approach are obvious in the case of social media, which relies on the energy and engagement of individuals who need the freedom to find their own way in to the online conversation.

CASE STUDY 13.1: UNICEF IN NEPAL – BUILDING BACK BETTER

In 2015 Nepal suffered two devastating earthquakes, leaving 2.8 million people in urgent need of humanitarian assistance, of whom 1.1 million were children. More than 8,000 schools were destroyed with thousands more damaged, while water, sanitation, and public health services were severely disrupted.

In the wake of major disasters, there is often an opportunity to upgrade infrastructure and renew policy – to 'build back better' – and avoid mistakes of the past. So, as well as mounting a humanitarian response to the disasters themselves, UNICEF began to push much harder on advocating the protection of children in Nepal.

UNICEF realised their advocacy efforts would be enhanced by building public pressure for change, not just in Nepal, but in influential markets around the world. Following the earthquakes, the organization globally went into 'high visibility mode', to raise funds for their humanitarian response, and to canvass international support for building better systems for child protection.

UNICEF's communication strategy mobilised digital channels, including social media and email, to great effect, outperforming previous appeals. In the first few weeks around half of their donations came from new supporters. Measured by media visibility alone, UNICEF was highly prominent during the global Nepal appeal, achieving 38% of the sector's share of voice in broadcast and digital media combined in target fundraising markets.

Efforts centred on stopping inter-country adoption and the transportation of children, and banning new registration of children's homes. Following the Nepal earthquakes, UNICEF's lobbying was instrumental to major policy breakthroughs in these areas.

CASE STUDY 13.2: WORLD VISION IN WEST AFRICA – LIFESAVING COMMUNICATIONS IN THE EBOLA RESPONSE

In late 2013 Ebola, the highly infectious fatal disease, struck in West Africa for the first time in several years, starting in Guinea, and spreading into Sierra Leone and Liberia over the following months. Local health systems were unprepared, and governments slow to respond, and it took several months to correctly identify the virus, allowing it to spread unnoticed across national borders. This made containment more challenging when the virus was finally identified in 2014.

Ebola can be contained, primarily by placing victims of the disease into isolation, and minimising contact with the bodies of those that have died. This, in turn, requires effective infrastructure with skilled health workers, adequate isolation facilities and – critically – community understanding of the disease and the behaviours that contribute to its spread.

Community distrust of authorities and foreign NGOs quickly emerged as a major issue, exacerbated by religious sensitivities. Some did not believe Ebola could be managed by medical means, preferring to rely on their own spiritual practices – including the laying on of hands – often resulting in more deaths. Communities were reluctant to change traditional burial practices, which again often involved contact with the deceased. A May 2014 burial of one traditional leader in Liberia resulted in 365 deaths, and many more new cases of the disease. In the international community, safe burials became a critical monitoring target in the Ebola response, and targeted, culturally sensitive communication with local communities would play a vital role in saving lives.

World Vision, the global Christian NGO, was a key actor in this effort. In partnership with other NGOs and local faith groups, the organization developed new, safer burial protocols for both Christian and Muslim communities, taking care to demonstrate sensitivity to local religious beliefs and practices. World Vision focused its efforts on directly engaging faith leaders, and equipping them with messages and materials to communicate with their wider communities. Their strategy ultimately reached almost 400,000 of the most vulnerable communities, and proved a game changer in the West Africa Ebola response (Marshall 2016).

Conclusion

Demographic shifts, political realignments, progress in poverty reduction, and developments in media and technology have all contributed to a changing context for international NGOs. For many international communications teams, this has led to a rethink – about their message, how they organize themselves and where they focus their efforts. Still an evolving discipline in the INGO sector, international communications has emerged as a sophisticated and vital component in the struggles against poverty, and for equality and the realisation of human rights.

Discussion questions

1. What are the main differences between national and international communications teams in large INGOs? Which would you prefer to work for and why?
2. How are the Sustainable Development Goals affecting international development narratives? What do you think needs to change about how international poverty and human rights are communicated?
3. How are changes in social attitudes presenting challenges for the INGO sector? How would you engage younger digital-native audiences?
4. How has progress in poverty reduction affected the role of INGO communications teams?
5. How would you communicate 'need' in a poor community powerfully enough to succeed in public fundraising, without reinforcing negative stereotypes of the developing world?
6. How would you convince donors in the developed world that they should fund a development programme in a middle-income country?
7. Can you think of three or four ideas for communicating with disaster-affected communities that might help save lives?
8. How would you ensure that the voices of poor and marginalised communities are heard and felt at international political summits?

Note

1 Eden Stanley's Trackers survey 2,000 members of the UK public each month, covering more than 400 questions relating to attitudes to international causes, and INGOs.

References

Associated Press (2017) World faces worst humanitarian crisis since 1945, says UN official. *Guardian* on-line. 11th March. Available: https://www.theguardian.com/world/2017/mar/11/world-faces-worst-humanitarian-crisis-since-1945-says-un-official

BBC Media ActionYour phone is now a refugee's phone. (Mobile only) https://www.youtube.com/watch?v=m1BLsySgsHM

Bone, J. and Baeck, P. (2016) Crowdfunding Good Causes. *Nesta.* https://www.nesta.org.uk/sites/default/files/crowdfunding_good_causes-2016.pdf

CDAC – Communicating with disaster affected communities (2017) Inspiring change. Available: http://www.cdacnetwork.org/inspiring-change/

Eden Stanley (2017) INGO Tracker: December 2016 to February 2017. Eden Stanley: London

Marshall, C. (2016) Case Study: Responding to the ebola epidemic in West Africa: What role does religion play? Berkley Center for Religion, Peace, and World Affairs at Georgetown University and the World Faiths Development Dialogue. Available: http://www.

wvi.org/sites/default/files/Berkley%20Center%20Religion%20and%20Ebola%20Case%20Study.pdf

Nielsen (2016) *Africa's Prospects.* www.nielsen.com/content/dam/nielsenglobal/ssa/docs/reports/2016/9573_Africa_Prospects_Report_DIGITAL_FINAL.pdf

Oxfam (2017) *MyOxfam: Oxfam's New App.* Available: www.oxfam.org.uk/donate/my-oxfam

Saxton, J. (2012) *Show and Tell: A Best Practice Guide to Portraying Beneficiaries and Service Users.* London: Charity Comms

Sumner, A. (2012) *Where Do the World's Poor Live? A New Update.* Institute of Development Studies. Available: https://www.ids.ac.uk/files/dmfile/Wp393.pdf

UN OCHA (2017) *Learning to Hope: Virtual Reality Film in Myanmar.* https://www.youtube.com/watch?v=QZhSPp0WBk0

United Nations (2015) *The Millennium Development Goals Report.* Available: http://www.un.org/millenniumgoals/2015_MDG_Report/pdf/MDG%202015%20rev%20(July%201).pdf

United Nations (2016) Global humanitarian appeal for 2017 requires record $22.2 billion in funding – UN Press release 5th December. Available: http://www.un.org/apps/news/story.asp?NewsID=55714#.WYilPGVeDgE

United Nations (n.d.) *Sustainable Development Goals.* Available: http://www.un.org/sustainabledevelopment/sustainable-development-goals/

WAN-IFRA (2016) *World Press Trends Survey.* Available: www.wan-ifra.org/articles/2016/06/12/full-highlights-of-world-press-trends-2016-survey

World Bank (n.d.) Data. Available: https://datahelpdesk.worldbank.org/knowledgebase/articles/906519-world-bank-country-and-lending-groups

World Humanitarian Summit (2016) *Commitments to Action.* Available: http://agendaforhumanity.org/sites/default/files/resources/2017/Jul/WHS_Commitment_to_Action_8September2016.pdf

14

NON-PROFIT PR IN INDIA

Prema Sagar, Rama Iyer and Nupur Chaturvedi

Introduction: the language of giving

There are over 1,500 languages in India; with 22 of them recognized in the Constitution of India. This linguistic diversity stems from India's large population and its rich cultural history. Yet, the authors believe that there is a common language in India – that of giving.

The cultural value of giving has been a constant bedrock. From the ancient days of mythology, philosophy and the scriptures, the concepts of *dana* (donation) and *seva* (service) have been fundamental to Indian culture. Formerly, altruistic concepts were conveyed orally. Folk and mythical tales of enlightened beings who followed the path of selflessness to salvation, were passed down generations. Over the years, countless voices have reinstated, revived or revised these ideas to suit the nation's changing cultural landscape. So, to understand how the non-profit sector communicates today, it is essential to first understand its evolution in a historical context.

India, a nation shared by over a billion people, is a beautifully complex land heaped with layers of culture. On the one hand, it has the second-fastest growing economy and industry in the world (International Monetary Fund 2017). On the other, disparity, the gap between the haves and have-nots, is increasing. The country provides a large and diverse base for non-profit organizations (NPOs) with its different issues, social units, regions, scales and stakeholders at play. For instance, issues can be considered on the scales of: village, town, city, a state, the nation, or a demographic segment. There is much to learn about the evolution, and communications, of the non-profit sector.

The authors of this chapter first trace the development of the non-profit sector in India. They then consider non-profit communications in India, focusing on media developments and grassroots communications. Following this, the authors highlight the importance of CSR in India. The all-important Companies Act 2013 made CSR obligatory for companies over a certain size. This was a milestone for philanthropy in India and its importance and impact on communications are considered. Finally, the role of advocacy is discussed.

Mapping the non-profit landscape in India

Tracing the roots of the non-profit landscape in India

With the dawn of the 19th century, older ideologies and practices of charity began to transform, as exposure to the rest of the world increased. During British rule, as more foreign travellers visited and more Indians made trips abroad, the country began to witness a shift in its social outlook. New perspectives were ushered in by reformers who sought to change the *status quo*. They included: Raja Ram Mohan Roy, Dayanand Saraswati, Rabindranath Tagore, Sir Syed Ahmed Khan, Vinobha Bhave, Ramkrishna Paramhansa, and Swami Vivekanand. The thought behind charity began to shift from simply being a 'good deed' or a 'respectable' thing to do, to a more socialist approach that was focused on societal improvements. This shift to the organizational increased the role of public relations in the sector.

With the onset of the Independence movement, society began experiencing major restructuring. Even as people mounted the fight for Independence, there was a need to consolidate the ideas of the country that India was to become once the Independence was won. This created the perfect conditions to set up several prominent non-profits. These included the National Council for Women in India, the Servants of India Society, Ramakrishna Mission, Arya Samaj, Brahmo Samaj, Royal Asiatic Society, All India Spinners' Association, and All India Village Industries Association, among others.

The challenges were aplenty, with issues coming to the fore. These included human rights, non-violence, women's rights, education reforms, child marriage and the *sati* practice, and religious reforms. The strength and success of all these social movements were only determined post-independence in 1947. With control back in national hands, it was up to the new Indian government to set precedents for modern Indian society. There was an urgent need for nation-building on various fronts like education, healthcare, industry, rehabilitation (given that there was a very painful partition between India and Pakistan), welfare, community development and infrastructure development. Several public-sector organizations were established in this period (though some continued from before independence). These ranged from heavy engineering and infrastructure oriented organizations to agricultural support, food and drugs manufacturing, and more. While the nascent Indian government developed the public sector, it was up to citizens to increase the breadth and depth of these efforts. There was some blurring in the lines between the roles of public, non-profit sector and commercial sector roles.

As industries developed wider and deeper roots, two different approaches can be identified. On the one hand, industrialists like Jamshedji Tata, Dhirubhai Ambani, and Baldeo Das Birla, much like the rulers of the past, acted as benefactors for their employees as well as the communities that surrounded the areas housing their businesses. This was as a way of giving back. So be it health, welfare, housing, children's education or retirement benefits; everything was provided for by them. For instance, Jamshedji established Jamshedpur, an industrial town around his manufacturing units, with housing, hospitals, schools and more. Contrastingly, there was a second kind of industrialist who only sought to exploit manpower and resources for profit. This resulted in the rise of unions, environmental activism and protests (Varghese 2010).

At this point, in the 1960s and 1970s, communications were being used for activism, paving the way for some of the country's most iconic social campaigns.

Over time, through different historical circumstances and a changing socio-economic landscape, the non-profit sector of the country began to take the shape we see today. Its role, whether led by icons, supported by international organizations, or independently, has never been so pronounced. The economic disparity has increased at an alarming rate. According to Forbes (2017), India is today home to over 100 billionaires – the fourth highest in the world. Contrarily, the country ranks a poor 131 on the UNDP's Human Development Index (UNDP 2017). This, of course, generates plenty of debates. Are these indicators always mutually contradictory? Should the government take complete charge of welfare? Do industrial organizations take charge of communities work? Where does individual giving take place in the system? India has seen successes and failures on both sides of these perspectives, simply because of the unique challenges such a multi-cultural and geographical land poses, as well as the intrinsic 'giving' attribute by its citizens. Perhaps the biggest problem then, is that all of this, has been unregulated and whimsical. Today's scenario is one where the majority of the causes gaining mileage are issue-based and driven by government agenda. So, the media and public relations have become the perfect mouthpiece to fill in the gaps left by this selective approach.

The non-profit landscape: number and types

One of the primary challenges of trying to understand India's non-profit sector is the difficulty in assessing its true size. The Supreme Court of India tasked the Central Bureau of Investigation with finding out the number of non-profits in 2015. They came back with a finding of 3.3 million; that is, one for every 600 people. According to an article by Johari (2014), this figure is likely to be an underestimate, given that it does not take into account trusts registered under the *Public Trust Act* (1950), *the Charitable and Religious Trust Act* (1920) or *the Indian Trust Act* (1882). Besides these acts mentioned, a non-profit can be registered under the *Societies' Act* (1860); *Indian Companies Act* (1956) (Section 25), *Religious Endowment Act* (1863); and the *Wakf Act* (1954), among others. Therefore, it is difficult to number non-profits in India with certainty. Nevertheless, an estimate is a useful starting point.

A defining factor for non-profit organizations is the relationship they have with the state. On-the-ground success is only achievable through collaboration. Nevertheless, this is not always an easy task, given that most non-profits are started with the intent of filling the gaps that the government leaves behind. Furthermore, in April 2017, the Government of India submitted an exhaustive list of draft guidelines to the Supreme Court of India for any non-profit that is planning to seek funding from the government (Mahapatra 2017). One of these provisions, journalist Mahapatra notes (ibid.) is that NGOs and their office-bearers are mandated 'to execute a bond, equivalent to the money received, promising to refund the amount with 10% interest if funds are misused or not used for the sanctioned purpose'.

With an array of non-profits, their agendas, government structure, geographic footprint to size and scope of work, it is difficult to define a common thread running through them – be that in terms of the challenges they face or the way they operate. It is this diversity that lends a complexity to the sector that makes it tough to regulate. Naturally, issues like trust, perception, credibility, capability and accountability are constant debates that pose another layer of challenges for non-profits to overcome. Especially with regard to accountability – which, at the end of the day, is what it comes down to. It was only a public interest litigation (PIL) filed in the supreme court on the lack of auditing among non-profits in India, that led to the government submitting guidelines for non-profits (Prakash 2017). This is what makes the role of communication so crucial, as a third-party medium monitoring the sector, with the power to speak out.

Non-profit communications in India

Getting heard in a country of a billion voices

NPOs' effectiveness is enhanced through communication. This is whether it is to help engage with or persuade existing donors and funders to continue their support, or attract new ones; raise awareness around causes, engender trust and credibility, or most importantly, to connect with and give voice to those in the community directly and indirectly affected by its work.

Public relations is so important in the Indian context, because there are complex labyrinths of stakeholders that NPOs need to engage with to succeed. For instance, government relations can be conducted at state or at a national level. Within different ministries, which departments should be targeted? Furthermore, what level of official should be contacted within them? Similarly, when targeting the media, decisions have to be made about whether or not to address the mainstream English-language media or the so-called **language media** (media communicating in Hindi or other regional languages); national or regional media; and digital, broadcast or print media.

The impact of media developments on non-profit communications

Non-profit PR has been affected by the rapid development of the media and communication industry of India. With today's abundance of private channels, including several news channels with 24/7 programming, various avenues for airing development-oriented content have opened up. Citizen journalism programmes that give voice to issues, like CGNet and The Viewspaper, documentaries, and social campaigns are all potential outlets for non-profits to employ for their cause.

Other mediums, like radio, have come a long way too. In 2002, the government released the guidelines for radio broadcasts by educational institutions, and extended this to include NPOs three years later. In 2015, there were nearly 200 community radio channels operational in India's cities and towns (Jain 2015). Even mainstream radio channels air citizen and social causes, with a popular radio channel, Red FM conducting multiple campaigns. For instance, one of the issues they covered was the lack of education for the children of sex workers. This went on to gain international exposure and support (BestMediaInfo Bureau 2017).

Journalists and non-profit communicators have traditionally treated each other with caution. They can perceive NPOs to be disorganized or corrupt and to have political, religious or 'anti-establishment' agendas. The non-profits on the other hand think that mainstream media is concerned with sensationalizing issues.

Media involvement and PR can lead to actual policy change. The public was mobilized after the brutal rape of a young girl by six men (including a minor) in a moving bus in December 2012. Referred to as the Nirbhaya (fearless woman) rape, the incident triggered widespread public outcry, which ultimately led to an ordinance being passed. The news media, both print and electronic fed this public sentiment with continuous reporting of the victim's condition as well as the outrage. The public outpouring of emotions was only a drop compared to the conversations on social media. Within days, a three-member panel of judges, led by Justice J.S. Verma, was constituted, and it submitted its recommendations in just a month, which has formed the basis of amendments to the law pertaining to rape (Express Web Desk 2017).

Looking ahead, it is the digital media that is perhaps the most promising area for NPO communications. Social media channels, blogs, online news portals and mobile applications are all important. It is one that is cost-effective, far reaching and direct. The non-profit sector of India recognizes this already, with digital occupying a substantial role in the communication strategies many NPOs now implement.

Achieving success through different communication strategies

Having to overcome a multitude of challenges makes India's non-profits develop diverse, interesting and innovative communication strategies.

Resourcing of communications

At larger non-profits, communication policies often reflect an organized corporate structure – they have a dedicated team in a usually well-defined communications department and sometimes engage with specialist communications agencies to give them both strategic as well as tactical support. The campaigns they roll out are usually 360-degree, employing all the latest tools of communication, from social media and media relations to advertising and activations.

Nevertheless, while communication is a core function of NPOs, it often takes a back seat amongst small-scale organizations that usually have a modest-sized team handling the entire operations.

Furthermore, non-profits can sometimes be reticent. This is, in part, because of the traditional belief that doing something good should not be something to talk about; that if it is promoted then it is not philanthropy but marketing. In addition, there is a fear that communications activity may be perceived to mean that the NPO is well-funded and therefore does not need further funding. There may be a conviction that all funds should be dedicated to the actual community work with no resources being spent on marketing. Finally, finding the people with the right communications competencies can be challenging. PR practitioners do not typically associate the non-profit sector with offering sustainable career options. This lack of specialist support is difficult for a NPO to overcome when seeking to deliver an impactful message.

Grassroots communications

Typical mass media outlets simply do not address grassroots communities. Given the rich diversity of the country, connecting with communities at this level, in both rural and urban areas, is of primary importance. For this, focused tools and innovative approaches are needed. Interactivity is key. Unless the community is co-creating the communication, the desired impact will not be achieved. Over the years, several tools have been employed to achieve things at this level in India. These range from folk forms and music, to street theatres, puppet shows and dances. These traditional forms of storytelling are impactfully used to deliver messages about causes. For instance, Health Care Foundation of India (HCFI) ran a 10-month nation-wide campaign on nutrition through the use of puppetry, folk songs and street theatre (Prasad 2013). A Maharashtra-based Indian development communication organization, Abhivyakti Media for Development, in fact, rolled out an initiative to identify those who are already using some of the folk forms so that they can be included in an informal network it has formed (Paranjape 2007).

Community radio is a powerful medium. Community radio stations (CRS) not only bring communities together; they also provide employment. Take the example of Radio *Nazariya* (perspective). The station was conceived by the Ahmedabad-based NPO Dhrishti, to 'deal with the urban question through dialogue and information sharing' (Radio Nazariya). Nazariya employs people from within the community it services.

One innovative approach is comic books. Utsah, a child rights and protection organization in the state of Assam, uses comic books to spread awareness about human trafficking and exploitation among school children so that they can recognise and protect themselves from it. Another NPO, My Choices Foundation that works on the same cause in the southern state of Telengana, also uses comic strips where heroes of a 'safe village' fight trafficking (Archana 2017).

Very often the medium itself is the differentiator. For instance, the Smile Foundation, which works with underprivileged children, youth and women, produces films and documentaries around the thematic areas it covers. Its most successful production, *I am Kalam*, is the first film in India to be produced by a development organization. The film has received 23 national and international awards and has been played in 40 film festivals across the world (Smile Foundation). The Smile Foundation was set up in Delhi in 2002 and has now scaled up to reach 23 states.

Celebrity engagement can also amplify message reach at grassroots level. Magic Bus, India for instance, works across 17 states with children who are under-privileged. It uses a sport-based model to motivate the children. This work enhanced through celebrity engagement, gives them the PR multiplier much needed with corporate donors.

Agastya International Foundation, one of the largest experiments in the world in science education, has reached over 8 million children. Imparting science education to children in villages, but more importantly nurturing creativity and grooming tomorrow's leaders of rural India, Agastya's scalable technology-driven lab has won it the Google Impact Challenge award among many other accolades (Pulakkat 2016).

The age of CSR in India: mandated CSR and its impact on communications

The mandate on corporate giving

A milestone in the development and support of the non-profit sector was legislation mandating companies of a certain size to spending at least two per cent of their average net profits on corporate social responsibility. This innovative government requirement, in Section 135 of the *Companies Act 2013* (Ministry of Commercial Affairs 2013), came into effect from April 2014. While the Act does not offer any punitive measures for companies that fail to comply, there is a provision for naming-and-shaming as a deterrent (Ramanathan 2015).

This law has attracted national and international interest in the CSR, non-profit and corporate fraternity (for example, Balaji 2013; Dharmapala and Khanna 2016).

The Companies Act was a defining moment in the journey of philanthropy of India on the whole. It has formalized the concept and put a structure to it. The Ministry of Commercial Affairs has notified what is popularly known as the 'CSR mandate' under Section 135 and Schedule VII of the Companies Act, 2013. In a nutshell, the mandate says that any company with a turnover of Rs 10 billion, or net-worth of Rs 5 billion or net profit of Rs 50 million every year has to spend two per cent of its average net profit of the preceding three years on CSR activities.

This formalization has driven the CSR sector to the forefront of the Indian story. While organizations are free to choose the issues they want to support, government development agendas also find legs as government, corporate organizations and NPOs align to affect real change. Take the example of the Swachh Bharat (Clean India) mission. The initiative is one of the flagships of PM Narendra Modi, who launched it soon after taking charge in 2014. Since then, through brand ambassadors, including Bollywood actors, continued promotions through all forms of media and behaviour change communication in rural and urban areas, the campaign has never slipped in visibility. Corporate India, in two years contributed Rs 4.76 billion to the fund created for the initiative, Swachh Bharat Kosh, (NDTV 2017).

Instances like this just make the stakes higher and the role of PR even more pivotal as mediators between the government, corporates and NGOs.

CASE STUDY 14.1: CSR WITHIN THE COMMUNICATIONS INDUSTRY

In a brief period of 12 months, WhiteKettle[1] and WPP (the world's largest communications group) have strategized and delivered a CSR mandate that has already seen measurable success. As with every innovation, the first step was a challenge – how to create a differentiated offering.

They sought to focus on the kind of approach, rather than the activity itself. So the decision was taken to launch a programme for underprivileged youth in Mumbai and Delhi NCR, but one that was clutter-breaking.

What distinguished this programme from others was the understanding that in India, education in isolation is not the answer to generating livelihoods – there needs to be holistic care and development. What is needed is balance between academic learning and softer skills, career counselling and livelihood options, proper nutrition, and awareness of personal hygiene.

The vision of E2L (Education to Livelihood) brought alive by strategic partnerships with Magic Bus, Hope Foundation and Genesis Foundation[2], has proven to be tremendously successful. With a reach of over 15,000 students and 38,000+ community members, the intervention has shown improved educational outcomes in terms of literacy, critical thinking, digital awareness, coding and design skills. Most importantly, early qualitative studies show success stories in terms of softer skills like confidence, team building, communication skills, enjoyment and fun in the learning process, and career linkages in terms of livelihood choices.

For now, this tightly monitored, deep intensive, holistic programme continues to gather momentum, and aims at generating livelihoods and the next level of bringing change in these children's lives.

The Companies Act effect on CSR communication

The relationship between the corporate sector and the non-profit sector in India has not been an easy one, with both types of organizations having inherently differing agendas. This legislation forces them to work together, with the hope that non-profits can learn processes and employ more systematic methods of working, and that companies can become more compassionate and find the right way to contribute to the development of society.

Communicating philanthropic activities is not new for companies in India, be that to gain corporate legitimacy or build reputation. However, they now have to be more thorough and nuanced about it. With the progress and documentation of CSR activities gaining importance for organizations, CSR and sustainability reports are sometimes part of companies' annual reporting. Then there are owned marketing and communication media like websites, brochures and newsletters; shared media like social networking sites; and paid media like advertising. While experts believe communication standards have gone up, the quality, content and extent of communication about CSR still varies. This has culminated in corporates playing a much more active role in CSR, as opposed to the cheque-book charity days of the past.

Advocacy campaigns

India's long history of public advocacy has always brought about change, from the 19th century days of Gandhi and other socio-religious reformers.

An iconic campaign was that of the Chipko Movement, a non-violent protest in the 1970s by tribal activists against deforestation. *Chipko* literally means to 'cling'. If you have ever wondered where the term 'tree-huggers' came from, it was from this peaceful act which saw activists cling to trees to stop demolishers from taking them down. Besides the forests, the movement also gave a platform to forest and tribal communities, who were being increasingly marginalized as the country marched down the path of development, to voice their concerns. Myths and legends abound about the movement, because it took place in remote villages. The tree-hugging enactments photos were captured in the media (Bandyopadhyay 1999). The Movement and the ideology of environmental activism gained a fillip with the involvement of activist Sunderlal Bahuguna, who invoked Gandhian tools of sitting on an indefinite fast and of marching for the cause. These brought the media spotlight onto the cause, with major publications taking notice of the unique struggle against deforestation and environmental exploitation (Gupta & Aggarwal 1996: 42).

Intricately entwined with these issues are the rights and culture of the people and communities who have for centuries given and taken from those natural resources. Take for instance, the Narmada *Bachao Andolan* (Save Narmada Movement), which was about protecting the River Narmada from extensive construction of dams that were slowly altering the river's natural course, leaving thousands of people displaced in the process. The movement came into the headlines under

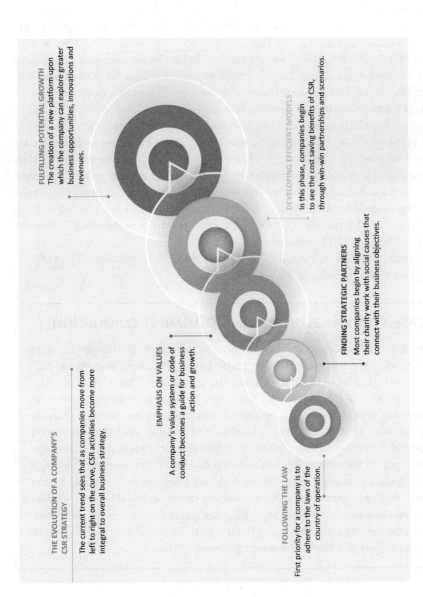

THE EVOLUTION OF A COMPANY'S CSR STRATEGY

The current trend sees that as companies move from left to right on the curve, CSR activities become more integral to overall business strategy.

EMPHASIS ON VALUES

A company's value system or code of conduct becomes a guide for business action and growth.

FULFILLING POTENTIAL GROWTH

The creation of a new platform upon which the company can explore greater business opportunities, innovations and revenues.

DEVELOPING EFFICIENT MODELS

In this phase, companies begin to see the cost saving benefits of CSR, through win-win partnerships and scenarios.

FINDING STRATEGIC PARTNERS

Most companies begin by aligning their charity work with social causes that connect with their business objectives.

FOLLOWING THE LAW

First priority for a company is to adhere to the laws of the country of operation.

FIGURE 14.1 The Evolution of a Company's CSR Strategy

the leadership of the now-iconic activists Medha Patkar and the late Baba Amte (a Gandhian activist). The movement was a great campaign. It had a strong message and multi-stakeholder involvement with both activist and celebrity influencers and mass mobilization.

Today, advocacy can be a tool for anyone who wants to posit a change in the policy framework for an issue. Examples include the movement against Section 377 of the Indian Penal Code on gay rights in India, the anti-corruption movement led by activist Anna Hazare and the public mobilization after the Nirbhaya rape in December 2012. The movement against Section 377 has been a frustrating one for LGBTQ activists in India, where homosexuality is considered illegal. The Indian Penal Code, which defines criminal offences in India, came into effect through an Act promulgated in 1862. In 2009, the Delhi High Court de-criminalized consensual homosexual acts, but in 2013, the Supreme Court overturned this verdict, saying that this needed to be tackled by the legislature, not the judiciary, because the law itself needed to change (Prakash 2016). NPOs and activists have been working to build public sentiment towards LGBTQ rights so that political will can be influenced. A coalition of NPOs in the area, called Voices Against 377, is at the helm of these efforts (Voices Against 377 2017).

Though, in such cases, it is the government that is the key stakeholder, with the media only affecting change in a supportive capacity.

CASE STUDY 14.2: CAMPAIGNING AGAINST CORRUPTION

In April 2011, Gandhian activist Anna Hazare went on hunger strike to persuade the government to table the Jan Lokpal Bill (citizen ombudsman bill). This was legislation to put in place an independent body to investigate corruption. The media propelled the cause, completely captivating the youth audience along the way. The 'revolution' was broadcast live on news channels as popular actors, musicians, celebrities and notably journalists also stood behind the crusading Anna. While Anna held his fast, a social media campaign took grip of the nation. This was truly the coming of age of online activism; it was India's own Arab Spring moment. Anna's mentions on Facebook, Twitter and YouTube went into millions, trending across India. What this kind of feverish conversation did was to mobilize the support of the urban middle class, who for the first time came out of the so-called comfort of their drawing rooms to participate in a citizen movement (Hanmer 2011).

The future of non-profit communication in India

India has the second-highest number of internet users in the world, after China, and a penetration of 34.4 per cent (Internet World Stats 2017). According to *The Future of Internet in India* report, released in 2016 by the National Association of

Software & Services Companies (NASSCOM) and Akamai Technologies, the number of users will go up to 730 million by 2020. Notably, the report predicts 75 per cent of the new users will come from the rural sector. There are also fundraising implications. The *Online Giving in* India 2015 report by Charities Aid Foundation (CAF) India, anticipates that by 2025, 50 per cent of all giving in India will occur online.

For non-profits, digital is not just about having social media accounts or fundraising, but also about having and leveraging an online presence, as well as using the tools of technology to streamline and speed up processes that have otherwise been resource and time intensive. While some of the larger NPOs do have digital strategies and dedicated social media experts, smaller NPOs can use digital less strategically. However, with an increase in employee volunteerism in corporate organizations under CSR, there are also instances when a smaller non-profit finds volunteers who come with expertise in digital marketing. An example of this is Genesis Foundation, founded by one of this chapter's authors. The Foundation is a non-profit working to support the treatment of critically ill, under-privileged children with heart disorders. Genesis Foundation's outreach is managed by volunteers from Genesis Burson-Marsteller.

There is an increased awareness of the role social media can play to support non-profits in their endeavours. Facebook now has a Donate button, while YouTube has a separate initiative to help non-profits not just tell but also promote their visual stories. Twitter is used extensively for influencer engagement.

An unsung hero among these platforms is WhatsApp, the mobile messaging application. In February 2017, WhatsApp hit the 200 million active users mark in India (Singh 2017), and as a peer-to-peer application, it plays a big role in building support groups and sharing information. CARE India, for instance, has used the platform to create peer networks through field workers in Uttar Pradesh, Bihar, and Odisha.

Looking beyond social media, the digital medium is seeing a remarkable rise in the proliferation and use of online crowdfunding platforms. Ketto.org, Milaap.org, Wishberry and Bitgiving are some of the popular crowdfunding platforms for non-profits to leverage in India. Besides streamlining online donations, these platforms support non-profits through their own promotion campaigns as well – something that smaller non-profits find extremely useful.

Conclusion

For now, non-profit PR and communications is still dawning in India. There is definitely a much higher awareness among non-profits about the advantages of PR and communications. This is more so with the increased interaction between Corporate India and NPOs, thanks to the CSR mandate. The journey is to go from awareness to implementation and ultimately outcome, but in the big picture, the challenges faced along this path have made the sector a global experiment that the rest of the world is keenly watching.

Discussion questions

1.   Discuss the evolution of philanthropy and the early stages of the non-profit
     sector in India.
2.   Trace the landscape of the sector in modern India.
3.   What are some of the communications challenges that the sector faces?
4.   How has the CSR mandate in the Companies Act 2013 impacted the non-
     profit sector and how it communicates.
5.   Research and elaborate on development and the media and PR aspects of any
     one of the following mass movements:

     a   Against Section 377
     b   Post Nirbhaya rape
     c   Anti-corruption movement of Anna Hazare.

6.   Discuss the landscape of grassroots communications in India.

Notes

1   Rama Iyer heads WhiteKettle and consults with WPP Foundation.
2   Prema Sagar is the Founder-Trustee for Genesis Foundation.

References

Archana, K.C. (2017) Indian social activists use comic books to raise human trafficking
    awareness among children, *Indiatimes.com*. Available at http://www.indiatimes.com/news/
    india/indian-social-activists-use-comic-book-characters-to-raise-human-trafficking-awa
    reness-among-children-273138.html (Accessed: 17 August 2017).
Bahl, E. (2014) An overview of CSR Rules under Companies Act, 2013, *Business Standard*.
    Available at http://www.business-standard.com/article/companies/an-overview-of-csr-rules-
    under-companies-act-2013-114031000385_1.html (Accessed: 17 January 2017).
Balaji, E. (2013) Companies Bill sets global benchmarks, *Hindu Business Line*. Available at
    https://indiacsr.in/companies-bill-sets-global-benchmarks-by-e-balaji/   (Accessed: 24
    August 2017).
Bandyopadhyay, J. (1999) Chipko movement: of floated myths and flouted realities. Avail-
    able at http://lib.icimod.org/record/10314/files/162.pdf (Accessed: 17 January 2018).
BestMediInfo Bureau (2017) Red FM's 'Bajao for a cause' supports 'Palna' initiative, *Best
    Media Info*. Available at http://bestmediainfo.com/2017/03/red-fms-bajao-for-a-cause-
    supports-palna-initiative/ (Accessed: 17 August 2017).
CAF India (2015) *Online Giving in India: Insights to Improve Results*. Available at http://ca
    findia.org/images/Online_giving_research_report.pdf (Accessed: 20 August 2017).
Dharmapala, D. and Khanna, V.S. (2016) The Impact of Mandated Corporate Social
    Responsibility: Evidence from India's Companies Act of 2013. University of Chicago,
    Public Law Working Paper No. 601; University of Chicago Coase-Sandor Institute for
    Law & Economics Research Paper No. 783; University of Michigan Law & Economy
    Research Paper No. 16-025; University of Michigan Public Law Research Paper No.
    526. Available at SSRN: https://ssrn.com/abstract=2862714 or http://dx.doi.org/10.
    2139/ssrn.2862714

Express Web Desk (2017) Nirbhaya gangrape case 2012: A look at what all has happened over the years, *The Indian Express*. Available at http://indianexpress.com/article/india/nirbhaya-gangrape-case-2012-a-look-at-what-all-has-happened-over-the-years-4641418/ (Accessed: 17 August 2017).

Forbes (2017) *World's Billionaires*. Available at https://www.forbes.com/billionaires/list/#version:static (Accessed: 26 June 2017).

Gupta, V.S. and Aggarwal, V.B. (1996) *Media Policy and Nation Building: Select Issues and Themes*. Concept Publishing.

Hanmer, M.S.L. (2011) India gives voice a case study of Anna Hazare's PR. Available at http://www.mxmindia.com/2011/09/india-gives-voice-a-case-study-of-anna-hazare%E2%80%99s-pr/ (Accessed: 20 August 2017).

International Monetary Fund (2017) *World Economic Outlook Update January 2017*. Available at https://www.imf.org/external/pubs/ft/weo/2017/update/01/ (Accessed: 17 January 2018).

Internet World Stats (2017) Top 20 countries with the highest number of internet users – March 2017. Available at http://www.internetworldstats.com/top20.htm (Accessed: 17 January 2018).

Jain, M. (2015) Why India has only 179 community radio stations instead of the promised 4,000, *Scroll.in*. Available at https://scroll.in/article/725834/why-india-has-only-179-community-radio-stations-instead-of-the-promised-4000 (Accessed: 26 June 2017)

Johari, A. (2014) Why India has one NGO for every 600 people – and the number is rising, *Scroll.in*. Available at https://scroll.in/article/657281/why-india-has-one-ngo-for-every-600-people-and-the-number-is-rising (Accessed: 26 June 2017).

NASSCOM and Akamai Technologies (2016) The Future of Internet in India. Available at http://www.nasscom.in/knowledge-center/publications/future-internet-india (Accessed: 20 August 2017).

NDTV Banega Swachh India News (2017) Corporate India has spent almost 500 crores for Swachh Bharat Abhiyan in past 2 years. Available at http://swachhindia.ndtv.com/corporate-india-spent-almost-500-crore-swachh-bharat-abhiyan-past-2-years-5922/ (Accessed: 17 January 2018).

Mahapatral, D. (2017) Tough norms for NGOs seeking government funds, *The Times of India*. Available at http://timesofindia.indiatimes.com/india/tough-norms-for-ngos-seeking-government-funds/articleshow/58038748.cms (Accessed: 17 January 2018).

Ministry of Commercial Affairs (2013) *The Companies Act*. Available at http://www.mca.gov.in/Ministry/pdf/CompaniesAct2013.pdf (Accessed: 20 August 2017).

Paranjape, N. (2007) Community media: local is focal, *Community Development Journal*. Available at https://doi.org/10.1093/cdj/bsm036 (Accessed: 17 August 2017).

Prakash, S. (2016) SC hearing on gay sex: All you need to know about Section 377. *Hindustan Times*. Available at http://www.hindustantimes.com/india/sc-hearing-on-gay-sex-today-india-s-struggle-with-sec-377-explained/story-PH220grrwgsw9mtNTBKXTM.html (Accessed: 20 August 2017).

Prakash, S. (2017) NGOs must register with Niti Ayog: Govt to SC, *The Tribune*. http://www.tribuneindia.com/news/nation/ngos-must-register-with-niti-aayog-govt-to-sc/387529.html (Accessed: 20 August 2017).

Prasad, N. (2013) Folk media: an active media for communication campaigns in digital era, *Global Media Journal-Indian Edition*. Available at http://www.caluniv.ac.in/global-mdia-journal/COMMENTARY-DEC%202013/Commentary_1_Neeru_Prasad.pdf (Accessed: 17 August 2017).

Pulakkat, H. (2016) How Agastya International Foundation is creating tomorrow's leaders in rural India, *The Economic Times*. Available at http://economictimes.indiatimes.com/indus

try/services/education/how-agastya-international-foundation-is-creating-tomorrows-lea
ders-in-rural-india/articleshow/50513945.cms (Accessed: 24 August 2017).

Radio Nazariya (2017) *Home Page*. Available at http://www.drishtimedia.org/RNZ.html
(Accessed: 2 February 2018).

Ramanathan, A. (2015) Fear of 'name and shame' will push firms to comply on CSR:
IICA's Chatterjee, *LiveMint.com*. Available at http://www.livemint.com/Companies/
EzwvbztSMQsyJ8Y26iaBrL/Fear-of-name-and-shame-will-push-firms-to-comply-on-
CSR-I.html (Accessed: 24 August 2017).

Singh, M. (2017) Guess WhatsApp's biggest market? India, *Mashable*. Available at http://ma
shable.com/2017/02/24/whatsapp-india-200-million-active-users/#ARP5qSV_Esq8
(Accessed: 8 July 2017).

Smile Foundation (2010) *I am Kalam*. Available at http://www.smilefoundationindia.org/
i_am_kalam.html (Accessed: 17 August 2017).

The Bridgespan Group (2017) Why Indian Non-profits Are Experts at Scaling Up. Available at
https://ssir.org/articles/entry/why_indian_nonprofits_are_experts_at_scaling_up (Accessed:
20 August 2017).

United Nations Development Programme (2017) India profile. Available at http://hdr.undp.
org/en/countries/profiles/IND (Accessed: 26 June 2017).

Varghese, M. (2010) *Historical Background of Trade Unionism in India*, Chapter 3. Available at
http://shodhganga.inflibnet.ac.in/bitstream/10603/610/11/11_chapter3.pdf   (Accessed:
20 August 2017).

Voices Against 377 (2017) Available at http://www.voicesagainst377.org/ (Accessed: 20
August 2017).

WPP (2015) Sir Martin Sorrell launches WPP India CSR Foundation. Press release. Available at http://www.wpp.com/wpp/press/2015/oct/07/sir-martin-sorrell-launches-wpp
-india-wpp-india-csr-foundation/ (Accessed: 20 August 2017).

WPP (2016a) *Annual Report & Accounts 2016*. Available at http://www.wpp.com/annualrep
orts/2016/how-we-behave-and-how-were-rewarded/sustainability-review/   (Accessed:
20 August 2017).

WPP (2016b) *WPP Sustainability Report 2015/2016*. Available at https://www.ungloba
lcompact.org/system/attachments/cop_2016/318041/original/WPP_Sustainability_Report_
2015-16.pdf?1474373885 (Accessed: 20 August 2017).

WPP (2017) *WPP Sustainability Report 2016/2017*. Available at http://www.wpp.com/susta
inabilityreports/2016/social-investment/ (Accessed: 20 August 2017).

15

NGO COMMUNICATIONS IN A ONE-PARTY STATE

The context and characteristics of non-profit advocacy communications in China

David Horton Smith, Sean Lang and Nicky Garsten

Introduction: China's constrained non-profit sector

China has one of the largest non-profit sectors in the world; likely the second largest. The sector has deep roots with NGOs dating back 8,000 years. In July 2017, there were about 700,000, or more, government-registered non-profits (Smith, Zhao and Xu 2017). This total has more than doubled that from a few years ago. Though speculative, estimates of the numbers of Unofficial Social Organizations/ USOs (mostly local associations) range from 8,000,000 to 10,000,000 circa 2008 to 2011 (Smith with Zhao 2016: 19).

The relationships between non-profit organizations and traditionally dominating government bodies are all important. Notably, the state impacts not only organizational survival but also on what messages can be communicated and through which channels. For instance, religious NGOs in China cannot communicate their spiritual missions (Kaltman 2007). Furthermore, whilst digital strategies are particularly important to advocacy NGOs, there are censors and controls on cyberspace. The Chinese government has, reports the *Financial Times* (Mitchell 2015), 'long maintained a "Great Firewall" between its … cyberspace and the rest of the internet, cutting off 20 per cent of the world's population from Facebook, Google, Twitter and other services'. Whilst laws about NGO registration and the media specify what is permitted, the interpretation of relevant legislation and regulations also requires expertise and cultural understanding.

In this chapter, the authors trace the development of non-profit organizations in China. They then identify the context to, and characteristics of communications in the NGO sector focusing on advocacy INGOs and national NGOs. The importance of using a variety of tactics to influence change, from an in-depth case report to digital communications, is illustrated through the case study about Greenpeace's Hungry Coal campaign. Some challenges of INGO communications are further explored in an unattributed case study.

Overview of the structure of the non-profit sector in China

David Horton Smith

China's non-profit sector before the reform and opening

China has had a strong and dominating national government for several millennia, most of the time under an emperor or a temporary substitute, such as an empress or regent (Keay 2011). As far back as 8,000 BC, non-profits arose in China and other territories of the world in the form of voluntary associations or membership associations in preliterate horticultural or village societies (Ross 1976; Smith 1997). When the unified empire arose in China in 246 BC (Keay 2011), after the agrarian revolution had greatly improved agricultural productivity, another associational revolution took place, as in other ancient agrarian societies (Smith with Zhao 2016: 9–11). In addition to kinship associations and social clubs, there now arose occupational guilds, religious associations, sports clubs, and other types of associations over the next two millennia in China (Smith & Ting 2016: 12). In the past two to three centuries, various other types of non-profit associations have also developed, as well as some non-profit agencies with paid staff serving nonmembers (ibid. 13). In the several decades after the fall of the empire in 1911 (Keay 2011), in the Xinhai or Democratic Revolution, China was briefly a democracy, but became an authoritarian state under Chiang Kai-shek from 1928 until the 1949 Communist Revolution led by Mao Zedong.

Mao established and ran a totalitarian one-party-state until his death in 1976, during which time there was effectively no Chinese non-profit sector or non-profits. The national party-state tightly controlled everything, so that non-profit-like **mass organizations** for the Chinese Communist Party (CCP), women, unions, youth, etc. were actually government agencies, not genuine non-profits or **nongovernmental** organizations (Smith with Zhao 2016: 14).

China's non-profit sector after Mao (1977+)

With Mao's death in 1976, under the leadership of Deng Xiao-ping there was a major shift in the power structure of China's national political regime, termed the Reform and Opening Up from 1978 on (Keay 2011; Smith with Zhao 2016: 13–14). China transitioned from a totalitarian dictatorship to an authoritarian regime – still a dictatorship, but with more civil and human rights and a newly emerging non-profit sector (Lieberthal 2003; Lin, Cai and Li 2003; Simon 2013).

This subsection describes briefly the recent associational revolution in post-Mao China, as well as the issues of NGO autonomy in this period. After Mao, some NGOs began to have significant autonomy from the government, but still often substantial constraints. Interestingly, genuine advocacy by NGOs is now possible, if done in a local, cautious, non-violent way respectful of the larger party-state hegemony. Government contracting with NGOs for services has become more common. And International Non-Governmental Organizations (INGOs) and other foreign-based NGOs have become more important.

New laws in 1988 and 1989 permitted foundations and other non-profits or non-profit organizations (NPOs) to exist, providing they registered with the national government and also avoided any political activity resisting the general party-state political regime. The Chinese Communist Party remains in strict control, and any unregistered non-profits are technically (*de jure*) outlawed. Paradoxically, the law forbidding unregistered non-profits is rarely enforced, effectively providing some *de facto* freedom of association at the local level.

Smith with Zhao (2016: 14) note, 'Beginning in 1978, and especially ten years later in 1988–1989 with new government Regulations legalizing NPOs ... party-state domination of NPOs began to lessen while still remaining substantial'. However, initially most non-profits and nearly all government-registered non-profits, were 'government stimulated and government controlled **GONGOs, or Government Organized Nongovernmental Organizations**', self-contradictory as this term is (ibid.). This situation persists in the present century at the level of **national** non-profit associations, but there are more genuinely independent non-profits at the provincial or district level of territorial scope. At the local or neighbourhood level, there is even more independence from government, always within the general limitation on opposition to the party-state regime.

Since 1988–1989, and especially since 1999, there has been an explosive growth of non-profits in China, which some call an **associational revolution** (Smith with Zhao 2016: 15). In 2017, there were about 700,000 government-registered non-profits (Smith, Zhao, and Xu 2017), up by 300,000 from a few years ago. Half of these non-profits are non-profit *agencies*, not associations, yet there are many millions of local (grassroots) associations in China, nearly all unregistered with the government Ministry of Civil Affairs. Though, as already mentioned, speculative estimates put the numbers of USOs in 2008 to 2011 at between 8,000,000 to 10,000,000 (Smith with Zhao 2016: 19). Thus, the numbers of non-profits in China circa 2010 are likely comparable to the numbers in the USA circa 1990 (ibid.: 20). China seems not only to have the second largest economy after the USA, but also the second largest non-profit sector, which few recognize, even academics.

The autonomy of Chinese non-profits is a key consideration. As suggested earlier, national associations in China tend to be tightly controlled by the party-state, hence being mainly GONGOs, organized by the government and often with government officials as top leaders and/or on their policy boards. Provincial level non-profits are more mixed, often freer from government control and management. Most importantly, at the local level, the millions of grassroots associations have a good deal of internal or operational autonomy, if they avoid challenging the national party-state regime (Smith with Zhao 2016: 20–22). The government has the legal right to intervene in the affairs of any non-profit, but rarely does so for unofficial non-profits (USOs) that observe the relevant boundaries on their conduct. Non-profit agencies, usually active at a local or municipal level, generally seek government registration eventually and tend to be carefully nonpolitical in their activities (Smith et al. 2017). However, even non-profit agencies often have difficulty in achieving government registration, and then may seek alternative forms of legitimation (ibid.). Most USOs do not bother to seek registration or other types of formal legitimation.

Some scholars argue that, rather than being dominated by the party-state, non-profit leaders sensibly seek positive relationships with government officials at various sub-national territorial levels (Smith with Zhao 2016: 18). In this process, non-profit leaders play a dynamic role, not a passive one (Teets 2014). Getting state resources for one's non-profit is crucial, in this view, and leaders who can do this are vital to non-profit success. The most successful non-profit leaders often are invited to become functionaries of the government and/or the Chinese Communist Party (CCP). Scholars often characterize this kind of government-non-profit sector cooperation as **corporatism**, or in China as **state-led corporatism**, emphasizing the dominant role of the party-state (ibid.).

There is cautious, nonviolent, local advocacy conducted by some non-profits. Openly activist social movement/resistance non-profits cannot get government registration, or even alternative formal legitimation, in most cases (Simon 2013). When such non-profits come to the attention of government authorities at any level, they tend to be disbanded by such authorities, and their leaders are often arrested and imprisoned. However, such activist/resistance non-profits are very rare, since most activists clearly understand the system and the dangers of active regime-resistance. But non-profit advocacy can nonetheless be successful in China, if done carefully by conventional, 'non-political' non-profits (Smith with Zhao 2016: 28–31). A special, limited kind of **orderly activism** can succeed if the advocacy observes certain rules. Aside from not challenging the general party-state regime, successful advocacy and even resistance by non-profits tend to require small scale, local focus, no public protest activities, non-violence, limited publicity, and limited claims and remedies sought. Protecting local residents' interests in cases of discrepancies between national party-state promises and the current local situation often works.

There are increasing government contracts for local non-profit services. In this century, the party-state has become gradually more favourable toward and accepting of contracting with local non-profit service agencies to supply relevant services that the government no longer wishes to provide or can provide (Smith with Zhao 2016: 21). Such non-profit service providers are nearly always government-registered local non-profit agencies, not associations, and definitely not USOs. Some registered (or otherwise formally legitimated) associations that help nonmembers (vs. only members) can also get these contracts. In this feature, China's government-non-profit sector relationships are approaching the situation in many Western nations, but with a much lower frequency or volume. It is worth noting that a survey of Chinese non-profits reported in 2009 found that most did not receive any government funds, for services or anything else (ibid.). This suggests significant independence from government for most non-profits in financial terms.

Since 1978, INGOs and other **foreign** non-profits have played a positive role in illustrating new ways that Chinese non-profits might operate and be successful (Smith with Zhao 2016: 22). Some Chinese scholars have suggested that foreign non-profits have led to 'more open governance structures, more transparent decision-making mechanisms, and more efficient service models' (ibid.). However, much of foreign foundation grant funds have gone to government-controlled organizations, not independent non-profits (ibid.: 23).

The economic, political, media and legal contexts of NGO communications

Sean Lang with Nicky Garsten

Current economic and political context in China

China is at a critical juncture with big shifts at the economic, political and social level creating potential for change. The current Chinese leadership, at the time of writing, has brought with it a stronger political will to introduce change and a stronger capability to enforce it. Strong action on a new scale can be seen in the tackling of issues ranging from air pollution (Reuters 2017; Yang 2017) to rebalancing the economy. There is also an ambition to influence through soft power. There is an economic transition from 'factory of the world' towards more domestic consumption and service-focused economy (Rhee 2015). Nevertheless, this is still in relatively early stages. The government has been responsive to public reaction on air pollution and the leadership appears to be more prepared to ride through short term or sectorial economic impact in order to deliver on its other goals. The advocates of this fundamental change are not only poli-bureau delegates (Bloomberg 2017), but also part of elite society and sections of the public with the rise of the middle class especially in tier one or two cities.

However, change has its challenges. There is active resistance by powerful vested interests that profited from the existing old economy model (Korsbakken et al. 2016). At a local level, key pillars of industry that are dependent on the old model, can find numerous ways to be obstructive. The policies designed to channel transformation face difficulties in real life partly because central and local government interests can differ. Meanwhile, the rhetoric of eco-civilization, and a healthier and better economy is not necessarily securing everyone's buy-in. Furthermore, new economic players championing for positive paradigm change are weak and dispersed.

China also finds itself under global scrutiny. The global audience is hungry for news and insights about China. On the other hand, Chinese officials and (a growingly nationalist) public have been historically sensitive about the face of China to the world.

The intersection of all these dynamics provides rich ground for those NGOs which are willing to campaign on critical issues in China.

Media censorship

'The Chinese government has long kept tight reins on both traditional and new media to avoid potential subversion of its authority' according to Xu and Albert (2017) in their discussion of media censorship in China. They observe that the government's controls include 'monitoring systems and firewalls, shuttering publications or websites, and jailing dissident journalists, bloggers, and activists'.

Citizens' freedom of speech is afforded in Article 35 of the Chinese Constitution (Xu and Albert 2017; Freedom House 2016). Yet, China has one of the lowest rankings in the 2017 World Index (176 out of 180). The research, published by a France-based watchdog, Reporters Without Borders (2017), reports 'more than 100 journalists and bloggers are currently detained'. In 2016, some detained and imprisoned professional journalists were, according to Freedom House, 'forced to air televised confessions'. Media regulations facilitate censorship of information deemed as harmful (Xu and Albert 2017). Experts privately observe that Chinese media outlets usually employ their own monitors to ensure political acceptability of their content.

Certain websites that the government deems potentially dangerous can be permanently or temporarily blocked. Well-known international platforms like You-Tube, Wikipedia, Facebook, and Twitter are 'permanently' blocked (Freedom House 2016). So too are some google services like Flickr and DropBox (ibid.). There can also be 'black outs' during periods of controversy, such as the 4 June anniversary of the Tiananmen Square massacre or Hong Kong's Umbrella Movement protests in the fall of 2014 (Ser 2016).

Specific material considered a threat to political stability is also banned, including controversial photos and videos, as well as search terms. The government is particularly keen on blocking reports of issues that could incite social unrest, like official corruption, the economy, health and environmental scandals, certain religious groups, and ethnic strife. Restrictions also have been placed on micro-blogging services, often in response to sensitive subjects like corruption.

Overseas NGOs can be seen as organizations which are hard to control. Hence, their communications, which relate to public social or environmental issues, are likely targets of censorship; particularly if they relate to hot topics.

Legal management of INGOs: overseas NGO Management Law

Any foreign NGOs, including foundations, now need to be registered to operate in China. The new Overseas NGO (ONGO) law in mainland China, called the *People's Republic of China's Overseas NGO Domestic Activities Management Law* came into effect on 1 January 2017 (China Development Brief 2017). Under it, INGOs need to **register** under the Ministry of Public Security (that is, the Police) and have a local sponsor to operate in mainland China (*The Economist* 2016). Alternatively, under the law, INGOs can engage in **temporary activities**, explains The International Center for Not-for-Profit Law (ICNL 2017). This, the ICNL explains (ibid.), 'requires notification' to the Ministry of Public Security and work with a local sponsor. Fewer than 100 international NGOs had registered out of the 7,000 active international NGOs in China by early June 2017 (ICNL 2017; Wu 2017). The ICNL (2017) attributed this low number to two main factors. Firstly, there appeared 'to be the unwillingness of many Chinese Professional Supervisory Units (PSUs) to vouch for foreign NGOs'. Secondly, there was 'considerable uncertainty' around the implementation of the law.

The law's requirements will affect INGO operations in China. The immediate impacts include the need for additional capacity to engage with the police and the supervising body (include meetings and more documentation). There are also resourcing constraints. *The Economist* (2016) notes that 'Foreign NGOs will also be banned from raising money in China, which they fear will limit their activities further.'

The full effects are still unclear. They will depend on the government's implementation details and the government's approach to implementing the law. *The Economist* reports (2016) 'Charities worry that ... sponsors, presumably public agencies, could keep them from activities the government does not like, such as those to do with human rights or labour law.' Hence, how INGOs negotiate the campaigning space is important.

Characteristics of communications in advocacy organizations in China

Sean Lang with Nicky Garsten

Millions of Chinese NGOs serve community support functions. They normally cooperate with government and local communities, working on poverty relief, disaster relief and other medical services. For them, the most important communication issue is applying the endorsement from government or obtaining public service contracts from government.

A small percentage of Chinese NGOs are advocacy organizations. These heavily rely on communications. Most of them are environmental protection organizations. The authors of this section highlight the importance of agenda setting digital and engagement strategies, meetings and printed research.

Agenda setting

Agenda setting is an important aspect of NGO communications that increasingly is moving into the digital sphere. Advocacy organizations tend to enrol support through digital and engagement strategies. There strategies are important given the state restrictions on communications.

Advocacy NGOs in many parts of the world have traditionally engaged in **agenda setting** with or though media. The **agenda,** according to communication theorists, Marianne Dainton and Elaine Zelley (2015: 229) is 'coverage by the mass media, which provides an indication of what events the public "should" consider important'. Agendas set through the media that sway public opinion can help influence political agendas. This established view of agenda setting gave prominence to mass media and made media relations a central focus of NGO communications. However, online communications are changing the dominance that the news media has in agenda setting (Merilainen and Vos 2011).

Media used to be the main communication channel for advocacy NGOs in China. However, securing coverage can be challenging. Journalists tent to be receptive to NGOs' activities that relate to topics endorsed by the government and that concern GONGOs. Effectively, this means there is little difference between the NGOs and with the government. The Chinese President has said (Associated Press 2016): 'All the work by the party's media must reflect the party's will'.

Digital communication strategies

In China, **digital communication strategies** allow grassroots movements to overcome the state managed control and censorship of the traditional media. NGOs can initiate social change processes online by creating salience using agenda setting, inviting the public to participate grassroots activism and debate. Social media are mainstream platforms in China. Large followings reinforce NGOs' legitimacy authority. Subsequently, NGOs can influence decision-makers, becoming part of the legislative process. However, this strategic approach is challenged by the Chinese government's awareness of the power of social media. The Government strictly controls all the channels and platforms. It disconnects the channels available for agenda setting and thereby weakens the influence and power of NGOs.

Many advocacy organizations in China use what can be called **a network model of digital communications** to communicate with the public and to build their networks of support. Networks increase NGOs' power to influence by spreading messages through tightly knit groups (clusters), or individuals (nodes), within the NGO's networks. They enable NGOs to extend their spheres of influence; to mobilize supporters and to inspire others to take action on social and environmental concerns. A network's intertwined nature makes it difficult to be destroyed; even if some relationships are cut off, others can emerge to replace them. Networks make campaigns messages 'louder' when there are large numbers of people spreading messages and taking action.

The power of networks can be measured by their breadth (variety of stakeholder types), size (numbers) and quality of layers. Having a broad network extends an organization's spheres of influence. The network can be conceptualized to have layers of stakeholder support. The first layer is supporters. NGOs can communicate to them directly, e.g. by e-mail and social networking sites (SNS) and encourage them to be active in the network. The second layer comprises allies, partners or social media influencers. The latter can be **change agents** who influence the adoption of innovations in networks (Rogers 1983 cited by Windahl et al. 2009) and who thereby can mobilize opinion. They are an obvious choice for

NGO's partners. To harness the power of these partner networks, NGOs have to consider them as possible campaign allies and incorporate cooperation in campaign plans.

Digital communications need to constantly evolve in response to technological, societal, legal and political change. Simultaneously, NGOs need to be at the vanguard of digital trends as they push boundaries to influence social and environmental change. People do not follow laggards.

Engagement to deepen relationships with supporters

A key engagement strategy is to focus on **depth of engagement** with supporters rather than on the numbers. The key is integrating online and offline communication with supporters. Advocacy organizations' evaluation metrics focus on the direct impacts of programmes as well as follower numbers. This strategy also reflects the shrinkage of traditional media and the popularity of SNS in mainland China.

This is also in response to the clear challenges for engagement work in mainland China. As INGOs cannot fundraise in China for the foreseeable future, critical players in their engagement networks are missing. Hence, INGOs need to reinvent what long-term relationships with **supporters** mean. More importantly, the political situation severely limits some avenues of engagement. Some tactics which many NGOs rely on in other countries are prohibited if they threaten national security and government's surveillance, like mass petitions and marches.

Therefore, engagement in mainland China needs to take on different shapes and strategies. To achieve depth of support, NGOs can focus resources to build three types of communication and engagement platforms as outlined below.

- Self-built platforms like websites and e-mail newsletters
- Official accounts on leading social media such as Wechat, Weibo, Zhihu and others
- Alliances with external partners (for instance, community groups) and opinion leaders like celebrities and influencers on social media.

Social media provides an important space in which NGOs can experiment. Currently, Wechat is a singularly useful SNS. This is because the platform's communication is based on a friend's circle, rather than open-access like Weibo (a popular platform that is a cross between Twitter and Facebook). Hence, the government still tolerates WeChat. The use of Weibo is becoming more constrained (Leob 2017). Weibo issued a statement in June 2017 stating that it would 'promote a "mainstream" discourse'.

Meetings and reports

Most Chinese NGOs utilize meetings and forums to influence stakeholders. This is because of constraints on public communications and limited resources. Often, government officials are key stakeholders and therefore they are invited to participate in such meetings.

NGOs produced printed reports, for reference or as policy advice, for government officers. Hence, print is an important communications tool with stakeholders.

CASE STUDY 15.1: SECURING ENVIRONMENTAL CHANGE

Sean Lang

The Thirsty Coal campaign was assessed to be a 'model for civil society action in support of the environment' (Feng Jie 2014) according to an article published by *China Dialogue*.

Greenpeace's report (2013d), *Thirsty Coal 2*, showed that the Shenhua Group, the world's biggest coal producer by volume, was exploiting water resources in Inner Mongolia. Shenhua's operations had caused severe ecological damage including desertification, which affected farmers and herders who faced severely reduced water supplies.

Alarmed by plans for an expansion of the Shenhua project, Greenpeace called on the company to end the water pumping and for the Chinese government to impose strict supervision and enforcement of the principles governing coal-to-chemical projects.

This report was the first time Greenpeace had challenged a Chinese state-owned enterprise and was based on 11 field trips to the Shenhua project in 2013. During the visits, Greenpeace produced content using photography, film and case studies to communicate with supporters and the public via different channels. For example, Greenpeace's (2013c) documentary-style video, *Thirst*, bore witness to changed landscape through images and interviews with local farmers. It had two million views before it was censored. Greenpeace's e-newletter (2013a) used powerful imagery of a farmer trying to work in a barren landscape. Greenpeace organized a press conference, media briefing, and a media-embargoed field trip. There was also a digital media push, as Greenpeace worked with key opinion leaders to forward its messages and report.

Following the publication of the Greenpeace report in July, the Shenhua Group invited the environmental ONGO to talks six days later. On 8 August 2013, Greenpeace then received another statement from the Shenhua Group, called *The Explanation of Wastewater Discharge*. The coal company appeared to be willing to communicate with Greenpeace; however, the solutions and explanations Shenhua offered fell short.

When the Shenhua Group (1088:HK) announced their financial Interim Results at a conference in Hong Kong in August that year, they were questioned by Greenpeace activists, one of whom held up an image of the 'creeping desertification' at the meeting (Greenpeace 2013a). Earlier, a Greenpeace representative submitted an open letter and the Thirsty Coal report to company board members. The petition action was picked up by many Hong Kong media without censorship.

In April 2014, the local government announced that Shenhua would stop pumping groundwater over the course of the year.

CASE STUDY 15.2: DISCUSSION WITH A CAMPAIGNER FROM AN INGO COMMUNICATING IN CHINA

Nicky Garsten

QUESTION: How do you grow your INGO brand in China when advocating 'sensitive issues'?

ANSWER: This is the challenge we, and many other leading international NGOs, face when the Chinese government deems our work 'sensitive'. The climate for international NGOs in China has never been tougher. I believe that new laws, including the National Security Law, Cyber Security Law and Foreign NGO Management Law, will make it near impossible for many INGOs (International NGOs) to operate within China independently from government control....Achieving a sustainable communications strategy [is] a daunting goal. Even with a relevant message, targeted content, and an appropriate tone, we adopt a less confrontational tone at times compared with other parts of the world.

QUESTION: How do you navigate censorship?

ANSWER: It is a constant game of cat and mouse with censors. When we began to grow our followers on the two main social platforms, Weibo (340 million active monthly users) and WeChat (938 million active accounts), our posts were removed and our accounts deleted. Our Chinese language website was blocked shortly after a successful launch. To self-censor in order to grow the audience goes against our values, and these values are core to our brand. We experimented with 'unbranded' issue-led accounts. These have a stay of execution from the censors but ultimately risk the same fate.

As a result, our mainland Chinese supporters have to find us using Virtual Private Networks (VPNs), and we have to find them. China's Great Firewall blocks an array of top websites including Google and news sites such as the *New York Times*. VPNs are the most common way for people in China to get past the Great Firewall, to access information including our Chinese language Facebook and Twitter profiles, as both platforms are currently banned.

With low brand awareness compared to elsewhere in the world, this core audience is relatively small but highly engaged. A recent directive to crack down on the use of VPNs means many users will have to adapt again [to circumvent the firewall], and so will we.

With increasing numbers of young Chinese diaspora across the world, there is a great opportunity to engage and build a sustainable audience via platforms like Facebook. For instance, we delve among niche audiences of arts and humanities students in Western universities as they are likely to be receptive to our messages.

The paramount consideration remains the security of our supporters, partners and staff. Communication tactics we use regularly elsewhere, such as stunts, are discounted for China due to the risks and possible consequences for the individuals involved.

QUESTION: What inspires your creativity and what motivates you?

ANSWER: We have learnt much from Chinese netizens who are incredibly inventive. The positive change we want to see is ultimately driven by them and that is why we remain committed to building an audience in China and to support them in achieving change.

The campaigner from the INGO is anonymous. The discussion was conducted with Nicky Garsten in 2017

Conclusion

Millions of non-profit organizations are working in China at grassroot and local levels. For these organizations there can be some autonomy when not challenging the state. A key focus of their communications is face-to-face liaison with local officials. Communication is more challenging for national and INGO advocacy organizations because of state controls. There are many reasons for INGOs to work in China given their important roles in responding to global and social environmental issues wherever they arise. A key issue for INGOs is how they can work in China with communications strategies that help turn challenges into opportunities in an increasingly digital world.

Discussion questions

1. How has the history of the non-profit sector in China influenced its current structure?
2. To what extent do you believe that the state influences NGO communications in a country that you are familiar with?
3. How can media censorship impact on non-profit communications?
4. How could depth of support be fostered amongst supporters of an NGO of your choice?
5. What are some of the communication challenges for INGOs working in China?
6. What factors helped the Thirsty Coal campaign's success?

References

Associated Press (2016) Xi Jinping asks for 'absolute loyalty' from Chinese state media. *The Guardian* online. 19 February. Available: https://www.theguardian.com/world/2016/feb/19/xi-jinping-tours-chinas-top-state-media-outlets-to-boost-loyalty (Accessed 12 February 2018).

Bloomberg (2017) In Xi's vision for China, 'environment' edges out 'economy'. Bloomberg New Energy Finance. 18 October. Available: https://about.bnef.com/blog/in-xis-vision-for-china-environment-edges-out-economy/ (Accessed 12 February 2018).

Browne, A. (2017) China Is the world's worst polluter. Don't expect it to be a climate crusader. *Wall Street Journal* online. 6 June. Available: https://www.wsj.com/articles/dont-count-on-china-as-next-climate-crusader-1496741425 (Accessed 12 February 2018).

China Development Brief (2017) China's implementation of the Overseas NGO Management Law. 6 March. Available: http://chinadevelopmentbrief.cn/articles/chinas-implementation-of-the-overseas-ngo-management-law/ (Accessed 12 February 2018).

Dainton, M. and Zelley, E. (2015) *Applying Communication Theory for Professional Life: A Practical Introduction.* 3rd edn. Los Angeles, London, New Delhi, Singapore, Washington DC: Sage.

Economist (2016) Charity ends at home. *The Economist*, print and online. Available: https://www.economist.com/news/china/21698292-chinas-leader-guards-against-nasty-foreign-influences-charity-ends-home (Accessed 12 February 2018).

Freedom House (2016) China. Available: https://freedomhouse.org/report/freedom-press/2016/china (Accessed 12 February 2018).

Greenpeace (2013a) Action at Shenhua Energy Conference in Hong Kong. Media archive. Available: http://www.media.greenpeace.org/archive/Action-at-Shenhua-Energy-Conference-in-Hong-Kong-27MZIFVXIYMP.html (Accessed 12 February 2018).

Greenpeace (2013b) China's coal industry is sucking the Ordos Grasslands dry! E-newletter article. Available: http://www.greenpeace.org/eastasia/news/ebulletins/2013/chinese-coal-company-overexploiting-groundwater/ (Accessed 12 February 2018).

Greenpeace (2013c) *Thirst*. Video. Available: https://www.youtube.com/watch?v=nMavdhg2f2c (Accessed 12 February 2018).

Greenpeace (2013d) *Thirsty Coal 2*. Available: http://www.greenpeace.org/eastasia/thirsty-coal-2/ (Accessed 12 February 2018).

Kaltman, B. (2007) *Under the Heel of the Dragon: Islam, Racism, Crime, and the Uighur in China.* Athens, OH: Ohio University Press.

Keay, J. (2011) *China: A History*. New York: Basic Books.

Korsbakken, J., Andrew, R. and Peters, G. (2016) China's coal consumption and CO2 emissions: What do we really know? *China Dialogue* online. 31 March. Available: https://www.chinadialogue.net/article/show/single/en/8780-China-s-coal-consumption-and-CO2-emissions-What-do-we-really-know- (Accessed 12 February 2018).

Leob, J. (2017) Weibo capitulates amid Chinese government's censorship crackdown. *E&T*. Available: https://eandt.theiet.org/content/articles/2017/06/weibo-capitulates-amid-chinese-government-s-censorship-crackdown/ (Accessed 12 February 2018).

Lieberthal, K. (2003) *Governing China: From Revolution to Reform*. New York: W.W. Norton & Company.

Lin, J.Y., Cai, F. and Li, Z. (2003) *The China Miracle: Development Strategy and Economic Reform*. Hong Kong, China: The Chinese University Press.

ICNL (2017) Civil Freedom Monitor: China. 9 June. Available: http://www.icnl.org/research/monitor/china.html (Accessed 12 February 2018).

Jie, F. (2014) How NGOs forced China's biggest coal company to back down over groundwater extraction. Available: https://www.chinadialogue.net/article/show/single/en/6977-How-NGOs-forced-China-s-biggest-coal-company-to-back-down-over-groundwater-extraction (Accessed 12 February 2018).

Merilainen, N. and Vos, M. (2011) Human rights organizations and online agenda setting, *Corporate Communications*, 16(4): 293–310.

Mitchell, T. (2015) China passes sweeping national security law. Available: https://www.ft.com/content/5dfa8360-1fdb-11e5-aa5a-398b2169cf79 (Accessed 12 February 2018).

Reporters Without Borders For Freedom of Information (2017) China: World's leading prison for citizen journalists. Available: https://rsf.org/en/china (Accessed 12 February 2018).

Reuters (2017) 'China vows big winter air pollution cuts in northern cities'. South China Morning Post. 24 August. Available: http://www.scmp.com/news/china/policies-politics/article/2108109/china-vows-big-winter-air-pollution-cuts-northern (Accessed 12 February 2018).

Rhee, C. (2015) Managing China's Economic Transition. *International Monetary Fund Blog*. 5 October. Available: https://blogs.imf.org/2015/10/05/managing-chinas-economic-transition/ (Accessed 12 February 2018).

Ross, J.C. (1976) *An Assembly of Good Fellows: Voluntary Associations in History*. Westport, CT: Greenwood.

Ser, K. (2016) How China has censored words relating to the Tiananmen Square anniversary. *PRI*. Available: https://www.pri.org/stories/2016-06-03/how-china-has-censored-words-relating-tiananmen-square-anniversary (Accessed 12 February 2018).

Simon, K. (2013) *Civil Society in China: The Legal Framework from Ancient Times to the 'New Reform Era'*. New York: Oxford University Press.

Smith, D.H. (1997) The international history of grassroots associations. *International Journal of Comparative Sociology*, 38(3–4):189–216.

Smith, D.H. with Ting Zhao (2016) *Review and Assessment of China's Non-profit Sector after Mao: Emerging Civil Society?*Leiden, Netherlands, and Boston, MA, USA: Brill.

Smith, D.H., Ting Zhao, and Jun Xu (2017) Chinese non-profit organization registration and other legitimation pathways: loosening restrictions in recent years. Paper presented at ARNOVA Asia Conference, Beijing, China, 6–7 June.

Teets, J.C. (2014) *Civil Society under Authoritarianism: The China Model*. New York: Cambridge University Press.

Windahl, S., Signitzer, B. with Olson, J.T. (2009) *Using Communication Theory: An Introduction to Planned Communication*. 2nd edn. Los Angeles: Sage.

Wu, D.D. (2017) More than 7,000 foreign NGOs in China: Only 91 registered so far. *The Diplomat* online. Available: http://thediplomat.com/2017/06/more-than-7000-foreign-ngos-in-china-only-72-registered-so-far/ (Accessed 12 February 2018).

Xu, B. and Albert, E. (2017) Media censorship in China. Council on Foreign Relations. Available: https://www.cfr.org/backgrounder/media-censorship-china (Accessed 12 February 2018).

Yang, Yi (2017) What will it take to clean China's air? The Diplomat. 22 June. Available at: https://thediplomat.com/2017/06/what-will-it-take-to-clean-chinas-air/ (Accessed 12 February 2018).

16

PUBLIC RELATIONS IN THE SOUTH AFRICAN NON-PROFIT SECTOR

Partnerships for social change

Dalien Rene Benecke and Lida Holtzhausen

Introduction

Partnerships are all important to the non-profit sector in South Africa, in a country where there has been major political change with the election in 1994 of a new government led by Nelson Mandela and where a rich diversity of culture means that communications are managed across 11 official languages. This chapter will discuss public relations in the non-profit organization (NPO) sector in South Africa from a partnership perspective as found in relationship management theory. Relationship management implies that public relations balance the interests of organizations and stakeholders through the management of organization–stakeholder relationships. Public relations serves to create mutually beneficial relationships built on trust and aims to create a two-way symmetrical platform for dialogue and open communication.

After specifying non-profit organizational definitions as they apply to the South African context, and after giving an overview of the NPO landscape, the authors examine some key foci of public relations (PR) practitioners in the South African context. They consider the importance of branding; relationship management; corporate social responsibility (CSR) and social return on investment (SROI); and social innovation through networks and partnerships.

NPO landscape in South Africa

Non-profit organizations in South Africa are defined and described according to their function and sources of funding (Patel, 2012; Statsa SA, 2014). The development of NPOs in South Africa is closely related to the historical development of the country. The term Non Profit Institutions (NPIs) is used by Statistics of South Africa (Statsa SA, 2014) to define all civic organizations such as Non-Government

Organizations (NGOs), Community-Based Organizations (CBOs) and Faith-Based Organizations (FBOs). These NPIs are characterized by being legal entities, having a not-for-profit focus and acting independently as self-governing entities with voluntary membership (Statsa SA, 2014: 5).

The Department of Social Development (DSD) refers to NPIs as Non Profit Organizations (NPOs) with approximately 125,000 registered with the department ranging from well-known and established organizations such as Child Welfare South Africa with offices throughout the country, to medium sized organizations such as the health activist group Treatment Action Campaign (TAC), to small local community based organizations such as the Klipspruit Community Centre which offers a day care facility to local residents in Soweto (Global Alliance, 2014). For the purpose of this discussion the term NPO will be used when referring to all not-for-profit organizations serving various communities, as it is the most commonly used term in South Africa.

In 2012, the SA Department of Social Development restructured the registration of NPOs which resulted in thousands of organizations losing their formal registration. Following this de-registration crisis (Wyngaard, 2013) the need for a different, innovative approach to NPO practice in South Africa again became an issue of social debate due to the significant role NPOs play in providing social services to South African citizens.

According to Patel (2012) the responsibility of service delivery to vulnerable and marginalized individuals and communities has mostly landed with NPOs, notwithstanding a governmental policy attempting a different partnership between government and civil society. In an attempt to change the legacy of Apartheid era social welfare services which was characterized by racialized and exclusive policies, the White Paper for Social Welfare (1997) was adopted with its 'rights-based approach, equity in the distribution of resources and redress through increased access to social services and benefits to those who have been historically excluded' (Patel, 2012: 603).

The NPO landscape in South Africa has seen dramatic changes since these early years of democracy with many more individuals having access to financial support in the form of social grants. However, at the same time many NPOs are struggling to survive due to a lack of funding, poor infra-structure, a lack of human resources and leadership capacity (Cheverton, 2007; Holtzhausen, 2014). Most services offered by NPOs are still centralized in urban areas and provided by mainly women who are often under-paid for their services or are volunteering (Patel, 2012). The implementation of policies seems to lack a developmental focus resulting in a discrepancy between what is proclaimed in government policy in comparison to what is actually practised (Patel, 2012). The involvement of public relations practitioners as relationship builders and cultural intermediaries should assist organizations and government structures in achieving objectives and influencing change in society.

Building relationships to obtain and strengthen the support of stakeholders and in the case of NPOs, support for their causes, are some of the key functions of public relations practitioners. Relationship management (RM) assumes an even greater importance in SA in the light of the foundation and development of many NPOs in the middle 20th century, and the present transformative agenda. RM and these issues are considered later in this chapter.

Research into the key characteristics of organizational public relationships (OPR), the measurement of relationships and the benefits for organizations have highlighted characteristics such as trust, levels of influence between members, relational commitment, relational satisfaction and control mutuality (Huang & Zhang, 2015). Based on the outcomes of OPR and the individuals' attitudes towards relationships, successful OPR is found to include the level in which organizations answer personal, professional and community relational needs whilst ensuring a culturally sensitive approach (Huang & Zhang, 2015: 36). In the case of NPOs as well as For-Profit Organizations (FPOs) the manner in which expectations are addressed through OPR is closely related to the effect and influence of public relations. One key benefit of effective OPR as a result of public relations activities includes dealing with crisis situations such as can be seen in a special request issued by the South African National Blood Services updating the public on available stock and appealing for more donations (see SANBS case study later in the chapter). Other benefits derived from effective OPR within the NPO sector found in a study by Kang and Yang (2010) include an awareness of OPR activities which leads to supportive behaviour and a positive view of organizational success. The mediating role of public relations in achieving effective OPR between donors (as well as other stakeholders) and NPOs is key to the success of these important social structures. In a study of five major South African NPOs Holtzhausen (2014) found a distinct need for more strategic communication efforts by PR practitioners in order for NPOs to ensure their corporate identity and reputation.

Branding

The concepts of branding and brand management are well known subfields of marketing management but although being addressed in the NPO sector in South Africa these are still emerging areas of practice. South African NPOs are faced with very distinct brand and brand management challenges which are overlaid with the reality of 11 official languages, rich cultural diversity, and the need to de-colonize policies and practices. These challenges include having to relate to a wide variety of stakeholder/customer/audience groups in managing their brands as well as the need to negotiate partner, sponsor, and donor relationships (Bruce 2011; Mort, Weerawardena & Williamson, 2007).

In the midst of competition with for-profit companies, the public sector and other NPOs (Lamb et al. 2015) often manage their brands with the aim of relationship building. For example, the NPO, Community Hours builds its brand through several partnerships and networks enabling various NPOs, volunteers and sponsors to work together on projects. These projects may be annual events such as Chief Executives Sleep Out SA or ad hoc events such as Operation Hydrate.

Brands are often associated with identifying the organization, differentiating it from similar institutions and creating a competitive advantage for the organization (Balmer, 2011). Brands are also used to create a sense of trust and credibility in the organization, which also forms the basis for building relationships with stakeholders/customers/audiences they relate to. Building trust, credibility and other aspects of brand such as brand personality and symbolic traits are crucial to NPOs but can assume a much greater importance in a country like South Africa, striving to decolonize and establish social justice. Take the example of the South African National Blood Service (SANBS). Its brand signifies the importance of giving life. Through blood donation, citizens in South Africa have the opportunity to give someone in need of a blood transfusion much more than mere blood – rather providing that person with the possibility to continue living, giving them the most precious gift of all: 'a lifetime waiting to be lived'. In this instance the SANBS brand portrays a brand personality that resonates with the essence of every person, i.e. life itself. This non-profit is also the subject of Case study 2.

In the South African (SA) context NPO brand development is characterized by limited budgets presenting a much bigger challenge than in the case of FPOs. As a consequence SA NPO brands need to constitute much more than mere organizational identification.

Challenges are dedicated staff communication management of multiple languages, which need to be included in all communication, and the organizational governance issues, which include affirmative action policies.

Some of the alternative aspects of NPO brands and their management include brand personality, brand history, stakeholder expectations and corporate branding as a service. These alternative aspects are discussed now in more detail.

Brand personality has received growing attention in the SA NPO context due to the shift from tangible characteristics such as the name, logo, signage and slogans, to more human characteristics associated with brands, thus referring to its personality. As is the case with humans, NPO brands are more and more being related to characteristics such as trustworthiness, integrity, credibility, caring and longevity, to name but a few (Holtzhausen, 2014; Bruce, 2011; Sargeant, 2009). The personality aspects of NPO brands are especially important when one takes into consideration that NPOs need to establish a credible and trustworthy relationship with their many stakeholders, so that they obtain what is needed for them to continue the work they have committed themselves to do. Stakeholders refer to the brand personality as one of the aspects necessary to determine whether they can relate to the particular NPO and continue their support, be it in the form of monetary support or time (Holtzhausen, 2014). Examples of effective brand personalities in SA NPOs can be found in the many NPOs focusing on education and employment where credible brand personalities are vital. This is due to the historical legacy of the struggle against apartheid which meant and means that many South African adults had to be supported through Adult Basic Education and Training (ABET) programmes.

The next brand element which assumes great importance in the SA NPO context is **brand history**. Having a history that is enriched by values, missions and strategic goals has enabled some organizations to stay afloat irrespective of turbulent times (Holtzhausen, 2014). Such NPOs boast histories filled with strong relationships between themselves and many stakeholders, built over time, and having a heritage which became much more than intricate organizational and managerial strategies, but rather a heritage built on trust and delivering on social promises made during engagements with stakeholders. Their history becomes the custodian of the NPO brand. Examples include South African Depression and Anxiety Group (SADAG), South African National Blood Service (SANBS), CANSA (Cancer South Africa) and Childcare South Africa. The SA National Council of the Blind (SANCB) has a brand history of active opposition to apartheid pre 1994, playing a leading role in encouraging activism by organizations of disabled people. This history is remembered and forms part of the SANCB brand in a de-colonizing SA. Conversely, the history of disability organizations who eschewed activism is remembered and is part of their brand history.

A third element is **stakeholder/customer/audience expectations** encapsulated in the marketing concept of positioning, .i.e. what do the different audiences think of the NPO. In the NPO context these individuals or groups include beneficiaries/ clients, donors, government agencies, businesses, volunteers, sponsors, and society as a whole and their respective perceptions of the NPOs might differ considerably (Holtzhausen 2014; Bruce 2011; Sargeant 2009; Andreasen and Kotler 2008). This complicates NPO brand management in any country but assumes an even greater challenge in South Africa – the Rainbow Nation – with its pre-1994 history, because organizations are faced with having to manage various, often conflicting perceptions of the brand. This challenge makes stakeholder engagement multi-faceted and a complex managerial function which PR practitioners need to deal with.

A further brand-related issue NPOs are faced with is linked to organizational culture, strategy and image. NPOs have to establish brands which are often not related to any product but rather **services** which are linked to the organizational mission and vision. NPOs need strong brands if they are to survive and fulfil their missions. The struggles NPOs face are intense and only those with competitive advantages seem to survive. Organizational brands provide NPOs with the opportunity to market the organization as a brand. Every aspect of the organization then becomes part of that brand which enables the stakeholders to hold a strong, favourable and unique association to the organization.

NPOs who address their brands and brand management in a strategic way, including their heritage, their vision and mission statements, culture, personality, stakeholders and their corporate brands, pave the way for relationship building, ensuring strong life lines needed in times of hardship and continuous struggles to survive financial challenges.

Relationship management

Building relationships to obtain and strengthen the support of stakeholders and, in the case of NPOs, support for their causes, are some of the key functions of public relations practitioners and have been the centre of many organization–public relationship studies. NPOs across the world are known for the wide variety of stakeholders with which they need to build relationships (Bortree, 2015). These stakeholders/customers/audiences include volunteers, employees, beneficiaries of their services, local communities, government, other NPOs, sponsors, donors and media. These stakeholders include various audiences (see p. 00).

In the case of South Africa, the historical segregation of welfare services needed to be decolonized and integrated after the democratic elections of 1994. The government needed to create policy aimed at partnering with civil society with access to services regarded as a constitutional right available to all South Africans (Patel, 2012; Skinner & Mersham, 2008).

The South African economic, social and political challenges have prompted NPOs to focus more on their relationships with numerous stakeholders and also corporate partners whilst building their brands to become a trusted entity between the different partners. This focus on relationships has caused South African organizations such as NPOs to renew their thoughts on what PR is: what it should do; its function and values within the organizational structure and the greater society; the benefits generated for the organization and the stakeholders those organizations serve, and the societies within which they exist (Ledingham & Bruning, 2000). Relationship management represents a renewed focus on building, nurturing and maintaining relationships (Ledingham & Bruning, 2000). It provides a platform for dialogue and discussion of issues, which is extremely important for NPOs where stakeholders can hold different values and often come to different conclusions concerning the organization. John Ledingham (2003:190) indicates that 'Effectively managing organizational-public relationships around common interests and shared goals, over time, results in mutual understanding and benefit for interacting organizations and publics.'

Relationship management, especially within the NPO context indicates how the organization and its stakeholders should interact with one another. This puts a priority on NPOs identifying their stakeholders as well as the nature of the current relationship between the organization and the stakeholders (Bruning, 2000; Grunig & Grunig, 2002). This will be followed by the NPO having to determine how the stakeholders view and experience their relationship with the organization. Strategies can then be developed to manage these relationships and the appropriate behaviour should be communicated to all involved in the relationship. Another aspect of relationship management in the NPO sector is measuring or determining the quality and outcome of the relationship between the organization and its stakeholders and this can be done by measuring dimensions of trust, control mutuality, commitment, satisfaction, as well as the relationship type (be it exchange or communal relationships) (Hon & Grunig, 1999).

Relationship management in the context of the NPO calls for joint partnership between the organization itself and its many stakeholders. NPOs thus act as socially responsible entities, creating a space for dialogue, accountability, involvement and relationship nurturing, whilst allowing the stakeholders to become the custodians of their brands.

Corporate social responsibility, environmental issues and reporting

The link between PR and corporate social responsibility (CSR) in South Africa was made by Skinner and Mersham (2008). They assigned the CSR developments in Africa to a well-established PR practice in South Africa, where the debate around CSR and corporate social investment (CSI) demonstrates the need for business and NPOs to review their motivations for CSR projects and their influence in society (ibid.: 240). The complex and pluralistic South African environment with its history of Apartheid, segregation and racial tension requires an understanding of corporates' motivation for supporting a specific cause, the strategic focus of project and manner of reporting. According to Skinner and Mersham (2008) CSR is practised along a spectrum ranging from simply gaining publicity for a corporate, through to a focus on social change which benefits society (ibid.: 241). Examples from all positions on this spectrum can be found in the wide variety of activities during the annual Mandela Day. Corporates will often mobilize their staff on 18 July to either assist with identified sustainable projects or allow them to choose their own charity to support. Many organizations lack a strategic focus for these events and often focus more on the publicity value and/or short term relief rather than sustained support.

In formal CSR programmes during the past decade a more strategic focus has developed with substantial resources being applied. The overall annual spend on CSR initiatives amounted to around $600 million in 2014/15, treble that when including the economic value of the skills development programmes delivered under Broad-Based Black Economic Empowerment (BBBEE) into account (Mersham & Skinner, 2016: 111).

What are the implications for good practice? PR practitioners in NPOs should understand and actively research social issues to ensure an inclusive and strategic approach to CSR in local African communities. As change agents and cultural intermediaries (Benecke & Oksiutycz, 2015; Benecke et al., 2017) they have the opportunity to educate and involve themselves in developmental issues, promote sustainable involvement of business in society and ensure integrated, triple bottom line reporting (Mersham & Skinner, 2016: 125). Movement in this direction is evident in the increase in corporate reports clearly indicating the increase in CSR spend by organizations who are motivated by a 'license to operate' and who often choose to focus on employment equity as part of CSR (Triloque, 2004 cited in Mersham & Skinner, 2016). Regular feedback given to identified stakeholders, and progress reports stating the influence of developmental projects are fundamental concepts in a contemporary reporting approach such as social return on investment (SROI) (Rossouw, 2010). Although various forms of reporting exist in SA, such as integrated reporting, SROI is motivated by the need to provide evidence of the social value which organizational CSR programmes have for society and organizations. Rossouw (2010) describes SROI as a process and an economic analysis which calculates the social value resulting from an investment made by an organization, and provides practitioners with the evidence needed of the financial value associated with their CSR efforts. It involves a complex process of listening to stakeholders, analysing environmental influencers to 'understand and valuing outcomes', and forming partnerships with NPOs in gathering such evidence.

Social innovation through networks and partnerships

As alluded to in the landscaping section, in 2012 the SA Department of Social Development restructured the registration of NPOs. Following this de-registration crisis (Wyngaard, 2013) the need for a different, innovative approach to NPO practice in South Africa again became an issue of social debate. Wyngaard called for partnerships to be formed, while Patel and Mushonga (2015) argued for CSR and community involvement to address issues associated with a developmental state such as South Africa. Stacks and Watson (2007: 80) ask the question as to what social networks in public relations look like, how can they be measured and what are their actual benefits to public relations. Other policy and governance matters affecting NPOs in SA also include equity in the workplace and skills development of staff. Moore and Westley (2011) offer a suggested approach, namely, a role within the NPO to address the complex social structures such as found in South African NPOs. Such agency roles can be found in NPOs which mobilize communities around social issues such as gender based violence. People against Women and Child Abuse (POWA) is an organization known for its ability to organize protest action whenever cases of abuse are reported on. Their actions have succeeded in placing gender based violence on the public agenda. According to Moore and Westley (2011) skills needed from change agents (such as PR practitioners) in these contexts include entrepreneurial 'relationship building and brokering, knowledge and resource brokering, and network recharging to ensure network development for human benefit and resilience' (n.p.). Social network theory and specifically the development of human networks to the benefit of NPOs should be based on the values described in organizational missions (Cheverton, 2007) as discussed on p.00. Social networks are described as specific social organizations with both horizontal and vertical lines of contact (Moore & Westley, 2011). PR practitioners as cultural intermediaries and relationship builders may have a key function in using their influence and expertise to promote social innovation to address complex problems experienced by NPOs in South Africa. This is an area of future research and knowledge development for PR scholars and NPO practitioners.

Current examples of partnerships and brand development are demonstrated with the case studies of the Community Hours SA and University of Johannesburg partnership followed by an example of a brand development exercise of the South African National Blood Services.

CASE STUDY 16.1: COMMUNITY HOURS

Community Hours (CH) was started in 2015 to connect volunteers, non-profit organizations, schools, youth and communities to actively address social issues. Managing and ensuring effective involvement of volunteers in communities are not only challenging tasks for NPOs but also schools and parents who want to ensure that the youth of South Africa develop as active citizens. The organization offers a coordination and management service to schools, volunteers and NPOs which includes a web based register of volunteering opportunities; complemented by needs posted by NPOs. There is a registration process, logging of hours volunteered, as well as certification and feedback to parents and teachers. Volunteers can register and join teams assisting with the development of art and culture, recreation, education, assisting people with disabilities, working with senior citizens and caring for animals. Volunteers are often mobilized during specific campaigns such as Operation Hydrate which addressed the water crisis experienced in many drought stricken areas in South Africa during 2016. Volunteers were mobilized to assist with collecting and distributing over 13 million litres of water to drought stricken areas throughout South Africa. To date CH has logged close on 100,000 volunteering hours of community work completed by over 10,000 volunteers.

In 2016 CH partnered with the Department of Strategic Communication at the University of Johannesburg (UJ) to assist NPOs and third year diploma students to develop a mutually beneficial relationship. PR students who are required to complete 400–600 hours of work integrated learning, were matched with NPOs who needed assistance with their public relations and communication functions. CH was instrumental in ensuring that specific objectives were developed, implemented and evaluated through their online system. Students and NPO mentors could log their experiences and feedback, hours completed and value derived from the collaboration. This provided much needed information to both NPOs and UJ as to the progress of students and the value they added to the NPOs. The 2016 pilot project will be followed with more extensive partnerships between CH, UJ and students.

> Malcolm Gladwell in his best-selling debut book *The Tipping Point* refers to 'The Law of the Few'. He writes that the success of social epidemics is heavily dependent on the involvement of people with particular and rare social gifts. CHSA offers young people, NPO, educational institutions and communities the opportunity to connect and share their talents to the benefit of all.
>
> *(Karen Landi, founder and CEO of CH)*

For more information visit https://www.communityhourssa.co.za

---

CASE STUDY 16.2: SA NATIONAL BLOOD TRANSFUSION SERVICE

Turning a Service into a Brand: Case study on Brand Building and Relationships

The South African National Blood Service (SANBS) is an independent non-profit organization and one of the leaders in the discipline of blood transfusion. It operates in eight out of nine provinces in South Africa. It also provides crucial support to countries in the southern Africa region. SANBS supplies over one million blood products annually and is rated among the top blood services in the world. Blood is collected from voluntary non-remunerated blood donors who lead safe lifestyles and meet the minimum criteria for donating blood; however this limits the potential donor pool. Blood is processed into its constituent components, which in principle can save up to three lives. SANBS is under constant pressure to deliver blood, other blood products and essential services. It also provides the medical industry with specialized products and services. The target audience stretches across the entire South African spectrum, with donors perceiving the organization as a service brand, while the medical fraternity views it as a product supplying brand. In order to grow its donor panel, it must appeal across a wider population dynamic, specifically to the youth market. SANBS has decided to focus its marketing communications efforts on attracting and retaining new donors from the large and growing pool in the youth market. SANBS campaigns are based on three pillars; awareness, education, and building a brand affinity. The overall long-term objective of SANBS is to maintain blood stocks at a five-day reserve, or at the least to not let this drop below two-day crisis levels. Underpinning these objectives is the urgent need to increase general awareness of the service and the important role it plays in South African society throughout the year. The brand is gradually moving from a 'crisis mentality' to a proactive approach, where the message is spread throughout the year.

https://www.businesslive.co.za/redzone/pages/2017-01-13-south-african-national-blood-service

Conclusion

The chapter has discussed some of the challenges and opportunities available to PR practitioners in the NPO sector in South Africa. The challenges include the multi lingual, pluralistic and richly diverse context in which NPOs provide services and the issues of limited resources, lack of infrastructure and adequate brand leadership. However these challenges create opportunities for more effective relationship development, more social networks, and development of social capital through strategic communication.

Discussion questions

1. Discuss the development of brand relations within a complex NPO context such as SA.
2. What are the particular PR challenges for NPOs in your country?
3. Describe the entrepreneurial skills needed by PR practitioners in an NPO sub-sector.
4. Identify examples of partnerships between NPOs, public and private organizations that you know of and discuss their effectiveness.
5. Explore SROI and its relevance to an NPO sub-sector of your choice.
6. Analyse the brand history of an NPO you know, in the context of the country's political, social and economic history.

References

Andreasen, A.R. & Kotler, P. (2008) *Strategic Marketing for Non-profit Organisations*, International edition, New Jersey: Pearson Education International.

Balmer, J.M.T. 2011. Corporate marketing myopia and the inexorable rise of a corporate marketing logic: perspectives from identity-based views of the firm. *European Journal of Marketing*, 45(9/10), pp. 1329–1352.

Benecke, D.R. & Oksiutycz, A. 2015. Changing conversation and dialogue through LeadSA: An example of public relations activism in South Africa. *PR Review*, 41(5), pp. 816–824.

Benecke, D.R., Simpson, Z., Le Roux, S., Skinner, C.J., Janse van Rensburg, N., Sibeko, J., Bvuma, S. & Meyer, J. 2017. Cultural intermediaries and the circuit of culture: The Digital Ambassadors project in Johannesburg, South Africa. *PR Review*, 43(1), pp. 26–34.

Bortree, D.S. 2015. Motivation of publics. The power of antecedents in volunteer-nonprofit organizations. In *Public Relations as Relationship Management*, J.A. Ledingham & S.D. Bruning (eds). New York: Routledge, Taylor and Francis.

Bruce, I. 2011. *Charity Marketing – Delivering Income, Services and Campaigns*. London: ICSA.

Bruning, S.D. 2000. Relationship building as a retention strategy: linking relationship attitudes and satisfaction evaluations to behavioural outcomes. *Public Relations Review*, 28(1), pp. 39–48.

Cheverton, J. 2007. Holding our own: value and performance in non profit organizations. *Australian Journal of Social Issues*, 42(3), pp. 427–436.

Department of Social Development. http://www.npo.gov.za

Edwards, L. (2009) Public relations theories: an overview. In R. Tench and L. Yeomans (eds) *Exploring Public Relations*. Harlow: Pearson.

Freeman, R.E. 2004. The stakeholder approach revisited, *Zeitschrift für Wirtschafts- und Unternehmensethik*, 5(3), pp. 228–241. Accessed on http://search.proquest.com/openview/5379084633f9e2f84308789523dcde92

Gladwell, M. 2015. *The Tipping Point: How Little Things Can Make a Big Difference*. London: Abacus.

Global Alliance of Public Relations and CommunicationsManagement. *PR Landscape Study*. http://www.globalalliancepr.org

Grunig, J.E. & Grunig, L.A. 2000. Public relations in strategic management and strategic management of public relations: theory and evidence from the IABC excellence project. *Journalism Studies*, 1(2), pp. 303–321.

Holtzhausen, L. 2014. Non-profit organizations bridging the communication divide in a complex South Africa. *PR Review*, 40, pp. 286–293.

Hon, L. & Grunig, J.E. 1999. Guidelines for measuring relationships in public relations. Paper presented to the Institute for public relations commission for PR measurement and evaluation, Gainesville, Florida.

Huang, Y.C. & Zhang, Y. 2015. Revisiting organizational-public relationship research for the past decade: theoretical concepts, measure, methodology and challenges. In *Public Relations as Relationship Management*, J.A. Ledingham & S.D. Bruning (eds). New York: Routledge, Taylor and Francis.

Landi, K. 2017. https://www.communityhourssa.co.za

Ledingham, J. 2003. Explicating relationship management as a general theory of public relations, *Journal of Public Relations Research*, 15(2), pp. 181–198.

Ledingham, J.A. & Bruning, S.D. 2000. *Public Relations as Relationship Management: A Relational Approach to the Study and Practice of Public Relations*. Mahwah, NY: Erlbaum.

Kang, M. & Yang, S-U. 2010. Mediation effects of organization: Public relationship outcomes on public intentions for organizational supports. *Journal of Public Relations Research*, 22(4), pp. 477–494.

Kotler, P. 2000. *Marketing Management. The Millennium Edition*. New York: Prentice-Hall.

Lamb, C.W., Hair, J.F., McDaniel, C., Terblanche, N., Elliot, R., Klopper, H.B. 2015. *Marketing*. 5th edn. Oxford: Oxford University Press.

Mersham, G. & Skinner, C. 2016. South Africa's bold and unique experiment in CSR practice. *Society and Business Review*, 11(2), pp.110–129.

Moore, M. & Westley, F. 2011. Surmountable chasms: networks and social innovation for resilient systems. *Ecology and Society*, 16(1): 5. [online] URL: http://www.ecologyandsociety.org/vol16/iss1/art5/

Mort, G.S., Weerawardena, J. & Williamson, B. 2007. Branding in the non-profit context: the case of Surf Life Saving Australia. *Australian Marketing Journal*, 15(2), pp. 108–119.

Patel, L. 2012. Developmental social policy, social welfare services and the non-profit sector in South Africa. *Social Policy & Administration*, 46(6), pp. 603–618.

Patel, L. & Mushonga, H. 2015. Corporate social responsibility and development: a study of stakeholder perspectives of listed South African companies. *Africanu*, 44(2), pp. 50–63.

Rossouw, R. 2010. Measuring social impact and return on investment. *CSI, Community and Social Development*. https://nextgeneration.co.za/measuring-the-social-impact-roi-of-csi/

Sargeant, A. 2009. *Marketing Management of Non-Profit Organizations*. Oxford: Oxford University Press.

Skinner, C. & Mersham, G. 2008. Corporate social responsibility in South Africa: emerging trends. *Society and Business Review*, 3(3), pp. 239–255.

Stacks, D.W. & Watson, M.L. 2007. Two-way communication based on quantitative research and measurement. In *The Future of Excellence in Public Relations and Communication Management. Challenges for the Next Generation*. E.L. Toth (ed.). New York: Routledge.

Statistics SA. 2014. Statistics of the non-profit sector for South Africa, 2011. http://www.statssa.gov.za

Wyngaard, R.G. 2013. The South African NPO crisis: time to join hands. *International Journal of Not-for-Profit Law*, 15(1), pp. 5–12.

17

THE RISE OF VOLUNTEERING IN BRAZIL

New perspectives, partnerships and paradigms

Paulo Nassar, Gustavo Carbonaro and Natália Tamura

Introduction

Brazil has the fifth largest number of volunteers in the world according to the Charity Aid Foundation's (CAF) *World Giving Index 2016*. By law, there is a national day of volunteering. Nevertheless, the percentage of volunteers is not high relative to the country's population. This chapter considers historical, social and cultural issues that impact on volunteering. In particular it examines the rise of corporate volunteering from the perspectives of companies and not-for-profit organizations (NFPs). Two case studies, at Vale and the Fazendo História Institute, illustrate contemporary practice. In addition, future trends and innovations are discussed.

The volunteering landscape

Brazil is the ninth largest economy in the world, with a GDP of US$ 1.8 trillion (World Bank n.d.) and a population of over 200,000,000 (World Bank n.d.). It is Latin America's largest country in terms of economy, population and geographical size. Brazil is the land of the 'cordial men', according to Brazilian historian, Sérgio Buarque de Holanda (1936: 76). This 'cordiality' is not linked to kindness or politeness of the Brazilian people but to a belief that the people are driven more by theirs hearts than by reason. Love and hate can both be expressed in a short space of time. Despite the scale of the population and their 'cordiality', limited research into the volunteer sector shows that Brazil is still shy when it comes to volunteer work.

A joint study by the Itaú Social Foundation and Datafolha Institute (Fundação Itaú Social 2014)[1], shows 72 per cent of people have never participated in any kind of volunteer work and that only 11 per cent volunteer regularly. Nearly a third (28 per cent) have engaged in voluntary actions at least once in their life. Silvia Naccache (2015) explains,[2] 'The Brazilian percentage [of volunteer work] is below the world average of 37%. In China and Canada, for example, they respectively have 55% and 50% of the population involved in voluntary activities'.[3]

However, levels of engagements have marginally improved in recent years. The *CAF World Giving Index 2016*, which provides an annual picture of charitable behaviour around the world, shows that Brazil had 29 million people volunteering in 2015. The is the fifth largest number of volunteers (Charities Aid Foundation 2016: 25) out of the 140 countries included in the index. The survey finds that 18 per cent of Brazilians (aged 15 years and older) engaged in volunteer activities (CAF 2016: 43). This represents a 2% rise compared with 2013 and 2014 findings of the same research. In the 2016 rankings, Brazil rose 37 places in one year, from 105 (CAF 2015: 35) to 68 (CAF 2016: 34). More than 54 per cent of Brazilians said they had helped a stranger in the previous month, compared to 41 per cent the previous year (CAF 2015: 35). Those donating money increased from 20 to 30 per cent (CAF 2015: 39 and CAF 2016: 41) in a year.

Historical patterns of giving in Brazilian give volunteering specific cultural context. Traditionally, religious beliefs have been more influential than civic participation. Natálio Kisnerman (1983) and Mike Hudson (1999) argue that volunteering is more linked to the act of giving than engagement in projects. Gino Giacomini and Ricardo Almeida (2016) believe that the association of giving as volunteering has created a 'paternalistic (model), which can be understood as an act of charity and unilateral, although worthy and contributory'.[4]

Gabriel Moura (Tamura 2017b), co-founder of the non-profit Atados (a small NGO that connects people to a variety of volunteering activities in Brazil) observes: 'We carry a voluntary informal concept that still has a strong elitist connotation, focused on hierarchical charity works'.[5] This stigma, he says, makes numerous volunteer actions invisible, especially **informal volunteering**. Informal volunteering is unpaid help to a non-family member that is not conducted through an organization.

History of volunteering in Brazil

Volunteer workers can be traced back to 1543 (Fausto 2009). The 'House of God for men' was established by Portuguese immigrants to serve exhausted adventurers arriving from Europe. It led to The Holy House of Saints, which provided assistance over many centuries. Support ranged from healthcare and lodgings to burial expenses. Today, The Holy House is one of the main healthcare institutions in Brazil (Piacentini 2015).

Until the 19th century, in Brazil, aid for people living in poverty was dealt with by civil society, based around religious institutions. The Brazilian state was not strongly present in civil life in this period. Historian Boris Fausto (2009) argues that it was not until the 1930s that the state started to become involved with the public life of Brazilians. This occurred at a time when Brazilian society was becoming more complex, urbanized and with bourgeoning industry. In the 1940s, the Government developed policies of social assistance for the Brazilian population (Pilotti and Rizzini 1995). Thereafter, wider society took more active participation in philanthropy and social movements emerged.

In the 1990s clearer definitions of voluntary work emerged. After more than 20 years of authoritarian rule, Brazil went through a process of re-democratization in 1985 and began the long process of stabilizing the economy, in the run up to the new millennium (Carbonaro 2009). In parallel, the neoliberal agreement reached in Latin America in 1989, known as the Washington Consensus,[6] removed part of the state from social actions (Abreu 2014). This opened space for more systematic action by civil society. Civil society grew considerably with the re-democratization of the country in the 1980s, and the new Brazilian Constitution supported and paved the way for wider civil participation (Schwarcz 2015).

New laws (Brazilian Government 1998) defined volunteering as 'non-remunerated activity, provided by an individual to a public entity of any kind, private or non-profit, which has civil, cultural, scientific, recreational, educational or social assistance objectives, including mutuality'.[7] Voluntary work is not treated as employment and participants are not required to make pension contributions. Legislation in 1985 established the 28th August as the National Day of Volunteering in Brazil. Since the 1980s, civil society began organizing itself more efficiently and started nationwide promotion of volunteering.

Volunteering and business communication

Like volunteer work, the evolution of Brazilian corporate communication followed the industrial development of the country (Nassar 2009). Business communication started slowly in the 1940s, grew with the arrival of multinationals in the 1950s and was consolidated in the 1960s. The first Brazilian PR Agency was founded in 1962. The Brazilian Association of Business Communication (Aberje) was founded in 1967. Nassar (2010) believes that it played a critical role in helping to shift working environments from being organized around scientific models to more human resource focused approaches.

Organizational communication, according to Margarida Kunsch (2003) is a strategic matter for companies. She believes public relations can help define and transmit values and facilitate organizational dialogue. Communicators have to work actively to engage people without, and within, organizations. Volunteers can act as vital conduits between society and organizations. Effective communications can add new levels of co-operation, understanding and advocacy.

The *Employee Volunteering Report* (Booth and Rodell 2015) is a global survey conducted by United Way in five countries (Brazil, India, USA, Canada and Australia). It shows that employees engaged in volunteering very often are six per cent more satisfied with their work. In Brazil, most of the actions related to corporate volunteering are organized and promoted by corporate communicators.

Company commitment and employee development

There has been growing corporate interest in, and commitment to, volunteering in the first two decades of the 21st century. Political and economic stability from 2000–2010 gave Brazil the capacity to shape what is now known as the **Decade of Volunteering** (2001–2011). During this decade, a new appreciation of the role of volunteerism in society emerged. The United Nations (UN) created a new focus for volunteerism with the International Year of Volunteers in 2001. The year gave impetus to the emergence of business volunteering programmes in Brazil from 2001–2011, according to Wanda Engel (CBVE 2013), CEO of the Brazilian Business Volunteer Council (CBVE). Increasingly, companies realized the importance of engaging their staff in volunteering, participated in practical discussions and launched initiatives around a range of social issues.

After this decade, Brazilian companies were also influenced by the UN's Sustainable Development Goals for 2030 that were launched in 2015 (United Nations n.d.). Silvia Naccache, coordinator of the Volunteer Center of São Paulo, and an advisor for many corporate volunteer programmes, confirms (Tamura 2017c) many companies have taken into account the UN objectives when shaping their programmes.

Data from CBVE (2016) points toward continued corporate encouragement of volunteering. Corporate intentions are usually linked to improving a company's image and illustrating its commitment to acting in a socially responsible manner; both motives and consequent actions have an impact on corporate reputation. Many companies invest in training volunteers. Initiatives range from **punctual actions** (these usually occur on a single day), through to long-term programmes designed to establish deep connections between volunteers and beneficiaries.

Comunitas is a Brazilian civil society organization for the improvement of corporate social investments. It highlights (2016) in its *Report of Corporate Social Investment Benchmarking* that 94 per cent of the Brazilian companies in the sample of about 300 companies have at least one volunteer programme. Those firms with programmes made an average investment of R$14,600,000 (about £3,730,000) in 2015. Typically, 10 per cent of workforces takes part in initiatives. According to Comunitas (2016) companies that adopt voluntary programmes usually released their employees during office hours. The most widely adopted corporate volunteer programmes involve group activities involving their own employees (81 per cent) or the formation and promotion of collaborative networks among volunteers (56 per cent). Such approaches from large companies foster volunteerism.

Engagement consultancy Santo Caos (n.d.) conducted research with more than 800 people and 80 companies. This research indicates that despite big companies' initiatives, only three per cent of Brazilians have first-hand experience of volunteering inside a corporation. Nearly 70 per cent of respondents have never worked for a company that offers a structured volunteer programme. It also showed that 56 per cent of volunteers are women, 61 per cent are young adults (18–33 years old), and those participating have family income around[8] US$ 1,000. One in four volunteers dedicate 80 hours per annum to volunteering. More specifically, according to this survey, a **corporate volunteer** is equally as likely to be a man as a woman. They have a family income around US$ 2,000 (68%), and dedicate themselves fewer than 40 hours per annum. Corporate volunteering is focused on employees in more administrative roles who have more money. They tend to be less dedicated and more involved with 'punctual' participation.

Bruna Ribeiro, a communications and sustainability researcher and PR consultant, observes that companies generally direct voluntary actions according to their social investment and business strategies (Tamura 2017a). The focus has been more directed to meeting the needs of the communities rather than the interests and preferences of their employees. One person is usually in charge of the volunteering programme. They usually report to Human Resources, or Sustainability and Social Responsibility or Communication and Marketing. She highlights challenges that companies with volunteer programmes face. There may be scepticism about whether businesses are genuinely going beyond a desire to generate profit. Secondly, employees need to be motivated to participate. Additionally, it can be complex to evaluate both societal and volunteer-generated gains.

Despite the difficulty in demonstrating results, over ten social programme managers, leaders and officials consulted by the authors asserted that the practice of corporate volunteering brings many benefits for participating companies. Improvements cited included those related to organizational climate, image and brand; talent retention rates, and internal engagement.

Volunteering can also contribute to the development of an individual's skills and outlooks. The development of skills when volunteering can be much more effective than traditional training. Silvia Naccache (Tamura 2017c) reflects that some companies want to include voluntary activity on the leadership agenda. As a minimum, they see it as an opportunity to discuss issues such as diversity, absenteeism and interpersonal communication. Corporate volunteering can allow employees to believe they are making wider contributions as national and corporate citizens and allow them to understand a wider range of global issues. It can widen the employees' understanding of where they work (systematic) and encourage people to make decisions after hearing alternative arguments and perspectives (weighting). Accepting and examining the perspectives of others regularly occurs (critical capacity). Volunteers often become more aware of the limits of their existing experiences (detachment). They may develop greater self-awareness and may become more humanly sensitive when helping people achieve their dreams.

Gabriel Moura (Tamura 2017b) believes that companies can provide an optional path for people to pursue their vocations as volunteers. Strong volunteering programmes can motivate individuals, as well as improve a company's reputation externally. Furthermore, Moura observes that some companies have expanded the complexity and diversity of their volunteering activities. It is now possible for employees to contribute according to their chosen causes and to flex the time that they give. The plurality of voluntary activities increases with employee involvement in the development of corporate volunteer initiatives and policies.

Democratic participation arising from volunteering can be a driver of internal cultural transformation. This can bring the values of equity and social justice to the fore and give visibility to groups to whom corporations may acknowledge but not actively listen.

CASE STUDY 17.1: THE EVOLUTION OF VALE'S GLOBAL EMPLOYEE VOLUNTEERING

Vale is a Brazilian multinational company that works in the mining sector. Created in 1942 as a State-owned company, the company is publicly traded on the stock exchange in São Paulo, Paris, Madrid and New York. Vale is the world's largest producer of iron ore.

The Vale Volunteers Programme (Voluntários Vale 2014) is an initiative to organize, promote and encourage the voluntary actions of its employees, contractors and family members. The company believes that volunteering can make a positive contribution to society. Vale encourages participation in volunteer activities that promote the exercise of citizenship and solidarity between its employees. Since 2004, Vale has run a programme to contribute to the company's social causes in the communities where it operates and where most of its employees live. It encourages employees to dedicate time, and skills, for causes of common interest.

In 2011, it created a department for Global Corporate Volunteering, with a remit to organize and mobilize volunteers, in order to stimulate the culture of volunteering within the company. By 2013, 37 local committees located in 11 Brazilian states helped shape volunteering. By 2015, 8,000 volunteers pursued 240 activities that have an impact on more than 40,000 people. The actions were divided into education and culture (12 per cent), quality of life (16 per cent) and service (62 per cent). The Vale programme has also been introduced in overseas markets including Oman, Malaysia, Mozambique and Australia.

The company has also developed a Global Corporate Volunteering policy that guides the participation of employees. The programme has a unique visual identity. The Vale Volunteer Portal is a repository of information on it.

Corporate communications plays a core role in the programme. It assists with the development of its global communication plan, co-ordinating local communication teams, applying the visual identity and promoting campaigns with employees and a series of external stakeholders.

The non-profit perspective

The Brazilian Institute of Geography and Statistics (IBGE), states the third sector represented 1.4 per cent of Brazilian GDP in 2007 (R$ 32 billion or £7,66 billion). However, the non-profit sector had little relevance in Brazil until the mid-1990s. Fisher and Falconer (1998) identify three core reasons why the change occurred.

Firstly, the influence of international organizations – mainly the World Bank; secondly, Government reforms between 1994 and 1998, and a legacy of neo-liberalism stemming from the Washington Consensus; thirdly, the business sector created groups to promote social investment such as Groups of Institutes, Foundations and Companies (GIFE), the Ethos Institute, and the Institute for the Development of Social Investment (IDIS).

This environment allowed the third sector to act in a more efficient and professional manner and to clarify their social demands. It also provided the opportunity to modify and frame communications between the Government, business and society (Calegare & Silva 2009). Simultaneously, the number of social organizations being established has risen (Avritzer 2012). Typically, they have sought to develop close relationships with the communities they serve. Therefore, people are increasingly looking for organizations and creating new ones to effectively meet social needs that the state does not address.Many non-profit organizations (NPOs) are highly active and need volunteers. NPOs are attractive to many stakeholders because they seek to assist distinct sections of society, or to remedy social problems, without focusing on profit. However, their lean structures can be perceived as insufficient to tackle the scale of the problems they are seeking to tackle.

Corporate volunteering is often perceived as highly attractive by non-profits, especially when it allows them to access corporate human and intellectual capital. It also enables the non-profits to expand their networks and to open paths to new fundraising and a fresh pool of volunteers. In the medium and long term, non-profits have the opportunity to promote their causes to important societal influencers, because of the access to political and social elites that large corporations can provide. Moura (Tamura 2017b) acknowledges that non-profits and companies often bring different objectives, contexts, realities, and many have to tackle uncertainty and suspicion from both sides. Yet, when objectives and plans are well aligned and understood, and limitations of a partnership are recognized, there can be strong synergy and commitment to delivering effective programmes. Non-profit managers often highlight the importance of fit between both parties and insist that corporates do not try to change a non-profits' model of operation. They will try to limit the way in which a corporate might seek to over promote the results it has achieved as a consequence of a partnership.

Nevertheless, non-profits need to administer their own body of volunteers without interference by corporates. Ribeiro (Tamura 2017c) asserts it is important that social organizations keep volunteers within their own structures. This should encompass roles and activities including project educators, administrators, and accounting. In many cases this will cause non-profits to think carefully, and creatively, on how to organize their internal structure and engage their volunteers.

Valdir Cimino, chairman of *Viva e Deixe Viver* (Storytellers in Health and Education) reflects (Tamura 2017d) there are a number of aspects that are vital to successful relationship between non-profits and volunteers. For example, it is important both parties value each other's volunteering expertise, work co-operatively, understand relevant legal frameworks and measure the impact of voluntary programmes on the balance sheet.

Innovation and alignment

Digital channels are being used to widen the possibilities for volunteering, enabling people to volunteer without leaving home or work, by the donation of hours, energy and talent. Joni Browne et al. (2013) refer to 'micro-volunteering', whereby people volunteer for an organization for a few hours. Social networks and other platforms have been widely used for performing digital and in-person volunteer activities. Atados (2017) offers a platform that connects non-profits to potential volunteers, enabling the latter to elect their preferred kind of work.

Reaching new sections of the community occurred with the *Abraço Cultural* project (Abraço Cultural).[9] The project is pioneering and has refugees acting as teachers of language and culture. The main objectives are to promote the exchange of experience, income generation, and the personal and cultural appreciation of refugees living in Brazil. At the same time, it enables students to learn new languages, help eliminate barriers and have direct contact with different cultural approaches. It also gives refugees employment opportunities.

Gamification is also being widely used in the field of volunteering. In addition to being a playful tool, platforms, applications and games are used to engage, mobilize and to manage the volunteer activities, and attract a young audience. An example is *Play the Call* (Alencar 2012), which teaches children to change the world in a fast and fun way. Players are challenged to perform different missions, from planting a tree to painting streets and parks, and cleaning beaches and rivers. Players can share their completed tasks via social networks. The Brazilian Scout network volunteered to launch the game.

CASE STUDY 17.2: FAZENDO HISTÓRIA INSTITUTE

The population of children and adolescents in Brazil is 60 million people, according to the Brazilian Institute of Geography and Statistics (IBGE) in 2010.[10] Around 17 million are at risk, living in poverty. According to the survey from the Institute of Applied Economic Research (IPEA) 20,000 of them are living in shelters (former orphanages), having experienced family separation (IPEA 2003).

Founded in 2005, the *Fazendo História Institute* is a non-profit with the goal of welcoming children and adolescents who have suffered a family separation, with a special focus on those living in shelters. Its objective is to rescue the affective memory of children and adolescents and encourage them to rewrite their own stories to redeem past memories; in turn helping to overcome their trauma. This pathway can provide a critical step in establishing communication and affection with possible adoptive parents.

Although its remit is still restricted to São Paulo, the non-profit has helped more than 12,500 children and adolescents since 2005. Today, there are 745 volunteers working on the programme, which has distributed more than 20,000 books and linked up with 7,100 professionals to assist children and adolescents.

Through the dialogue between the volunteers and the child, and the narrative construction of children's life stories, (particularly with the use of storytelling) traumas can be overcome. There is a great care in preparing volunteers' communication skills to deal sensitively and humanely with these issues, which often generate repulsion and aggression in the child.

Final considerations

The voluntary sector in Brazil is growing and enjoying increasing wide support from the commercial sector. The value to employees, corporations and non-profits is increasingly accepted and ways of working effectively are being developed. Professional communications increasingly play a role in attracting employees, highlighting the worth of programmes and providing kudos for corporations.

However, the evolution of volunteering still bumps into cultural issues that can hinder the rapid development of this type of action, although there is growing acceptance of its benefit, including a recognition for employees who make their contribution as global citizens.

New generations are facing new social issues, whilst the ways in which it is possible to contribute are wider, and more diverse, than ever. Communications are crucial in allowing the volunteers to see the impact they can make. New technological tools are opening open up a new range of ways to perform volunteer work. Young people who possess technological expertise can help in ways never thought possible. The focus on convincing the young people that is important to be involved with volunteering is what will define the future of volunteerism in Brazil. Non-profits, companies and any organization that promotes voluntary actions should focus on raising the awareness among young people.

The creation of bridges between companies and the non-profit sector helps clarify the modern role that an NPO plays, and importantly challenges historical views of volunteering. The growing number of programmes has expanded the vision of ordinary people about how they can participate in civil society and illustrates that voluntary contributions can go far beyond financial donations.

The company that sets free its employee for volunteer work for a certain number of hours usually ends up creating a new paradigm that equates help with time, skills and knowledge transfer, as well as financial contributions. This new thinking allows for a wider range of often sensitive issues, such as work with abandoned children, to be tackled in fresh and sensitive ways.

A population conscious of its social problems can help focus an individual's attitudes to volunteering. It can also lead to more being required of the public authorities. For developing nations, it can be advantageous if their populations are conscious about what challenges lie ahead and are aware of how change can bring about collective improvement. There is still a long journey for volunteering in Brazil, but the benefits are increasingly being understood.

Questions for discussion

1.   How do religious beliefs affect how volunteer work is seen in Brazil?
2.   What are the main differences between charity giving and volunteering in Brazil?
3.   How do big companies view the benefits of volunteering?
4.   How can global companies expand their volunteering programmes beyond the borders of the country in which they operate?
5.   What can non-profits do to attract more young people to their volunteer programmes?
6.   How does the training and the expertise of people in volunteer work (how to deal with abandoned children, for example) influence wider society?

Acknowledgements

Silvia Naccache graduated in biomedical sciences, is coordinator of the Volunteer Center of São Paulo (CVSP) and is responsible for coordination of partnerships with civil society organizations, Governments, schools, universities and businesses.

Gabriel Moura graduated in business administration, and was founder of the non-profit Atados, responsible for tying volunteer opportunities to volunteers. Today he is researching and studying the topic of volunteering and acting as one.

Bruna Ribeiro is a public relations and researcher in the areas of communication and sustainability. He has experience in national and multinational companies in projects aimed at socially responsible management, private social investment, sustainability reporting (GRI) and training of multipliers.

Valdir Cimino holds a masters in Health Sciences, is Chairman of Viva e Deixe Viver (Storytellers in Health and Education). He is author of the books: *Viva e deixe viver, É formiga o barata?, Um tesouro a descobrir no barco que naufragou, O papel do educador na era da Interdependência, Viva e Deixe Viver e Humanização em Saúde,* and others.

Notes

1 The results are based on: (a) an online survey with their partner institutions, representing a universe of 299 companies, 23 business foundations, 1 independent institute, 1 private non-profit institution and a Federation of companies of the industry sector of Rio de Janeiro; (b) interviews with social managers and leaders of a small group of companies/ business institutes; and, (c) evidence gathered at meetings of the BISC (Benchmarking of Corporate Social Investment) Discussion Group.

2   This refers to the 2012 IBOPE Intelligence research, which was done in partnership
    with the Worldwide Independent Network of Market Research (WIN), conducted in
    59 countries, with 53,433 respondents. In Brazil, IBOPE Intelligence heard 2,002
    people between December 8 and 12, 2011.
3   'A porcentagem de trabalho voluntário brasileiro está abaixo da média mundial de 37%.
    Na China e no Canadá, por exemplo, há 55% e 50% da população, respectivamente,
    envolvida em atividade voluntárias.'
4   '[...] um modelo paternalista, que pode ser entendido como um ato de caridade e uni-
    lateral, embora digno e contributivo'.
5   'Carregamos um conceito de voluntariado informal que ainda traz forte conotação eli-
    tista, focadas em obras de caridade hierarquizadas.'
6   The Washington Consensus is the informal name of a meeting held in November 1989
    to discuss neoliberal economic reforms in Latin America.
7   '[...] atividade não remunerada, prestada por pessoa física a entidade pública de qualquer
    natureza, ou a instituição privada de fins não lucrativos, que tenha objetivos cívicos,
    culturais, educacionais, científicos, recreativos ou de assistência social, inclusive
    mutualidade'.
8   This sum represents three times the medium income of Brazilian population according
    to IBGE. For further information see: http://www.ibge.gov.br/home/estatistica/indica
    dores/trabalhoerendimento/pnad_continua/default_renda_percapita.shtm.
9   Abraço Cultural (n.d.). Sobre o Abraço, available at: abracocultural.com.br
10 For further information see: http://7a12.ibge.gov.br/vamos-conhecer-o-brasil/nosso-p
    ovo/caracteristicas-da-populacao.html

References

Primary sources

Tamura, N. (2017a) Interview with Bruna Ribeiro, PR consultant, in São Paulo. March.
Tamura, N. (2017b) Interview with Gabriel Moura, co-founder of Atados in São Paulo.
    March.
Tamura, N.(2017c) Interview with Silvia Naccache, co-ordinator of the Volunteer Center
    of São Paulo in São Paulo. March.
Tamura, N. (2017d) Interview with Valdir Cimino, Chairman of Viva e Deixe Viver São
    Paulo, Brazil. March.

Secondary sources

Abraço Cultural (n.d.) *Sobre o Abraço*. Available at: abracocultural.com.br (accessed 2 January
    2018).
Abreu, M. P. (2014) *A ordem do progresso: dois séculos de política econômica no Brasil*. 2nd edn.
    Rio de Janeirol: Campus-Elsevier.
Alencar, V. (2012, 4 December) A brincadeira é a única maneira de mudar o mundo.
    Available at: http://porvir.org/a-brincadeira-e-unica-maneira-de-mudar-mundo (accessed
    4 March 2017).
Associação Viva e Deixe Viver (2017) Quem somos. Available at: www.vivaedeixeviver.org.
    br/ (accessed 4 March 2017).
Atados (2017) Sobre nós. Available at: www.atados.com.br (accessed 4 March 2017).
Avritzer, L. (2012) Sociedade civil e Estado no Brasil: da autonomia à interdependência
    política. *Opinião Pública*, vol. 18, no. 2, pp.383–398. ISSN 104–6276. http://dx.doi.org/
    10.1590/S0104-62762012000200006 (accessed 17 August 2017).

Bondal, M.R. (2001) The human face of globalization: implications in education, *Estudios Sobre Educacion*, 1, pp. 81–89.

Booth, J.E. and Rodell, J.B. (2015) *Employee Volunteering Report: A Global Study of Employee Motivation to Engage in Corporate Volunteering Programs*. Alexandria, USA: United Way Worldwide.

Brazilian Government (1985) Lei n° 7.352, de 28 de agosto de 1985. Institui o Dia Nacional do Voluntariado. Available at: http://www2.camara.leg.br/legin/fed/lei/1980-1987/lei-7352-28-agosto-1985-356953-publicacaooriginal-1-pl.html (accessed 17 August 2017).

Brazilian Government (1998) Lei n. 9.608, de 18 de fevereiro de 1998. Dispõe sobre o serviço voluntário e dá outras providências. Available at: http://www.planalto.gov.br/ccivil_03/leis/L9608.htm (accessed 17 August 2017).

Brazilian Institute of Geography and Statistics (IBGE) (2007) Notícia Terceiro Setor: finalmente no PIB. Available at: http://www.ipea.gov.br/acaosocial/article926d.html?id_a rticle=388 (accessed 2 January 2018).

Browne, J., Jochum, V. and Ockenden, N. (2013) *The Value of Giving a Little Time: Understanding the Potential of Micro-volunteering. Summary Report*. Available at: https://www.wcva.org.uk/media/739801/micro_volunteering_full_report_071113.pdf (accessed 2 February 2018).

Calegare, M.G.A. & Silva Junior, N. (2009) A "construção" do terceiro setor no Brasil: da questão social à organizacional. *Revista Psicologia Política*, 9(17), 129–148. Available at: http://pepsic.bvsalud.org/scielo.php?script=sci_arttext&pid=S1519-549X2009000100009&lng=pt&tlng=pt (accessed 10 June 2017).

Carbonaro, G. (2009) Brazil: correspondentes internacionais no Brasil. Trabalho de Conclusão de Curso, Escola de Comunicações e Artes da Universidade de São Paulo. Orientação Rosana de Lima Soares. Brazil: USP.

CBVE (2013) *Voluntariado Empresarial: do conceito à prática*. Brazil: CBVE. Available at: http://www.cbve.org.br/?p=2747 (accessed 17 August 2017).

CBVE (2016) *Censo CBVE*. Brazil: CBVE. Available at: http://www.cbve.org.br/?p=3928 (accessed 17 August 2017).

Charities Aid Foundation (2015) *CAF World Giving Index 2015*. Available at: https://www.cafonline.org/docs/default-source/about-us-publications/caf_worldgivingindex2015_rep ort.pdf?sfvrsn=c498cb40_2 (accessed 16 July 2017).

Charities Aid Foundation (2016) *CAF World Giving Index 2016*. Available at: https://www.cafonline.org/about-us/publications/2016-publications/caf-world-giving-index-2016 (accessed 30 March 2017).

Comunitas (2016) *Relatório 2016 Benchmarking do Investimento Social Corporativo*. Available at: http://comunitas.org/wp-content/uploads/2017/01/relatorio_bisc_2016_internet1.pdf (accessed 30 March 2017).

Fausto, B. (2009) *História do Brasil*. São Paulo: Edusp.

Fisher, R. and Falconer, A.P. (1998) Desafios da parceria Governo Terceiro Setor. *Revista de Administração*, 33(1/2), 12–19. Brazil.

Fundação Itaú Social (2014) *Pesquisa sobre voluntários no Brasil: Resultados 2014*. Realizada pelo Datafolha. Available at: https://d13q7w9s0p5d73.cloudfront.net/uploads/itau/document/file/614/a082e3a3-993a-4bd4-a29e-9e1eb82ee0f7.pdf (accessed 30 March 2017).

Giacomini-Filho, G. and Almeida, R. (2016) O novo voluntariado e a comunicação de ONGs no contexto da América Latina. *ECCOM – Educação, Cultura e Comunicação*, v. 7, pp. 191–204. Brazil: ECCOM.

Holanda, S. (1936) *Raízes do Brasil*, São Paulo: José Olympio.

Hudson, M. (1999) *Administrando Organizações do Terceiro Setor*. São Paulo: Makron.

Instituto Fazendo História (2016) *Institucional*. Available at: www.fazendohistoria.org.br (accessed 4 March 2017).

IPEA (2003) *Levantamento nacional de abrigos para crianças e adolescentes da Rede SAC*. Available at: http://www.mpsp.mp.br/portal/page/portal/infanciahome_c/acolhimento_institucional/Doutrina_abrigos/IPEA._Levantamento_Nacional_de_abrigos_para_Criancas_e_Adolescentes_da_Rede_SAC.pdf (accessed 4 March 2017).

Kisnerman, N. (1983) *Introdução ao trabalho social*. São Paulo: Moraes

Kunsch, M. (2003) *Planejamento de Relações Públicas na Comunicação Integrada*. São Paulo, Brazil: Summus.

Martinez Soria, A.B. (2001) Voluntariado: 2001, proyecto global de acción. *Estudios Sobre Educacion*, 1, 91–97.

Moreno, A.S. and Yoldi, I.S. (2008) Avances recientes en la investigacion econômica sobre el voluntariado: valoración econômica del trabajo voluntario, costes de gestión del voluntariado y voluntariado corporativo, *Revista de Economía Pública, Social y Cooperativa*, 63, 191–225. Available at: http://www.redalyc.org/pdf/174/17412307008.pdf (accessed 30 March 2017).

Nassar, P. (2009) A Aberje e a comunicação organizacional no Brasil. In M. Kunsch (Org.). *Comunicação Organizacional: histórico, fundamentos e processos*, vol. 1. São Paulo, Brazil: Saraiva.

Nassar, P. (2010) The evolution of Brazilian organizational communication in the business context. In M. Marchirori (Ed.) *Comunicação e Organização: reflexões, processos e práticas*. São Caetano do Sul, Brazil: Difusão Editora.

NCVO (2016) *Alamanac 2016*. London: NCVO.

Piacentini, P. (2015) *Trabalho voluntário no Brasil: parcela pequena da sociedade se engaja nesse tipo de iniciativa*. Available at: http://pre.univesp.br/trabalho-voluntario-no-brasil#.V3x05bgrLIU (accessed 25 March 2017).

Pilotti, F. and Rizzini, I. (1995) *A arte de governar crianças: a história das políticas sociais, da legislação e da assistência à infância no Brasil*. Rio de Janeiro: Editora Universidade Santa Úrsula.

Santo Caos (n.d.) *Além do bem: um estudo sobre o voluntariado e engajamento*. Available at: http://santocaos.com.br/alemdobem/ (accessed 30 March 2017).

Schwarcz, L.M. & Starling, H.M. (2015) *Brasil: uma biografia*. São Paulo, Brazil: Companhia das Letras.

V2V (n.d.) Quem somos. Available at: http://www.v2v.net/ (accessed 4 March 2017).

United Nations (n.d.) *Sustainable Development Goals*. Available at: http://www.un.org/sustainabledevelopment/sustainable-development-goals/ (accessed 14 July 2017).

Voluntários Vale (2014) Sobre o programa. Available at: www.voluntariosvale.com/ (accessed 30 March 2017).

World Bank (n.d.) *Data Brazil*. URL: http://data.worldbank.org/country/brazil (accessed 14 July 2017).

INDEX

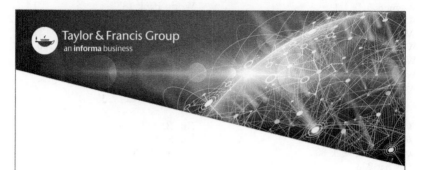